You Are Loved
. . . an email memoir

Lisa Lucca & Mark Mathias

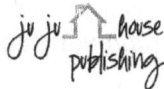

ju ju house publishing

JuJu House Publishing
Alameda, California
www.youarelovedthebook.com

ISBN-13: 9780615686615

Library of Congress: 2012948223

I Ching excerpt source: The I Ching Workbook, R.L. Wing, Immedia 1979

Films discussed and/or quoted in this book:
Fight Club, 20th Century Fox 1999, adapted screenplay by Jim Uhls
Carolina, Miramax 2004, written by Katherine Fugate
Phenomenon, Touchstone Pictures 1996, written by Gerald Di Pego
Prime, Universal Pictures 2005, written by Ben Younger
Bridges of Madison County, Warner Bros. 1995, adapted screenplay by Richard LaGravenese
The Curious Case Of Benjamin Button, Paramount Pictures 2008, adapted screenplay by Eric Roth

Book cover design: Lisa Lucca
Book photos: Shutterstock.com | Dreamstime.com | Depositphotos.com

Introduction

It's not a lack of love, but a lack of friendship that makes unhappy marriages.

-Friedrich Nietzsche

We did not fall in love or rush into a romantic relationship after first meeting thirty years ago. Neither did we project onto one another naive fantasies of an idealistic future together. It was much simpler and more honest than that: we liked each other a lot, and took our time discovering why.

Whether love endures or falls apart seems to have a lot to do with how it started. In spite of beautiful ceremonies and promises made, even the most sincere attempts at long-lasting love can crumble and fall under the weight of unfulfilled expectations, dramatic life changes, or simple mediocrity. We've learned the hard way that the allure of financial ease or the sensuously warm sand of romance are poor foundations on which to build something as big and heavy as a *life* together. If love is to remain standing, relationships need to be built on something more substantial and solid.

We recommend friendship.

This is our story . . .

one

Subject: Hi!
Date: Sat, 3 Nov 2001 5:03 PM
From: Lisa
To: Mark

Mark,

Hope all is well with you and your family! Things have been hectic here. I got laid off from my job shortly after 9/11, and while that's scary, I've taken this time off to write. I know it will take several months to get a new gig in this economy, so I'm actively pursuing my dream.

I've designed a website with a survey to research my subject - relationships, of course (write what you know, they say). I thought you might enjoy it. Fill out the questionnaire, share it with Mariah if you like, and feel free to pass it on to anyone you think may be interested in participating. Let me know if you have suggestions for content, etc.

I hope you are happy and well.

Take care.

Lisa

Subject: hey
Date: Sun, 23 Dec 2001 3:02 PM
From: Mark
To: Lisa

Just read your last email again and wanted you to know that I intend to stay in touch with you as the years go by. It'll be in snippets though, till more space opens up in my life.

That's a big subject that's up for me these days: *space.* I so miss being alone, with time for writing and self-reflection. Everything feels more like *doing* . . . lots of have-to's and suppose-to's these days.

I am not enjoying being married. It's rarely fun or wonderful, and never romantic. My commitment energies go into "hanging in there" and toughing it out in the face of unpleasant ways of relating. Being a parent to Savannah, however, is a great source of joy for me and I cling to the idea that it's really about her that Mariah and I have come together. The rest is just spiritual stamina.

Put THAT in your book . . .

I've looked over your website and have some suggestions for your questionnaire. That will come later. WELL DONE on doing it!

Merry Christmas and much love to you, my dear friend. We shall endure.

Mark

_____
Subject: re: hey
Date: Mon, 24 Dec 2001 8:50 AM
From: Lisa
To: Mark

I was so glad to hear from you this morning.

It makes me smile to know that you will not let our friendship slip away as the years go by. It's rare to have a connection like ours that transcends time and distance, and I believe we have more to learn from each other. Thanks for looking at my site and please send your suggestions.

I hate to hear that so much of your life is "getting through it". It's good that you recognize that and are trying to find time for reflection. You are such a deep and spiritual person with an abundance of love, Mark. Savannah is blessed to have you for her dad. Your relationship with her seems to be the way to keep a spark alive in you.

I feel the same about Zac in that I always have a force of love in my life, even when I am 'alone'. Being free from my unhappy marriage, available to explore new relationships, hasn't yielded as much joy as I had believed it would. Navigating the murky waters of single-parent dating for nearly six years has not been all fun and games. Yet I still have hope that

5

something long-lasting with someone wonderful is out there for me. With every 'failed' relationship I feel further away from my dream of Great Love, yet I persevere with wary optimism. Ever the hopeful romantic, me.

Write back when you have a chance or give me a call. I would love to hear your voice sometime. And keep trying to find space. It's a right, you know. At this stage in our lives we need to be living as fully as we can and *enjoying* it!

Hang in there, have fun over Christmas, and I wish you a new year filled with time to reconnect with yourself.

Lis

Subject: Hi there
Date: Thu, 3 Jan 2002 2:33 PM
From: Lisa
To: Mark

Can I say how wonderful (!) it was talking to you after so long? I'm so glad you called and I hope another year won't pass before I hear your voice.

Happy New Year! Things here are getting back to normal after the holidays although Zac is still off from school. I'll get in the swing for real next week.

I'm job hunting and working pretty heavily on the book. It feels good to do it, but I'm so insecure about my talent. Oh well. I wrote a press release which I'll send out to magazines, newspapers and radio stations to see if they will plug the website. Wish me luck! One good PR hit and I could be flooded with responses.

Well, I just wanted to say hey and tell you again how great it was to hear from you. Hope to again soon.

Subject: Hey
Date: Sat, 5 Jan, 2002 9:35 AM
From: Mark
To: Lisa

Got back last night from a few days on the land up north. Stormy and rainy on our arrival Tuesday night, but quite nice on Wednesday and Thursday. The big storms of the last month have brought spectacular water energy to the land. Streams and creeks are noisy and gushing.

6

I feel much more connected to myself when I'm doing work on the land, especially when I'm alone up there. I had a couple of hours to myself Wednesday afternoon, walking the length of our new road to the lower half of the property (50 acres), sculpting trails and clearing out trenches for water run-off. Mariah lived off the grid with her first husband on this property in the 70's in their homemade "hippy house". The house and property have been pretty much neglected ever since. There are trails, bridges and sheds to be built, and, hopefully, a small cottage . . . if we can ever agree on the size and design. (sigh)

Do not doubt your talent as a writer. If it helps, think of yourself as a messenger, delivering information a great many people have been searching for. Most people our age don't need to read or learn something *new*, as much as we need to be reminded of what we already know, but have forgotten or neglected.

So go ahead and remind us. We could sure use the help.

___

Subject: re: Hey
Date: Sat, 5 Jan, 2002 5:35 PM
From: Lisa
To: Mark

It sounds like you fed some of your hungrier parts being in nature. That's wonderful. It sounds like a cool place.

It's very cold here in Chicago. It's been a sweet, lazy day with Zac and we snuggled up with each other watching *Back To The Future* movies. He's nine now, and such a remarkable kid. I just love him so much.

Thanks for the encouragement about the writing. I do agree that there's nothing new for my book to report about relationships. It's just my observations and experiences. *Reminders* . . . that's a good way to put it.

I need to stay focused and keep true to myself while job hunting. I sent my resume' to a book publisher yesterday who expressed interest in my project management skills but has a hold on hiring right now. After working in direct marketing for the past several years I would be very happy to find a job in a field I'd enjoy, like publishing. I have a couple months to pursue new possibilities before I *have* to get a job doing just anything. Here's hoping.

Take care and keep in touch. Hope the effects of being out on the land last for a while.

Lis

Subject: Hey
Date: Thu, 31 Jan, 2002 7:30 AM
From: Lisa
To: Mark

Hope all is well. I've often thought of you lately while reading *The Unimaginable Life* by Kenny & Julia Loggins. Have you read it? It was written while he recorded the *Leap of Faith* album (one of my faves). It's so deep and pretty far out there, but their relationship concept is compelling and more in line with what I believe love can be, as opposed to what I've experienced. Reading it makes me yearn for that deep soul connection. Their story gives me hope.

What I like about it is that it addresses all the areas of love that we don't like to talk about: jealousy, self-image, beauty (or lack thereof), surrender, insecurity, sexuality. . . and this coming from a guy who APPEARED to have it all going on. He's *Kenny Loggins*, for God's sake! Yet underneath he was as screwed up about love as anybody. I see a little bit of us in them. The characters are real and flawed and lovable. Check it out.

I've been dating someone new, and though the whole process is fun I still feel like I'm missing someone I have loved forever. Somehow I sense that when the *right* person comes along it will feel like coming home.

Anyway, I hope you are taking care of you. I did something you will be proud of: I quit smoking! A week now and no urge at all. I had hypnosis and it was a miracle. I wish I'd done it years ago.

Let me know when we can chat. Soon?

Lis

_____
Subject: call
Date: Fri, 1 Feb, 2002 8:24 AM
From: Mark
To: Lisa

I should be available for a chat on Monday morning. Try me then.

_____

Subject: re: call
Date: Fri, 1 Feb, 2002 10:20 AM
From: Lisa
To: Mark

I noted Monday on my calendar and will plan to call you. I'd love to chat.

Have a great weekend! We just got a foot of snow so I think there may be sledding on my agenda. :-) Take care.

_____
Subject: re: call
Date: Fri, 15 Feb, 2002 7:03 AM
From: Mark
To: Lisa

Sorry I haven't been able to talk with you. On Monday I got the remodeling Job From Hell, arriving at the house at 7:30 every morning, hacking and sawing on steel frames to make the new windows fit. Four days of that and I was ready to kill myself. Hope all is well with you. I've enjoyed our talks.

Mark

_____
Subject: re: call
Date: Fri, 15 Feb, 2002 11:08 AM
From: Lisa
To: Mark

Sorry to hear about the bad week! It will get better . . .

I've had an interesting week myself. New Guy Jack and I decided that there's not enough fire to really keep this going, yet now he wants to see me tomorrow night. I'm still undecided. I've been keeping in touch with someone else I met online who wants to meet in person. We'll see.

In the meantime, I had a psychic reading which blew me away. She had a lot of intriguing things to say about my love life. Let's talk soon.

Lis

_____
Subject: Good morning
Date: Wed, 6 Mar, 2002 7:51 AM
From: Lisa
To: Mark

I saw you were online when I logged in and wanted to say hello! Hope things are better than when I talked to you last. I was sorry we couldn't chat long but I'll call again soon. Cool to hear that you have old friends coming back into your life. Good for the soul . . .

_____
Subject: mornin'

Date: Mon, 18 Mar, 2002 6:48 AM
From: Mark
To: Lisa

Hi there . . .

We'll need a long phone call to get caught up on all that's going on. We'll chat during my next long drive to a job.

Hope all is good with you. Spring is GORGEOUS here in the Bay Area!

love, Mark

_____
Subject: re: mornin'
Date: Mon, 19 Mar, 2002 8:46 AM
From: Lisa
To: Mark

Hey Mark!

Things are good. Still no job (came close but didn't get it). We should definitely talk soon. I want to hear the latest!

_____
Subject: Mark says hi
Date: Mon, 1 Jul, 2002 6:50 AM
From: Mark
To: Lisa

Greetings, earthling . . .

So . . . . where are you, and what's been happening?

_____
Subject: re: Mark says hi
Date: Tue, 2 Jul, 2002 5:56 PM
From: Lisa
To: Mark

Hey you.

I am currently in Canada for the month with my boyfriend Alex and am doing good! He's a man I met online in February who lives in Toronto. We're spending time together, talking about the future and working things out. I'm happy, yet there are obstacles that make this a challenging endeavor. The challenge: he has cancer. I know, it's scary, but he's doing well and could be healthy for years. It feels worth it to not let it stop us from exploring our relationship. We are good together and there's every sign that we can have a future if his health continues to be stable.

Zac is great, spending time with my family while I'm up here. He will be down in Tennessee with his dad in August. I miss him and we talk every day. This time apart is a chance for him to bond with others who love him. All is good.

I hope you are happy. I smiled to see your note. Please share what's going on with you and yours. I hope you're enjoying the summer, my friend. Be in touch.

Lis

Subject: re: Mark says hi
Date: Wed, 3 Jul, 2002 5:40 PM
From: Mark
To: Lisa

Lis,

Thanks for responding. Your note describes pretty much what I suspected, and I'm happy for you and Alex. Man, the idea of feeling genuine enthusiasm and love for your partner must be glorious . . . (sigh)

I quit the window job in exchange for a home remodeling company. MUCH happier in this job, doing and learning all kinds of new things, stretching me a bit and expanding my skills, all of which affects my ability to make things happen up on the land. We'll be up there for ten days starting tomorrow. I'll be more newsy when I return.

Take care.
Mark

Subject: re: Mark says hi
Date: Wed, 3 Jul, 2002 10:45 PM
From: Lisa
To: Mark

Good to hear back from you. Yes, it's a wonderful feeling to be in love, yet new love has its challenges, too (as you know).

Have a great time up on the land. Your new job sounds good. I hope to find a good job when I return home. It's so important to enjoy your work.

Write when you get back.

two

Subject: From Lis
Date: Tue, 8 Apr, 2003 11:50 PM
From: Lisa
To: Mark

Hi Mark,

How are you my friend? It sure has been a while. You've been on my mind, and after watching the movie *Phenomenon* I just had to write . . .

Things have changed in my world significantly. I'm now working for a chiropractor, booking wellness lectures for him. It's not a bad gig, but hardly my heart's desire. I'm still researching my book. I have a meeting next week with a couple who have a life coaching center and I hope to do some freelance marketing work with them. Zac is doing great in school, karate, band (playing drums!) and drama. He won first place in his recent geography bee.

On the love front, Alex and I broke up after the holidays :-(It's been very hard to move on. We still talk. There are so many reasons why we can't be together, yet I miss him. Life goes on. It was not meant to be for the long haul, though we had a profound purpose for our time together.

How are things with you? I hope all is well and that you're all happy. Please drop a note to say hi and let me know how you are doing. I miss our chats. Take care of you.

Lis

Subject: Re: From Lis
Date: Wed, 9 Apr 2003 7:37 AM
From: Mark
To: Lisa

I was wondering what happened to you. I was sure I wasn't hearing from you because you were married and blissed-out in Canada. I'm surprised it didn't work out. You've been on my mind the last couple of weeks, mostly trying to imagine what you've been up to. I've been unhappy lately, mostly re: my marriage.

We're more into horses than ever, trailering our horse 'DJ' all over, and are looking to buy a second one. The new job is great. I'm a foreman now.

The girls will be up soon, so I'll send something more newsy later.

Gotta go.

Mark

_____
Subject: From Lis
Date: Wed, 9 Apr, 2003 2:28 PM
From: Lisa
To: Mark

So good to hear from you! I'm happy that you're doing so well work-wise and that you're finding joy with DJ (and Savannah, of course). As for your unhappiness, well, that's been an ongoing condition for you that I have hoped would work itself out. Maybe in time?

Ah, "blissed out and married" . . . it was a thought, though with him it would not have been so blissful. As it turns out there was a very dark side there which took time to reveal itself. At first I attributed it to his illness (which plays a part absolutely), but there are other demons I could not slay.

He came down for three weeks over the holidays. It started out great but by the end I was miserable. In some ways he couldn't accept my devotion to Zac; in other ways he was just having a pity party over his cancer, despite his optimistic prognosis. In the end he wanted Zac and I to move up there, but I couldn't do that for many (including legal) reasons. Along with all the other red flags I just couldn't take the risk of fighting with Zac's dad and my family to go to a place of isolation with someone more focused on dying than living.

But when it was good . . . boy, was it good. Letting go has been hard. We're trying to stay friends (he called last night) but the contact may be making it harder to move on.

So now I'm back 'out there', the place I hate (a place which you probably long for!) where anything can happen and my next love may be around the corner. *Maybe.* It's been three months and I've just started looking up from my sadness, focusing on me & Zac and moving my career in a new direction.

I believe God will send me the person I'm meant to share my life with. God was at work in meeting and coming together with Alex, and had a hand in our undoing as well. In my heart I believe this is for the best. There were many things that would have been so hard for Zac and I to go through had I married Alex. We are now free of that pain, and I'm grateful for that. Especially for Zac.

Tell me about you. How you are feeling? Tell me about Savannah and what she's up to. Call me anytime, if you can. I would love to hear your voice. You always help me put things into perspective, my friend. How good a feeling it is to reconnect with you.

Hugs,
Lis

———

Subject: Re: From Lis
Date: Sat, 12 Apr 2003 2:43 PM
From: Mark
To: Lisa

Finally, a moment to myself to write a bit. Things around here are pretty much the same relationship-wise. Mariah and I continue to engage in arguments and head-bashing over so much little bullshit, and I am utterly bewildered by how mean-spirited an unhappy wife can be sometimes. It must be that this is some sort of cosmic payback for the pain I caused women in my past.

It can be so fucked up here, so sad to have to live like this . . . what a waste of life. Divorce? What? And give up half of everything, including Savannah? Forget it. That's a hell that couldn't possibly be better than the one I'm in now.

OK . . . got that out . . . so how are you?

Most other things are good for reasons that have nothing to do with my marriage. This is especially true for my work, which has moved to center stage as of late. I'm way into this remodeling thing, running a crew that just recently grew to 7 guys. We start a 2-month remodel of my mom's house on Monday, which is going to be the coolest thing for all kinds of reasons.

Savannah has become a truly great rider. She's nine years old now, doing well at events and in classes with her horse club. So much so that we're now shopping for a second horse, one that's more suited to English-style eventing. DJ has been a trail horse most of his life, and even after extensive training it looks like we'd be better off with a horse that already knows that stuff, making it more fun and less effort for Savannah. This also means we could take some nice family trips with two horses, hiking and riding in all kinds of cool places. I'm way into Friesians, big black horses with long manes and huge, feathered hooves . . . and SO sweet! There's one at the barn and I always go to his stall to love him up. He hangs his massive head over the stall door and lowers it into my chest. I rub his face and head and talk in his ear real sweet. I put my face against his and stroke his nose . . . oh, man, it's the best!

Sorry to hear of your love life dilemma. I thought for SURE you were living happily-ever-after in Canada . . . you were so sure that this was IT, and then you disappeared. Let's talk about that one over a drink or two someday.

Gotta go. The girls will be home soon.

Take care of you, too.
Mark

_____

Subject: Hi
Date: Tue, 18 May 2003 6:35 AM
From: Lisa
To: Mark

Hey you,

Been thinking about you and wanted you to know that I took your advice of making *me* the center of my universe and so much has changed! I have let Alex go completely, started dating (nothing serious) and Zac is doing great. I am on a good path.

I've been working with the life coaches I recently met. They've written a book on relationship boundaries - something I could use! I help them market their book in exchange for their coaching services and plan on starting coaching school myself.

Zac and I went to their house for dinner tonight and had an amazing evening of insightful conversation, hearty laughter, wine and Chinese food. As Zac slept in the backseat on the way home I was thinking: *of all the men I've known, who would have fit in the scene tonight? Who would have enjoyed the evening and appreciated the dynamic energy?*

You.

Subject: (no subject)
Date: Sat, 24 May 2003 8:51 PM
From: Mark
To: Lisa

Just a quick note to say I got your email re: your work with the life coaches. You'll do well with them. I'm happy to hear you've moved on from Alex and the doc's office.

The big news here is that we will be making a trip to Ashland, Oregon to check out the possibility of moving up there, perhaps as early as summer. We need a house that we can afford, a quieter life, and a small-town community. There's even a horse club up there. We keep hearing great things about this area so we're gonna go see if the reality matches the fantasy. House prices in the Bay Area continue to be a joke, and now that we're ready to buy we thought it best to blow off California and seek out a new life elsewhere. More later . . .

Oh! James Taylor is touring with my favorite drummer, Steve Gadd. This is such a great match that you *must* see this show if you can.
Mark

Subject: (no subject)
Date: Sun, 25 May 2003 8:59 AM
From: Lisa
To: Mark

Hi Mark,

Great to hear from you. Things are moving along with the coaches, and though I am still at the doc's office (to make a living) I have a different perspective about that job. Viewing it as an opportunity to gain more experience in the lecture world, knowing that it will benefit my coaching career, makes the work more interesting.

As for Alex, yes I have moved on, though not without some pangs of sadness from time to time. I poured a lot of love and energy into our relationship yet had to walk completely away because of his erratic moods and rage. We can't even be friends. It's sad but I'm fine. I've been seeing someone I like, but am approaching this relationship differently, stating my needs and establishing boundaries without hesitation or apology. I'm willing to walk away if we are not on the same page. Focusing on the new things in my life, and on Zac, continues to keep us at the center of my universe.

Thinking of a change of venue, huh? I hope it works out for you. I just talked to Cathy (remember her?) and they have been thinking of moving out of the Bay Area, too. Funny, this is the time in our lives that should feel the most 'settled' and it seems so many of us are working towards following a new path.

Look forward to hearing from you soon, my friend.

Lis

three

Subject: Hey
Date: Wed, 28 Jan 2004 4:11 AM
From: Lisa
To: Mark

Hi Mark,

It was great to talk with you again after so long . . .

It sounds like things are good with you. I can't tell you how much my life has changed this past year and the fulfillment I have found by being still and listening to what I really want in my life. I spent so much time chasing after external relationships to fill the void I felt, and I only needed to look within. Like Dorothy in Oz.

Please take a look at my coaching website when you have a chance. I would love your feedback. I realize that I have been doing this work all my life. Now that I've studied it and taken it seriously, all is coming together, although I know in my heart my *real* conscious study began with you many years ago in California.

Lis

Subject: hey yourself! From Mark
Date: Wed, 28 Jan 2004 5:36AM

From: Mark
To: Lisa

Nice website! Well done! Nice picture, too. You'll do well with this.

More later . . .

_____
Subject: Hi
Date: Wed, 10 Feb 2004 6:57 PM
From: Lisa
To: Mark

Hope all is good with you!

You have been popping up recently . . . in my thoughts, in a dream, and then I ran across an old photo of you last night. Hmmm. Makes me think about what a positive impact you have made on my life and that you still continue to show up. I am grateful.

Hope we get a chance to talk soon. Write when you can.

Lis

_____
Subject: Hey, it's Mark
Date: Tue, 17 Feb 2004 9:31 PM
From: Mark
To: Lisa

Here's a link to a commencement speech by Pat Metheny for Berklee College Of Music (where I went to school for a year in Boston) . . .

Lisa, you have to read this, and be sure to read Chick Corea's and James Taylor's. Very inspiring. I wanted to share it with you . . . makes me want to run downstairs and play my drums and record an album of the songs I've written. Enjoy.

Mark

_____
Subject: Hi
Date: Wed, 18 Feb 2004 2:34PM
From: Lisa
To: Mark

Hey Mark,

Thanks for sharing that with me! I read Pat's and Taylor's and Sting's so far and am working down the list. I'm glad you're inspired. Music is one of the fundamental things that make you YOU.

Hope all is well. Things here are good. A bit slow, and I am starting to market my coaching practice. I have been really into yoga and love the changes in me and my life as a result. As a happy byproduct I am working with my yoga instructor on his personal training/nutrition website in exchange for personal training sessions at my house. How cool is that?

Subject: Hey
Date: Fri, 30 Mar 2004 1:24 AM
From: Lisa
To: Mark

Haven't heard from you . . . hope all is well.

Lis

Subject: Re: Hey
Date: Wed, 31 Mar 2004 2:20 PM
From: Mark
To: Lisa

Sorry, things got pretty fucked up since we last talked. Almost quit my job on Friday, then stressful weekend of horse stuff. Got home late Sunday night and took Monday off from work, then had a meeting with the Calico band (music and old friends). Doing much better now. I'll be in touch . . .

Subject: Hi
Date: Tue, 18 May 2004 2:01 AM
From: Lisa
To: Mark

What's up, my friend? Been thinking of you and hoping life has taken an upward turn.

Things are good in my world. Started writing in earnest. Had an article published and did my first motivational speaking engagement! Woo Hoo! Mark, I am loving what I'm doing. My clients are kicking ass and creating amazing things in their lives. I feel so blessed to be a part of it. Zac is great and looking forward to the end of the school year.

Oh, by the way, we will be in the Bay Area August 10 -16 . . .

Lis

Subject: Hey Mark
Date: Thu, 26 Jul 2004 3:21 AM
From: Lisa
To: Mark

So . . . what's up? I hope you are doing good, enjoying summer. Haven't heard from you since my last note.

We will be in your neighborhood in a couple weeks and would love to see you. Hope there's a chance we can get together even if it's to stop by with Zac and say hi to all. Please let me know. It would not feel right to be in the Bay Area and not see you.

So much good is happening! My coaching practice is starting to slowly grow. I've done a few speaking engagements and am publishing my second article! I actually spoke last weekend about dream collages as a way of using visualization and affirmation in achieving goals. You've been there since the beginning, turning me on to creating collages in the early '80's. Remember all those hours clipping things out of magazines on my living room floor, listening to albums and drinking wine? We manifested a lot back then . . .

There is also a new man, a good man that you would like. He's ridiculously smart and fun and we are really enjoying getting to know one another.

Anyway, please let me know that you got this and if we can say hey. If not, that's cool, too. Just let me know.

Lis

Subject: Hey
Date: Wed, 11 Aug 2004 5:03 PM
From: Mark
To: Lisa

Sorry for the delay in reply. Things here are not good and it doesn't look like a visit will happen this time around. Maybe next time. Sorry.

Mark

Subject: re: Hey
Date: Thu, 12 Aug 2004 9:21 AM
From: Lisa
To: Mark

Aww . . . that's too bad. We're here in the East Bay till Sunday then off to Nan's in Marin. If anything changes, let me know.

Lis

Subject: The Universe has other plans. . .
Date: Fri, 13 Aug 2004 5:21 AM
From: Mark
To: Lisa

Turns out the girls will unexpectedly be off to a horse show for the weekend. I'm free. What are you up to tonight?

Subject: re: The Universe has other plans. . .
Date: Fri, 13 Aug 2004 9:21 AM
From: Lisa
To: Mark

Well, whaddya know? I'm going out for dinner with Mary to Bruno's in downtown Lafayette if you want to meet us for a drink after 8 . . .

Subject: re: The Universe has other plans. . .
Date: Fri, 13 Aug 2004 3:30 PM
From: Mark
To: Lisa

I'll be there.

Subject: Article
Date: Thu, 9 Sep 2004 2:33 PM
From: Lisa
To: Mark

Hope all is well with you. Just want to touch base. Here is the article I just had published! Unfortunately for me, the article has a better ending than the reality of my latest relationship (sigh). Guess I'll have to think about Plan B and the dream you had about us meeting up in Italy someday . . . LOL

Hope you and yours are very well.

Lis

Subject: Hi from Mark
Date: Mon, 13 Sep 2004 12:53 PM
From: Mark

To: Lisa

Hi Lis . . . read your article the other day. Where'd you get it published? Nice job!

Still busy as all get-out here. Started playing drums with a blues band as of last Saturday night. Man, that was fun! Looks like they play a couple of times a month, so music is back in my life again.

Had a powerful experience with a South African shaman/medicine man at an event held at a friend's house. I was asked to bring my djembe (drum) to play during the event. Later I received a personal blessing from him and it seems my drumming ancestors are calling. More on that another time.

Again, well done and congrats on your article. A published author!

Subject: Hi
Date: Tue, 14 Sep 2004 1:40 PM
From: Lisa
To: Mark

Very cool to hear that you are playing music again. It is such a part of your spirit. Your encounter with the shaman sounds incredibly powerful. Indeed, the ancestors are calling. I'm thrilled you listened.

My article was published in Chicago Suburban Woman magazine. That's why it had a slant toward women, though the principles are true for us all. I give my first workshop in November. I am excited about all the developments in my work. Autumn is here . . . one of the (few) benefits of the Midwest.

Started reading *Bridge Across Forever* again.

Be well and happy.

Subject: Re: Hi
Date: Wed, 15 Sep 2004 5:20 AM
From: Mark
To: Lisa

I just finished reading *One* by Richard Bach again after finding it in a box of giveaway stuff. I've been reading a lot of manifestation and human potential material lately. Currently reading *The Life We Are Given* by Michael Murphy and George Leonard. Also have been sucked into Savannah's world of reading all the Tamora Pierce stuff. Really fun. Horses, magic, nature, women knights. . . excellent! Savannah has recently wanted to add a (plastic) sword to her horse play as she gallops around the yard.

We leave for New Mexico and Colorado next week. I SO can't wait!

Hugs to you . . .
Mark

_____
Subject: Hi
Date: Wed, 15 Sep 2004 5:21 PM
From: Lisa
To: Mark

I will pick up *The Life We Are Given* and check it out. I have accumulated quite a library of books on personal growth which I love sharing with my clients. One of my fave authors is Miguel Ruiz and his *The Four Agreements* and *Mastery of Love*. Both very powerful.

Glad to hear about your trip. Sounds awesome. I remember saying once that I would spend my twilight years in New Mexico, finally with my soul partner.

Though the coast of Italy sounds good, too.

_____
Subject: Hi
Date: Wed, 15 Oct 2004 12:10 PM
From: Lisa
To: Mark

Hope you had a great Friday! Mine was awesome. Met with my coach first thing (which is always enlightening) and then had a couple of clients, worked on my final exam, then got a call about speaking for the Women's Club in November. My workshop is filling up, too. Whew. All good.

Lis

_____
Subject: PS
Date: Wed, 15 Oct 2004 5:25 PM
From: Lisa
To: Mark

I've just been invited to contribute a chapter to a book about purpose and passion!

The hits just keep on coming. ;)

Subject: OK . . .
Date: Wed, 5 Nov 2004 7:05 AM
From: Lisa
To: Mark

Good to chat with you. Love that you are writing a drum article for
Modern Drummer magazine. Can't wait to read it.

Subject: Hey
Date: Fri, 3 Dec 2004 12:52 PM
From: Lisa
To: Mark

Here is the chapter so far for the Purpose and Passion book. It needs work!
Talk with my editor today.

Subject: drum article
Date: Tue, 11 Jan 2005 3:26 AM
From: Mark
To: Lisa

Finished the drum article yesterday while sitting in a Starbucks. It
was a nice day.

Mark

Subject: re: drum article
Date: Tue, 11 Jan 2005 2:52 PM
From: Lisa
To: Mark

Wow, great story about working in the drum shop. It pulls in the reader
and gives a glimpse into your drumming history.

More later . . .

Subject: re: drum article
Date: Mon, 17 Jan 2005 9:52 PM
From: Lisa
To: Mark

Hey! How are you doing? Would love to chat about your article. Got the
final on my chapter today. All is a go. Write or call . . .

Subject: re: drum article

Date: Fri, 21 Jan 2005 9:52 PM
From: Lisa
To: Mark

What's up? Haven't heard from you at all. Hope all is good. Interested in hearing how the writing is going. Have you sent the article out?

Things here are cooking in the New Year. Busy with clients, I have the workshop next week and have 10 signed up for it. I spoke last week for Chicago Coaches Alliance and it went great. Finished my chapter, and the book goes to press next week. I can't wait to have it in my hands. I will be on my friend's radio show *Let's Talk Relationships* on February 2 which will be fun. We'll be talking about my You-*don't*-complete-me theory. LOL

Zac is great. Finished this quarter with good grades after a slight slump. We have lots of snow so he's going snowboarding in Wisconsin this weekend with my sister. Unlike me, he loves the winter! I'm still dating Jerry, that's all good, though he is in Barcelona this week working a show. I have some time to myself the next couple days.

Please tell me how things are in your world. I miss you.

Subject: ???
Date: Thu, 27 Jan 2005 6:37 PM
From: Lisa
To: Mark

Hey. What's up? Puzzled by your disappearance.

Lis

Subject: re: ???
Date: Fri, 28 Jan 2005 1:58 PM
From: Mark
To: Lisa

Sorry 'bout not staying in touch . . . lots to deal with around here since quitting my job, including a HUGE blowout with Mariah a week after I quit.

We went to Yosemite the weekend after that - Savannah's birthday snow trip with one of her horsey girlfriends - which was great. Rented a condo a half-hour from the valley. Monday, MLK holiday, we packed up and went cross-country skiing. We had perfect weather, the kids did great, fun for all. I took my laptop, but not enough alone time to accomplish anything.

Tuesday, Wednesday, laid low, did a bit of writing . . . oh! The Modern Drummer article . . . I had already sent it in just before emailing it to you . . . two days later they emailed back saying it was well written but they already had a bunch of similar first-person stories on file, so thanks but no thanks.

That Thursday was the big blowout with Mariah. Lots of yelling, name-calling, tears, with me letting it all out about how I'm just trying to have a good life, to just live and work in a way that feels connected to who I am. Part of quitting my job was to take the time to figure that out. Her nudging me to find work and buy a house and all that was absolutely the wrong version of support that I needed right now. It became an argument about how I don't understand her, which led to an argument about something else, which led to an argument about something else, which led to me driving to the coast, walking the beach and journaling . . .

Came home to everything having calmed down and things being actually nice for the next few days. Helped get the girls out of town for a weekend horse thing last Saturday. Did a side job that afternoon before a blues band gig in the evening. Sunday morning went to Sacramento to rehearse for tonight's gig, as well as reconnect with long-time musician friend, Bill. Had breakfast with him before rehearsal, which was great since we hadn't had a heart-to-heart for way too long. Rehearsal was good, then a long, back roads drive home.

Had an Odyssey Of the Mind meeting Monday night with my group of kids, then went up to our land Tuesday morning to look in on the property and take some space. I thought this would be a great writer experience - alone on 50 acres in a small shed during a two-day rainstorm - but I did more journaling and reading than story writing. In fact, I got so frustrated about feeling so blocked and uninspired that I tried writing a simple children's story just for fun: *Once upon a time there was a little girl who loved horses . . .* and got stuck there. Nothing. I had the laptop in front of me for an hour and a half and wrote absolutely nothing. Tried re-reading some previous stuff in hopes of adding to it. Nothing.

Then came the depression about how hard writing is, that I really can't write, and what could I possibly have to say that anyone would want to read. This was all late Wednesday night. Finally I thought I'd write a long letter to you, letting you know all that's gone on since we last talked, but aside from not knowing where to start, feeling depressed, and it being midnight, I was spent, and crashed. Packed up yesterday morning and spontaneously went to a hot springs on the way home, hoping that would make me feel better, or help me shift my mood. It didn't. The last two hours of the drive home I listened to Michael Meade's "The Water of

Life", which reminded me that sometimes not knowing where one is going is exactly the correct way to get one's self back to the kingdom.

I leave soon for Sacramento to set up for tonight's gig so I'll close for now. This may be the best I can do about staying in touch. Calls to Chicago would be a red flag to Mariah, and in the meantime I'm just trying to do my life. Sorry 'bout not keeping you in the loop more frequently.

Sounds like all is well with you, but no surprises there. I can tell you're on a big roll into a bigger life, and I enjoy hearing from you how well you're doing. Take care.

Mark

Subject: Hey you
Date: Thu, 3 Feb 2005 5:15 PM
From: Lisa
To: Mark

Hello, my friend . . .

Hope the work situation has landed you where you want to be. Any new developments?

Things here are great. Zac and I are both doing well. The radio show was a blast and quite good from the feedback I received! Very fun and I'll be their guest again on March 2. I'm gearing up now for the Women's Expo and have been working on my booth. I am excited to have a place to meet lots of women to talk about coaching and promote workshops, etc. My last one went so well that I am looking forward to many more! Things are good with Jerry and he is really supportive of my work, which is great, especially given his resources at his office to create things for me like banners and booth display pieces and such. Very cool. We have a nice relationship and it continues to develop. I am being open and am consistently intrigued by his integrity. There is a synergy that works, which includes my being somewhat reticent. A good thing.

Keep me in the loop. Let me know what comes next for you and keep sending what you write. You are in my thoughts and I want to always be a source of support though it all. I miss you . . .

Hugs,
Lis

Subject: Hey you
Date: Thu, 10 Mar 2005 5:02 PM

From: Lisa
To: Mark

There is some new writing in the works and while going over these notes from an essay I wrote a year ago, I read this:

I can still feel that overwhelming sense of being alone. During that time I had so many people around me but felt adrift. One of the most important people then was my friend Mark. He brought such a pure love to my life. Mark and I met at a gig he was playing the week I moved to San Francisco in October of 1982. We became instant friends. I had a crush on him, but over the years I accepted that a lifelong friendship would be more valuable than being one of his six-month love affairs. He resurfaces in my life over and over, just when I need him. He always answers my cosmic page.

Beep, beep, beep . . .

Are you there?

_____
Subject: Re: Hey you
Date: Fri, 11 Mar 2005 8:20 AM
From: Mark
To: Lisa

Now I understand the reaction you got from one of your former loves who had a hard time "showing up" for you as your personal star began rising ever higher. There's only so much cheerleading he could do for you from the ground before feeling left behind, feeling small and insignificant as the distance between you increased . . .

From way down here the sight of you and your great life going higher and higher means that, eventually, I need to get back to my own rising star project. Problem is, when I open the door to my workroom, the sight of all those parts strewn everywhere, the partially completed sections lying on their sides, the well-worn instruction manual with its missing page . . . I just can't look at it all without feeling a little tired, a little stupid, like there's something wrong with me. You're out there flying through the clouds with that I-can't-believe-how-great-this-is smile on your face, and I'm back here trying to get my own flying machine built so I can fly with you. I just let out a big sigh, turn on some music, get on my knees, and start in where I left off before you called to say: "Hey, I'm flying again! Come watch what I can do NOW!"

No excuses, no explanations, no justification . . . I just turn the beeper off so I can concentrate on getting this flying machine built.

_____

Subject: Re: Hey you
Date: Fri, 11 Mar 2005 9:37 PM
From: Lisa
To: Mark

Thanks for your beautiful words, Mark. Your plane will fly. Seems you could benefit from my workshop, my friend. Wish you were here. Please keep the cosmic pager on silent and look at it once in awhile in case I really need you, 'k? I still do. Call me, please.
Lis

___

Subject: Re: Hey you
Date: Wed, 16 Mar 2005 3:41 PM
From: Lisa
To: Mark

I have read your email over and over. I miss you.

Please call.

___

Subject: Re: Hey you
Date: Tue, 4 Apr 2005 2:29 PM
From: Lisa
To: Mark

Hi Mark,

I wanted to tell you that I got my book. I am officially a published author! My first book signing is in a couple of weeks at Transitions Bookplace in the city. This is pretty exciting and I go there today to bring over a box of books so they can display them. I would love to send you one.

While I am excited about this book, it's still a co-authored achievement. I want to create my own work, so that is what I am doing. The work is hard and slow, and, well . . . you know. Going through a lot of really personal material has feelings come up that are very cathartic. You are the one I wish I could talk to now.

So I will leave it at that. I have asked to speak with you twice now, Mark, and I won't persist. I know that you hear the page even with the pager off. I know that you are where you are and if you wanted to speak with me you would. I have to admit I hate that I don't get a say in whether I can talk with my dear friend now. You are the one who understands me and holds so much history with me.

I miss you so much.

Subject: Re: Hey you
Date: Mon, 9 May 2005 2:04 PM
From: Lisa
To: Mark

Hi, it's me again . . .

I hope you weren't angry with my last message. I was really missing you
and had a lot to share and I was frustrated that I couldn't call you. You
were there when the seed was planted for that book and I wanted to
celebrate the harvest with you. Lots of great opportunities are coming to
me. So exciting, a little scary.

Jerry and I broke up. That sadness has been an energy drain but has
opened my heart. My, I have learned so much in the past year.

I would love to hear from you . . . and wish all things good for you.

beep, beep

Lis

Subject: read when you have a few minutes
Date: Wed, 17 Jun 2005 1:44 AM
From: Lisa
To: Mark

I read the last email from you periodically, to hear you again, your voice,
your spirit. I've been picturing you on your knees in your workroom,
trying to build your flying machine. God, I miss you. Lately I have been
licking my wounds, trying to write, enjoying the bursts of flight with the
book, then feeling a bit let down when I land, not knowing when I'll get to
go up again. It's addictive, you know, speaking, teaching, inspiring others.
I love it, yet it takes a lot of work to keep getting opportunities to do it.

Last night I made a list of the Men Who Have Mattered and their
contribution to my path. I bolded the ones that Really Mattered. Your
name is bold, of course (It's a short list).

Hoping you receive this with all the warm intention I send it with,
knowing that I can't help myself but to continue to share with you, unless
you ask me to please stop.

Lis

PS: Maybe my dimly-shining star is easier to respond to? Hoping so. I'm learning to embrace the dark times, the painful stuff and the moments stuck on the ground due to technical difficulties, for it is then that we get to repair, plan and revise our flight plans (and maybe catch a great lightning storm). Please just let me know you're okay . . . (hug)

_____

Subject: Re: read when you have a few minutes
Date: Tue 28 Jun 2005 3:31 PM
From: Mark
To: Lisa

Yeah, I'm fine. Got back late last night from 2 weeks in New Mexico and Colorado. I feel different, hence this email.

Can't and don't want to explain the long silence. It's all there in my last email. The work-in-progress metaphor (scattered parts, missing page from manual, etc) was dead-on accurate, and has nothing to do with you. It's just me, paying attention to my instincts, with little desire to justify or explain myself and not feel guilty about it.

I see you soaring, and I can't seem to get my own flying machine off the ground. Fly on. I'll be up there eventually, you know I will. We will one day drink much wine and tell many stories.

Thanks for your concern. And by the way, please don't equate not hearing from me with not thinking of you. You of all people should know better than that.

You are STILL in my heart, Lisa.

Mark

four

Subject: Hello from Mark
Date: Sat, 8 Oct 2005 3:31 PM
From: Mark
To: Lisa

Send me your mailing address asap. I've been writing an ongoing letter to you for a month and I want to send it.

Mark

_____

September 12- October 10, 2005:
Excerpts from a handwritten letter from Mark . . .

Monday morning, Sept. 12, 2005

I'm stopping in the middle of my routine morning to reach out for help. I thought it might be a good idea to write a journal entry *to* someone in the hope it would help me get a handle on what it is that, for weeks now, has me spinning out into feelings of depression, uncertainty, and . . . well . . . suicide.

But hey, hold on . . . I'm not planning my death. It's just that my most recent attempt at book material began with writing down the truth of where I'm *at* and what came out was a quick description of a bunch of things I have going for me, things which on the surface or in the eyes of others appear to be points in my favor: looking five to ten years younger than I am, musical talent, skilled carpenter being well-paid to make beautiful things, good cook, good friends, and potential, potential, potential. Following this description comes the line: *So why would I want to kill myself?*

It appears that God is not listening to my pleas for guidance. *Hello?!? HELLO!? Anybody in here? It's me, Mark, the guy with all the talent and creativity who can't punch through to the other side of himself to make contact with his life's purpose. What? I'm LIVING my life's purpose? Are you NUTS? How much longer do I have to go on feeling like some great life is just around the corner only to find out I was wrong? Is that YOU inspiring me to keep going, or is that some part of me that can't let go of a false self-image? I'm so DONE with the struggle and the waiting. Hello? HELLO?!!?*

I'm waiting for the ah-HA!, the flash of inspiration and vision that makes moving forward *effortless*, the feeling of *wanting* to do what I need to do because I'm so certain of the outcome I want to produce.

It's very important to me that I *feel* God working through me, that the work I do, the music I play, the relationships I have, the actions I take towards creating my life's path . . . all these things ring hollow if I'm moving through life by *my* cleverness, *my* planning and efforting to give myself the life that *I* want. I've been living that way for quite awhile and as time passes it all begins to feel more and more selfish . . .

I go to the gym instead of going home; I sit on the couch watching a movie when I could be filling out loan papers; I read the newspaper online when I could be studying for my contractor's license. And here I am, *right now,* sitting in my truck, writing, instead of working on my customer's house for the last hour or more. I could go to the ocean to write, pray, cry, and no one would know: daughter in school, wife at work, customer out of town until Thursday. . .

I notice a mental battle with feelings of guilt: blowing off work in the pursuit of some cathartic breakthrough that will push my reset button so I can return home a new and focused man. Shit, how can a guy be fifty, not own his home, and *still* be looking for a connection to his life's purpose? I've read the books, I wrote down the feelings, I went to the workshops, I fell to the earth, sobbing . . . but it's been what feels like a long dry spell since I was in "contact" (hmm . . . this metaphor could easily be superimposed on you . . .)

Tuesday, September 13 - 7am

I ended up at the ocean yesterday after all, sitting in the sand, talking out loud to God, asking for help, guidance and stamina to get me through the coming changes: new job, house-buying, contractor's license. But isn't this "let go, let God" stuff just a bit immature for a fifty year-old?

My evening ended with an argument with Mariah about the *details* of how and when these changes are going to take place. On and on with the *push, push, push.* I tell her that all will be well, that it's important for me to pick the right company, that getting upset with me for not having better answers to her fear-based questions just makes me feel like she doesn't trust or support me. Well, we just get louder and angrier until finally I have to withdraw from what becomes a totally useless conversation. *Ugh.* After she and Savannah left for the evening barn chores I called a friend of mine - nearly called you - to help me out of my despair. He helped me realize that perhaps Mariah and I are on different spiritual paths, and that my faith needn't be shaken by her fear and insecurity . . .

So enough of the wife-bashing stuff. My spirituality is deepening, these changes are necessary and temporary, and a new-and-improved life is coming.

Thursday, October 6 – 7am

At the barn to walk our horse as part of the rehab for a hoof injury, but the horses have just been given their hay so I'll write to you while they eat.

I've called four different remodeling companies this week—all of them advertising that they're looking for help—and I haven't heard back from any of them. It's a bit strange. So of course I begin thinking: *there must be something else trying to come through.* Whatever. I feel like I've spent most of 2005 trying to make contact with the "eventual me".

Monday, October 10 – 7am

Got your email with your address this morning but forgot to bring the envelope I'd set aside, so one more page before sending off all this writing.

I'm sure you were surprised to hear from me after all these months. At this writing I haven't re-read any of the earlier stuff I'm sending you. I only remember going to the beach that one day and essentially talking to you on paper to help put my thoughts in some sort of context. Please forgive my disappearing act - it helped to keep my energies focused around home and family while I sorted out my stuff. As you can see I still turn to you when I've needed to work out some of my more personal and intimate issues. If I thought I could get the support I needed by discussing these things with Mariah, I would have . . . but I'm not willing to be let down again by opening up to the wrong person. I'm 50 now, and I feel pretty confident about where I can and can't go for the support I need.

During part of this past summer I even went through a phase of not caring if anyone thought I was being a selfish jerk or not. I just made a point of not *intentionally* hurting anyone. There was some freedom in that, but one aspect of living that way was that it came with a certain level of isolation . . .

I trust all is well with you. Don't think I haven't thought about you or wanted to call. You may have a lot to say after reading all this stuff, as well as filling me in on what's been up with you.

Blessings & love to you,
Mark

_____

Subject: photos
Date: Mon, 5 Dec 2005 7:18 AM
From: Mark
To: Lisa

Phone minutes on my truck phone are expensive, so haven't added any since our talk in October after my letter. I have a music CD to send you, along w/ stories about each song. I'll tell you when it's coming.

Here is a picture of the blues band I've been playing with, taken at the hot rod show we played last Saturday night. Just saw the one of you and I taken by your friend Mary last year during your visit. o*offf!* The first thing I noticed was how tired my eyes look, and how badly I need a haircut. But YOU! Hubba-hubba . . .

Mark

_____

Subject: re: photos
Date: Fri, 9 Dec 2005 6:55 AM
From: Lisa
To: Mark

Hi there. . .

Thanks for the pix. Here is a picture of my latest dream collage. I'm trying to pack a lot into the coming year, huh?

Subject: Hey
Date: Sun, 11 Dec 2005 7:55 AM
From: Mark
To: Lisa

Random thoughts without editing . . .

The first attempt at writing you (at 4am on Friday) included the return of old feelings of being trapped and frustrated by making the wrong choice of partners. Became a bit despondent and even angry with myself when I don't write, drum, or otherwise move with my creativity when the moment inspires me because my wife is nearby, or coming home soon, or expecting me to do something else, or whatever. I'll spare you the complaint session - I know how you feel about that - but I find myself turning over and over in my mind the feelings of self-repression - the ACTS of self-repression - and the frequency with which they come up. I'm keeping some part of myself prisoner . . . son of a bitch . . .

Saw the picture of your collage, which brought up memories of you and I doing them together, and wow, I want to do one now and oh shit, my wife will want me to explain the meaning behind everything I put on it and won't it be a drag because there's not likely to be a significant portion of it having to do with love/relationships/family. I sense it will mostly have to do with finding deeper meaning, getting the writer in me to come out, *what am I here to do?* questions, and shit, how much longer can I go on living in the shadow of someone I rarely enjoy being with? Made a 200-mile drive south to a niece's graduation yesterday, a solid half-hour of which was spent considering the long-term effects of divorce. Even now I type as quietly as I can (it's 7:48am) so as not to be asked, "What were you doing on the computer? I heard a lot of typing . . . who were you writing to?"

Gotta work today. The new kitchen refacing company is looking more and more like too much work for too little money, but I'll give it 10 jobs and this is only my first for them. I work alone (my preference) and I just love the old couple whose kitchen I'm doing.

Nice collage. I'll take a pic of mine, too.

Mark

Subject: Hey
Date: Mon, 12 Dec 2005 6:27 AM
From: Mark
To: Lisa

Our phone conversation about your relationship with this guy Jon had me thinking . . .

Relationships are such a crap shoot. How many times have we felt that he/she is The One? I was so sure, so many times through the years, learning from the most recent break-up in those days, thinking I was now clear and informed as to what my real needs were, but lo and behold, wrong again . . . and again. Now I'm jaded and cynical. My memories of being truly happy and enjoying the quality of my life are almost entirely void of being *with* someone. It was during my road trips to the Southwest that I felt truly happy; the gypsy-like wandering through towns and vast expanses of nature, finding special, magical places to explore, write, take pictures . . . always comfortable and at home in the middle of some beautiful nowhere.

You used to tease me about how I wanted everything to be "effortless" - including my hair - but it's not such a bad way to live. It's much better than efforting and striving to *become:* to get to a place, a person, a position. This job I'm doing is mirroring exactly what I'm talking about: efforting my ass off to get at the *money* (and not very much, relative to the amount of energy expended), at the expense of a quality of life which is infinitely better for my Being.

Live and learn, live and learn, live and learn . . .

Mark

_____

Subject: Hey
Date: Tue, 13 Dec 2005 6:58 AM
From: Mark
To: Lisa

Sorry to cut our chat short . . .

Two things, referring to Jon's level of involvement as "passive fear". . .

That's probably accurate. Also, how long have you known this guy? Is it too soon to decide if it will work out or not? I mean, people get married after knowing each other 5, 7, or 10 months, only to discover a few YEARS later that *whoops! I was wrong about that one!*

It seems clear as to your intentions and desires re: Jon. Your frustration with his fear is well founded, especially if you're certain that he will never really come around, staying stuck in "wait-for-me-while-I-decide-what-I'll-do" mode. It's possible you're expecting too much too soon, OR what you're responding to is some aspect of your soul or spirit which knows what the future holds with this guy. Pretty good bet you've spent way more time at the Soul Gym than he has, "working out" and getting in shape to know what your strengths and limitations are.

I wonder what would happen if he *pretended* to not be afraid for a week, and just tried on what it would be like to be 100% *with you*, and not listen to the voices in his head talking him out of you. Gotta go . . .

Subject: Hey
Date: Sat, 24 Dec 2005 7:57 AM
From: Mark
To: Lisa

Merry Christmas to you and thank you for the e-card. Hope your birthday was great! Thought about you.

We are so, SO far behind with Xmas here. The tree's not even decorated yet - nothing - and I just sat down to wrap gifts and listen to some music. I still need to shop some. Got my poster board for my collage and started cutting stuff out. Contractor's license by Spring!

Working my ass off at the new job - long hours but not enough money - so I'm already planning to move on. Love the people, getting all kinds of side job offers, so in general all I do is work, eat and sleep. Not much fun going on.

You got tons of snow, right?

Blessings

Subject: re: Hey
Date: Sun, 25 Dec 2005 6:44 AM
From: Lisa
To: Mark

Merry Christmas, my friend! Yes, we have snow and it's really pretty. Christmas is one day of the year that I don't mind it. LOL

Birthday was good . . . 45! Time sure flies. Looking forward to a new year and all that it will bring. Hope it has good things in store for you, too.

hug.

Subject: Hey
Date: Fri, 30 Dec 2005 7:14 AM

From: Mark
To: Lisa

Rains are here, big storm today and tonight. Would love to spend the day sipping tea and exchanging stories with you on days like this. Called a friend a few days ago, asking him to pray for me. Been depressed and pessimistic about almost everything. This "meaningful work" thing haunts me.

This job with this company ain't it, and efforts to adopt a spiritual perspective lack inspiration. I have been getting up early and clipping out stuff for my dream collage, even pulled out the laptop at 5am a couple of mornings ago to write a bit. Thought writing The Truth would be an inspiring approach, and ended up with one long paragraph about how I used to think I was this compassionate, spiritual guy, capable of loving my wife no matter how she looked or acted but turns out I'm full of shit because I'm also a pig-asshole-jerk who can't stand being told that I need to get over myself and love her for who she is. Oh great, another whining session. Poor me, etc. with some anger thrown in. That's when I started clipping stuff out for my collage; a better use of my time and my head. Then I read an article in the business section of the paper about the realities of getting one's book published . . . *fuck* . . .

So how are you ? :-)

Mark

_____
Subject: Hey
Date: Tue, 3 Jan 2006 6:37 AM
From: Mark
To: Lisa

Thank you! Talking to you last night woke me out of my stupor, and things are moving a bit. Began really reading and studying for my contractor's license.

Had a very interesting breakthrough the other night after causing a scene with the wife when, out of the blue and for no justifiable reason, I cancelled myself out of a dinner date we had with another family, an hour before we were supposed to be there. Instead I stayed home, spontaneously writing a letter to a backpacking/musician buddy from high school days who I haven't had any contact with for ten years.

So a shift of some kind has taken place. I like the direction I'm pointed in, and your support was an influence. If I can just stay committed and focused.

Subject: Hey. . .
Date: Tue, 3 Jan 2006 7:49 AM
From: Lisa
To: Mark

Happy New Year!

You're welcome. Glad to hear you are pointed in the right direction :-)
Here are a few pix of Zac from Christmas. Send some of Savannah when
you have a chance.

Hugs.

Subject: re: Hey. . .
Date: Fri, 13 Jan 2006 7:59 AM
From: Mark
To: Lisa

Thanks for the pics of Zac. Haven't seen one since he was ten or
something. Holy cow, he's big now, and he *really* looks like you.

The next movie you rent will be *Carolina*, with Shirley MacLaine and
Julia Stiles. Funny, sweet. Love, friendship, writing, family. . . parts of it
will make you think of us.

Had the day off yesterday. While I was waiting for new tires to be put on
the truck I had the laptop and started in on "Mr. Hang In There", about a
guy who has felt, his whole life, that great things were just around the
corner - some of them Divinely inspired - but always seemed to take much
longer to materialize than he thought they would.

Off to work now. We leave for our weekend horse thing at 6am Saturday
morning, then home Sunday for the premiere of *24*.

Big ol' hug to you

Mark

Subject: wow
Date: Thu, 19 Jan 2006 2:19 PM
From: Lisa
To: Mark

I watched *Carolina*. Thank you for suggesting I see it. You were
absolutely right.

When Albert handed her the galley of his book and she opened the page, something opened in me. When he said, "It's about us, Carolina. It's a love story", a sob rose up from deep in my soul. I wept for what was, what could have been and what will never be. And for what still *is* after 25 years of knowing you. I trust that what *will* be is our continued friendship and understanding of each other. That is timeless.

I send you a long hug and a tearful smile.

Lis

Subject: re: wow
Date: Fri, 20 Jan 2006 9:12 AM
From: Mark
To: Lisa

I knew you'd enjoy that movie. I didn't think it would affect you the way it did, but the emotion was clear - I felt it in your email. You know, if it wasn't for your encouragement I doubt I would be writing what little I do. I've got this collection of bits and pieces of stories and attempts at what I think are good ideas, but reach a dead end after a paragraph or two. Wednesday nights I take Savannah to her piano lesson and usually wait in the truck for her, using the hour to read or write. This last week I made an effort to write as though I would later send it to you, the subject being about how *everything is temporary. EVERYTHING!* The good stuff, the bad stuff, the times in life when things are going great, when the world comes crashing down with a personal tragedy or loss . . . it won't be permanent . . . none of it.

I got through about one long paragraph then fell asleep. Oooh, but it was raining the whole time, and there I was in my leather seat, writing/talking to you, so comfortable, quiet and pulled inside my Cancer crab shell, cozy and dry, the rain coming down through the dark . . .

I notice that I write differently with pen and paper than keyboard. It seems more personal and spontaneous with a pen. The keyboard makes me stop, read, and edit more. Can't seem to get a long enough flow going. Also, I rarely get more than an hour of writing time, especially now that I'm squeezing in study time for the contractor's license. Other times I *choose* the gym, drum practice, light reading, or a movie . . . like *Carolina*.

So I re-read your *Purpose & Passion* chapter this morning and come away - this time - with the reminder that I'm constantly *choosing* what to do with my time, like getting up @ 5am to make tea and write to you instead of studying, getting my tax info in order, or read the Chronicle online. It's after 6 now, and I have to shift gears in a half hour, get ready for work and Savannah off to school . . .

I'm proud of you. I like what you've written and that you're connected to what you're passionate about. I shall keep on keepin' on.

. . . hug . . .

Mark

_____
Subject: more wow
Date: Sun, 22 Jan 2006 8:59 AM
From: Lisa
To: Mark

I grabbed my journal and wrote while watching *Carolina*. I was glad that I responded to the moment and wrote down the emotion while I was feeling it. It surprised me. I wonder if it was partly because you told me to watch it and I knew you connected them to us? That movie made me think of all the choices we've made over the years and how even one small difference in those choices could have led us to a very different place.

hug.

five

Subject: Big Hey
Date: Thu, 09 Feb 2006 9:10 PM
From: Lisa
To: Mark

Where have you been? No news lately . . . what's up?

Busy here. Good stuff. My speaking gig for the teens went great and now I'm looking to speak for other teen outreach chapters. I loved being able to talk to kids about finding their passion and being true to themselves long before they get fucked up and have to hire a coach when they're middle-aged. LOL. There was amazing energy working with 100 teens. Zac will be attending the retreat next year. Wow.

My trip to Florida with Karen was great and I think it loosened something in me to be at the beach, allowing all this new stuff to flow through. I feel fluid. I wrote some there, though haven't written since I got back.

In the same space with Jon, doing more letting go than anything else. Most of the time I see that we are headed nowhere, then we'll have a great time together, a moment will catch me by surprise and I will think . . . *hmmm, maybe?* Keeping it in proper perspective and low on my energy food-chain feels like the best choice while I just focus on everything else in my life.

That movie really moved me. It brought up some really old feelings that I hadn't taken out and looked at for awhile. There are some similarities between how I feel sometimes with Jon and how I felt with you when we were young and would hang out for hours and *just be*, although I have changed a lot since then, I think.

And in some ways, not at all.

Hugs, my friend. Write back.

Lis

_____
Subject: Hey!
Date: Sun, 12 Feb 2006 9:28 AM
From: Mark
To: Lisa

This sentence is being written on Sunday morning, 9:30am, letting you know that the letter below was started a 1/2 hour after you sent me your last email on Thursday morning. I have way more to write, but the message below tells the story. . .

Good morning . . .

Two weeks ago I had The Job From Hell. It took several days longer than maybe it should have, but one thing after another had to be dealt with. For those two weeks I was pretty much a very grumpy guy . . . just ask my family. We celebrated finishing the job with a great dinner at a cool, crowded, noisy family restaurant last Friday night. After a glass of wine, some pasta and a pizza, all was well.

(7:45 pm.) I got cut off this morning when Mariah got up to see what I was doing up so early after going to bed so late. I've got side jobs going on for the next three days, and we're preparing for a four day trip to a horse event next week. I hope you got great weather for your trip. Man, the beach in

Florida musta been heaven, yes? Sounds like something changed for you a little bit during that trip . . .

(Friday, 6 am) Your reaction to the movie was stronger than I anticipated, I'll admit, but it moved me that it affected you so.

This storyline in my life where I secretly write you, go to the gym, or to a coffee shop to write - this "stealing" of moments and time to spend an hour or two doing some self-pleasing thing - is an inauthentic way to live. I make a choice whether or not to tell the truth about what I do based on the reaction I'm certain to get.

Now it's Friday night, 9:30pm. Just came in the door, the girls will be home soon, so I have a few minutes. Where was I? Stealing moments of "Me" time doesn't exactly suck because I get a few hours to myself for writing or working out and that's all good . . . but . . . I just don't get much - if any - positive reinforcement or support to go off on my own to do some pleasurable or nourishing thing. It's just easier to TAKE the time. So I write you when I can.

Hi there. It's 9am on Sunday morning and my first thought when I woke up @ 8, hearing the girls trying to get out of the house, was: *ahhh . . . they're leaving soon, and I can finish writing to Lisa before I head out . . .*

The last four days have been like the busy day ahead of me: zooming around, having to be someplace else, and not having enough down time to just hang out and relax. Even my visit to the gym yesterday was wedged in between the completion of another side job and having to get ready for the gig instead of getting home early enough to write to you some more.

So of course NOW I've lost the flow of where I started this letter, and all the stuff I wanted to get into has pretty much been forgotten. Can we just meet for drinks and dinner and breakfast and tea and coffee and lunch and drinks and dinner somewhere cool . . . like Tuscany?

Gotta run . . . again.

Subject: Big Hey
Date: Sun, 12 Feb 2006 9:10 PM
From: Mark
To: Lisa

I stand on the rotting back deck, look out over the back fence into and beyond the pasture behind our house, and as the lamb sausages cook on the grill I think: two glasses of wine are just the right amount to put my head in a place where I can laugh at how hard I am on myself about my so-called shortcomings and failures. Will I ever OWN my own house? Am I burning out on playing music? (The gig last night was good for about six songs, the rest of the night I watched the TV behind the bar AS we were playing) - and thank God I've had the last few hours to myself to cook, straighten up the house, take a bath, and write Lisa . . .

Been thinking about God a lot these days. Some part of me is calling out for help and guidance to overcome my critical and judgmental thinking about my work, my wife, and my situation in life. My good and longtime friend, Bill, came to my rescue one night last week. We had dinner together at the end of our respective work day and talked long about music, God, and well . . . all kinds of stuff.

This is the place I find myself in: big chunks of my life are not working for me, and I'm fragmented by attempting to please myself with whatever I decide I need at any given time, and fuck everybody else. Selfish? In part, yes. Do I care? In part, yes. The other part of me is calling out to clean up an emotional mess and get integrated and whole, instead of being split between *sometimes* acting one way, while being consciously aware that I want to act *another* way, to be a better human being, a higher-quality man.

In conclusion I own up to having had two glasses of wine to mellow me out after an intense several days of coming-and-going-and-coming-and-going . . . and then making time to write you to say: *You are one of my few and rare sources of true friendship, spiritual connectedness, and inspiration for a better-quality life . . . and my love for you cannot be defined in human terms*. Thank you, Lisa.

Mark

———

Subject: re: Big Hey
Date: Mon, 13 Feb 2006 6:32 AM
From: Lisa
To: Mark

You're welcome, Mark. That's all I can say right now. You've left me speechless (not an easy thing).

Lis

———

Subject: Yo
Date: Thu, 16 Feb 2006 6:02 AM
From: Mark
To: Lisa

I'll be out of town til Sunday night, leaving in a couple of hours. Check with you then.

_____

Subject: re: Yo
Date: Thu, 16 Feb 2006 6:17 AM
From: Lisa
To: Mark

Have a great time . . . a horse thing this weekend, right? Luck to Savannah!

Broke it off with Jon, by the way. Got your last emails a couple hours after I did that. Nice timing. I'll write more later for when you return about how your words struck me in just the place that needed comfort. No coincidences.

_____

Subject: re: Yo
Date: Sun, 19 Feb 2006 11:39 AM
From: Lisa
To: Mark

I hope you had a good trip. This has been an emotional week for me, culminating in having energy work done at a Body, Mind & Spirit expo yesterday that has left me cracked open and raw. Every feeling is at the surface after going deep. This has been a very good thing as I sift through all that has been dredged up: fear, anger, resistance, love, hope, truth, faith . . . the biggies. Since deciding about moving on from Jon I have felt fragile and exposed. In my openness to possibilities it feels like I had to do this for bigger ones to show up. I know that I have grown in ways that I couldn't have anticipated and he has drawn out some part of me that I needed to feel. I did the same for him, and while we desire to be friends, I find myself wanting to detach completely for awhile. It's incredibly painful to do so. I don't let go of people that I love very easily, as you know. . .

Getting your email hours after my decision was perfect, of course, reminding me that I am loved by someone who is also at a distance, making me face that. Jon loves me from an emotional distance, you from a physical one. Neither are my lover. Both more than just a friend. This hurts me and makes me wonder why it is that I have not drawn to me the man who can love me up close, face to face, completely. Whether it is miles or fear that separates me from the men who love me, it is separation just the same. This is not a pitiful feeling (mostly) but more of an observation that makes me look inside myself and wonder *what is it about me that creates this?*

Maybe it is all about timing, and 'he' is out there getting ready for Great Love. With me. Maybe. *Yes*.

Thank you for sending your love and gratitude. It means so much and I know that you are the man you want to be under all your feelings of obligation, limitation and inauthenticity. You are already him. I have seen him. I know him. I love him. That I have been inspiring to you is the greatest gift I can offer. You were the one who twenty-some years ago asked what I wanted most and I said, "inspiration." You connected that with my having asthma. *To breathe is to inspire.* I have learned to breathe since then. Deeply and intentionally. It is in breathing deeply that I feel most calm and centered, most inspired. Thank you for the gift of connecting me to my own inspiration, even if I didn't see that for many years. I see it now and you inspire me to not settle for a less spiritual, less connected, less contemplative, less passionate man than I deserve. I know such a man exists because I know you.

My intention now is to attract the man I can share authentic love with who is available to me in every way. It may take some time, yet it will be worth the wait.

Lis

Subject: Good luck with this one
Date: Mon, 20 Feb 2006 6:10 AM
From: Mark
To: Lisa

Interesting timing, your breakup and my email. I have to admit that the poetic license I took professing a "love that can't be defined in human terms" made me wonder how it would be interpreted, but even *that* attempt at describing my connection to you didn't hit the mark, though it was pretty close. And I hear your frustration that something so good, so desired, and so rare should continue to elude you. It eludes me, too, so I turn my attention and energies to other things that fulfill me: nature mostly, which intersects with horses and photography, which brings me in contact with other people, most of whom are genuine and interesting to know. Intimacy is missing - *my* choice, I would add - but I'm not in a place where seeking out and building some great intimate relationship with Miss Right is an option . . . again, my choice.

I notice that I'm making more of an effort to exorcise my own demons, take more responsibility for my shortcomings, and *not be so hard on myself* about it all. I can point to a whole bunch of stuff that *proves* I'm a dick or a slacker or a failure, but it's mostly in comparison to other guys my age who all seem to it have it so much more together than I do. Of course, I also have the ideal partner for pointing out or bringing up any failings I may have missed . . .

Your experiences come from your beliefs, right? (from *The Nature of Personal Reality*) so *not* having what we really want equals holding (probably unconsciously) a belief which is working at cross-purposes to our efforts to manifest a given desire. It's a whole, long rap, and the book sits dog-eared and heavily highlighted on the dresser next to my bed.

I'm starting to run out of gas, getting frustrated that I can't really put my finger on what I want to say here, or where I want to go with all this. I don't have any answers for my own goofy life, and I suppose at some level I'm choosing my private little hell because of the rewards and nourishment some part of me is receiving by living this at-times inauthentic way. Must be that more things than not are going *well enough* to keep from making any major changes. So much of life seems stupid, unfair and pointless . . . a *belief* which keeps me stuck, you see. So complaining about being stuck is ridiculous.

Even after we meet and join up with who we believe to be The One, there will follow doubt, disappointment, and dark times. Those moments, as well as all the great and way cool ones, will be temporary. So the question becomes: *who would be the most fun to ride that roller coaster with?*

This may serve as a clue as to why you and I continue, in the face of physical distance and apparent diverging life trajectories, to stay connected.

. . . then again, maybe not. There's still a page missing from my instruction manual, so . . . consider the source.

Mark

———

Subject: re: Good luck with this one
Date: Mon, 20 Feb 2006 3:05 PM
From: Lisa
To: Mark

Well, this one will require some contemplation. In the meantime, know that your confession hit the mark that it needed to and was not interpreted in a way that holds any expectation. In fact, it's the opposite. It is precisely the kind of love that just *is* and defies the labels and boundaries we put around love that seeks to possess or limit us. The distance between you and I has always given us good reasons to not project an outcome whatsoever. More later . . .

———

Subject: re: Good luck with this one
Date: Mon, 20 Feb 2006 7:48 PM
From: Lisa
To: Mark

I keep re-reading your last email and each time I have a different reaction:

Right on!

You're full of shit.

What are you really saying?

It's kind of fun really. Mostly I think you are in complete clarity about where you are, that it is all about the choices you've made and yes, we do create our own reality from our beliefs. What observations! HATE that you feel any of life is stupid or pointless. AGREE that complaining about being stuck is pointless (since you choose it)! Keep the stream of consciousness flowing . . . there's gold to be mined from that river.

And by the way, what are you trying to say to me?
". . . but even *that* attempt at describing my connection to you didn't hit the mark, though it was pretty close. This may serve as a clue as to why you and I continue, in the face of physical distance and apparent diverging life trajectories, to stay connected . . . then again, maybe not. There's still a page missing from my instruction manual, so . . . consider the source."

What do you really mean?

_____

Subject: re: Good luck with this one
Date: Tue, 21 Feb 2006 6:37 AM
From: Mark
To: Lisa

What I meant was I'm not clear enough or grounded enough to have a definitive answer to the question: *what is the significance of this connection between you and I? How can it be defined?* If, during the process of building my own "flying machine" I discover there's a page missing from the enclosed manual, I can hardly speak with any real authority about what it means to fly. Any thoughts I may have on the subject are based on having flown in machines *built by other people* . . . So if my words confuse you, *consider the source*, which is me: the guy who made a bunch of choices which led to the sometimes inauthentic life he now lives.

Also, I'm figuring it out as I go . . . and part of that process takes place when I write *you*. I have so little idea of what I'm going to say when I start writing. It's like taking a solo when playing in a band: I do the best I can with the ideas that come to me in the moment, doing my best to make it sound interesting while at the same time having it fit and make sense within the context of the music being played. You've been around bands enough to know that not all solos are interesting or make sense.

off to work . . .

hug

Mark

_____

Subject: re: Good luck with this one
Date: Tue, 21 Feb 2006 6:57 AM
From: Lisa
To: Mark

You don't give yourself enough credit. You have flown solo plenty and some of it was in a self-created machine. Remember your life before you felt like this? I do. You lived from your heart, did work you were passionate about at the time . . . music, cooking, massage. You wrote and studied a *lot* when we first connected. Maybe it's when I hear you forgetting that time in your life that I feel you are full of shit, when you sound like you have never lived from that place . . . ever! Maybe that's why we are still connected, because I help remind you of that time, that feeling, of who you were then. It's hard to define what it is, so let's not try.

You aren't missing a page in the manual. You misplaced it. Maybe it's the page that said:

Step 1. Live from your heart.
Step 2. Trust yourself.
Step 3. Make choices which honor that.

The choices you have made since then led to the life you have now. New choices are being made daily, in each moment. That you choose to write me is choosing to remember and connect with who you really are, and have been. I believe that is what happens when you sit down and spill it all out to me, knowing there's someone at the other end who *gets* you and knows you. That's part of the significance of our connection.

Hug back.

_____

Subject:
Date: Wed, 1 Mar 2006 10:15 AM

From: Lisa
To: Mark

Where have you been?? Say hi soon.

_____
Subject: Hey
Date: Thu, 9 Mar 2006 6:40 AM
From: Mark
To: Lisa

Got a call out of the blue the other night from a guy I knew in my high
school jazz band. He's now married to his high school sweetheart. They
married and divorced other people, looked each other up after some 15 or
20 years had gone by . . . and are now married to each other. Mind
blowing, and totally fun! I really liked these two a lot in high school, and
it's so perfect that they're together now.

I'm off today, and will be home making a cabinet for Mariah's new office.
It's been kind of a cool week . . . gigged last night in SF, worked every day
last week . . . enjoying the rainy days . . . real, real busy but I've been in
some sort of groove where I've enjoyed the work and accomplished a lot . .
.

So what's new for me is this unexpected feeling of enjoying the carpentry
work and the extra time I've put in to help remodel Mariah's new office
space. On weekends the medical building she's in is pretty much deserted,
so while it was cold and rainy outside, I was inside an empty building with
my CD player and tools, grooving and creating. The way-early morning
fits me like a glove, and doing fine woodworking while others were
sleeping was kind of cool.

Still waiting to hear how you've been and wutzup. Snow there, right? Hope
all is well . . . my intuition tells me you're struggling with something . . .

hug

another hug

Mark

_____
Subject:
Date: Thu, 9 Mar 2006 11:18 AM
From: Lisa
To: Mark

Good radar, my friend. I admit to feeling blue as I release the remnants of

50

this last attempt at True Love. I know now that he was never the right guy for me, but he was really smart and made me laugh—and was stable and successful. *That* is something I have not attracted much of, opting for passion and excitement instead. Anyway, life goes on . . .

Glad to hear you are enjoying your building project. What a great story about your old friends ending up together after all those years! Must have been fate.

hug.

_____

Subject: Hey
Date: Fri, 10 Mar 2006 12:54 PM
From: Mark
To: Lisa

Good morning . . .

I was going to include, in my email to you yesterday, a reiteration that even the good times are temporary . . . a reminder to myself that in spite of my current streak of good vibe and optimism, it would eventually change into effort and/or hard times at some point, and back again later still . . .

An hour after I sent you my glowing report of how I was doing I was in the garage building a cabinet when my nail gun rubbed against my right calf and discharged. I dropped everything and headed to the ER, freaking out at the thought of having to fillet open my calf muscle to remove the nail, and not be able to work or play drums for a month or two. *Shit*!

Played the stupid waiting waiting waiting waiting STILL waiting game to get an x-ray and see a doctor, which ended with a surgeon telling me to leave it in there, like a piece of shrapnel. He was pretty sure he would have a very hard time getting it out, cutting through perfectly fine muscle, which would take a while to heal. The doctor said that in a few days I probably wouldn't even know it was there. WHEW!

I was relieved to know all would eventually be well by leaving it alone. So, I am being slowed down, since I would not slow myself down . . . even though I was rather enjoying *handling* the pace I was going at.

And as for you, my dear . . . I'm a bit relieved to hear that the struggle I was intuiting is not TOO serious, though I don't know the particulars of your heart's immunity to lost love. I see you as a warrior-ess, coming through the smoke and mist of yet another battle with whatever demons stand between you and The One . . . no blood or scars on you, no hindered mobility . . . but sweaty chestnut hair plastered to your cheek and forehead, soot smears on your neck and sword hand from close proximity to flame and heat. You are walking back to camp, disappointed and weary, but not beaten, not broken, oh no. . . Lisa of Lucca will eventually head back to her castle to bathe, contemplate, and rest. Later, she will confer with her aides about the battles' details, assess her experiences, then eat a fine meal with good wine, and soon enough will laugh in the company of good friends.

She imagines a break from demon-slaying, traveling to a place where there is sun, water, a villa perhaps . . . a chance to remove her armor, expose her skin to the elements, her personality to the locals, her soul to the gods. She will leave her sword behind, sheathed, oiled, and sharp, but unnecessary for a time.

There will be music, fresh produce from the village marketplace, a small child's laughter emanating from an upstairs window above a bakery . . . the early morning walks along the dirt roads just beyond the villa will be a glorious assault on her senses: tall grasses hissing in the light breeze, the subtle warmth of the morning sun penetrating her sheer cotton blouse, horses snorting as they graze in an expansive, grassy field . . . the smell of coffee and bread as she draws closer to the village . . .

She will sit at a small, round table in front of the bakery, order coffee, and pull out her journal. The coffee arrives. She wraps both palms around the fragile cup, and leans in with closed eyes to take in the aroma. She sits back in the sculpted iron chair, kicks off her thin sandals, and rubs the bottoms of her feet on the worn, ancient cobblestones. Folding her hands in her lap, she sits motionless, letting the moment seep in. A minute passes . . . then another . . . and without knowing why, unaware that she was even thinking about anything at all, tears begin to well up in her eyes. This moment - all this beauty and perfection - it's too much, too much . . . She has been heading for this place, this moment, from the day she was born . . . and she is here now, rested, nourished, safe . . .

Mark

six

52

Subject: Hey
Date: Sat, 11 Mar 2006 7:08 AM
From: Lisa
To: Mark

Wow. I woke up early thinking about our time together talking on the phone last night and journaled about it a little (deep breath, slow smile . . . shaking my head . . . *sigh*).

More later, need coffee. ox

_____

Subject: mornin'
Date: Mon, 13 Mar 2006 8:29 AM
From: Lisa
To: Mark

Hey,

Very interesting weekend. Jon was here Saturday night and there was such a different (indifferent?) feeling that I had towards him. Of course, as a result, the computer problem that he had been helping me with for months magically fixed itself. One less reason to be connected.

Moving on, moving on . . .

_____

Subject: Hey
Date: Fri, 17 Mar 2006 7:07 AM
From: Mark
To: Lisa

The new job on the coast will be finished Tuesday, but I'm telling everyone it'll take til Wednesday so I can spend the whole day at the ocean, writing. Then a one-day job on Thursday - which I'll announce as a two-day job - and use Friday as a writing day.

Credit where credit is due: I wouldn't be so motivated to write if it wasn't for your feedback and encouragement.

Thanks so much.

Mark

_____

Subject: re: Hey
Date: Fri, 17 Mar 2006 12:17 PM
From: Lisa
To: Mark

Hey,

I have thought about our long talk, all week, and how good it felt. I have been feeling a bit melancholy this week while pulling back from Jon, thinking about you, then being propositioned by a former (now married) lover who is remembering me way too fondly. It is nice to be lusted after, I admit, since it *has* been over a year since I've been intimate . . . I miss it.

Last night I felt very lonely. Watching a movie on my new, big comfy couch, missing someone I may not have even met yet. Missing Jon. Missing every man I have ever loved. Missing what could have been. Wondering why I'm not the one chosen to be loved and cherished. It is also not me that is cheated on or lied to. I suppose that's the good news. They just leave, or withdraw . . . or I do. Funny thing is, I am grateful that I am not with any of them now.

Waaaaaaa. Poor me. I'll snap out of it! One day there will be a great guy lying on my couch with me, snuggled up, my hair falling on his cheek, his hand caressing my face as he tucks it behind my ear. Or we'll be like bookends, our feet touching, animatedly discussing the movie we just watched and how the screenwriter must have felt when he sat for hours, writing a story so personal, so deep, and yet so comically, tragically funny.

You could have been that guy. Only not. A glimpse of you on my couch serves as a space holder till the real one comes along. You are *the kind of guy* who belongs on my couch, in my life, in my heart, in my world. I know there is a great guy who wants to be here, and when he is he will feel like there is nowhere else he'd rather be.

Thank you for holding that space . . . I feel better now.

Lis

––––––
Subject: Hey
Date: Fri, 24 Mar 2006 7:03 PM
From: Mark
To: Lisa

Oh boy, are the wheels ever turning . . . god, I wish I could see you tomorrow. . . drinking whiskey tonight (!), saw a movie, gonna disappear tomorrow. . . don't know where to go, though. Any suggestions?

Been writing you a long letter around the CD I'm about to send you . . . give me your address again . . .

––––––

Subject: re: Hey
Date: Fri, 24 Mar 2006 11:12 PM
From: Lisa
To: Mark

Hey . . . Yeah, that would be cool. Hang out all day . . . sharing all the turning wheels.

I will be doing a photo shoot tomorrow with a professional photographer for my new website. I'm excited about the new site but it is a lot of work with people who don't quite grasp my vision. What do I suggest for *you* tomorrow? Write!

How fun, a CD and letter!

_____
Subject: Some that I like
Date: Sat, 25 Mar 2006 7:12 PM
From: Lisa
To: Mark

Pictures attached for my new website. What do you think? Be honest.

_____
Subject: re: Some that I like
Date: Sat, 25 Mar 2006 10:49 PM
From: Mark
To: Lisa

These pics are all great, especially the first two. I really like the one of you in the blue blouse . . . and I can see a Sandra Bullock thing in the last one with the hat. Oh yeah . . .

_____
Subject: re: Some that I like
Date: Mon, 27 Mar 2006 6:20 PM
From: Lisa
To: Mark

I LOVE the one with the hat, too.

Got the CD and letter today. Thanks, I can't wait to hear it!

_____
Subject: hey
Date: Mon, 3 Apr 2006 8:24 AM
From: Lisa
To: Mark

what's up?

Subject: re: hey
Date: Tue, 4 Apr 2006 8:42 AM
From: Mark
To: Lisa

Coming up for air . . . then gotta go back down . . .

Had a Tarot reading the other night, having to do with divorce. The next night, after prodding me about my mood shift, I told Mariah that I was going to file for divorce. My daughter came down with a fever the next day - sick at school, had to come home - and Mariah has been a different person ever since: agreeable and pleasant. Well, great, but twelve years too late, right? We're going into counseling soon to get to the bottom of all this.

Now, overlapping all of this are my ten and twelve-hour workdays, every day for two weeks, including weekends, on a tricky, frustrating job. Started a new one Monday, the same day our horse got sick, rendering her un-rideable, requiring shots four times a day. Now I'm up at five, gone by six, coming in the door at seven pm. Call me Mister Hang In There.

That's what's up.

Mark

Subject: re: hey
Date: Thu, 6 Apr 2006 9:04 AM
From: Lisa
To: Mark

Wow. Lots to handle. Glad to hear you made a decision and it led to a shift. Just keep in mind that people don't become different people overnight. They change behavior in extreme situations. Counseling is a good idea, whether this decision ends the marriage or brings you closer.

Lots on this end, too . . . big emotional shifts. Jon blowout. Health scare. I'll be ok. Talk soon if we can . . .

Subject: hey
Date: Wed, 19 Apr 2006 6:02 AM
From: Lisa
To: Mark

We watched *Dreamer* last night and I thought of you and Savannah. Wonderful film! It made me think a lot about my grandfather who owned a racehorse and practically lived at the track. I wish he had shared that with us more as kids. When he died we took his ashes to the track and spread some of them in the flower beds of the Winner's Circle (he was also an avid gardener) and I ran down the track with the rest, letting him fly in the wind and land in the hoof prints of a thousand horses.

How are you? I have been thinking of you while listening to your CD in my car. I love it. Have you started counseling? I hope this brings clarity and healing to you both regardless of the outcome. It can only bring good.

I talked to my friend Mary the other night and there is a possibility of a visit to the Bay Area this summer. I would love to come out, or maybe go to New Mexico or Sedona, places I've been drawn to and have yet to see.

Things have settled for me after an emotional week with Jon awhile back. That is finally over and a friendship remains. I finished my finals for my advanced coach degree and I graduate in June. Glad to be DONE! Got a couple of cool new clients. The new website will be up next week and I can't wait.

Yesterday, with my music in my ears and the sun on my face, I ran through the park and flew my kite. There is something about flying kites that I just love . . .

I hope you are writing and happy and growing. Miss you.

Lis

Subject: re: hey
Date: Wed, 19 Apr 2006 6:45 AM
From: Mark
To: Lisa

Growing, yes . . .but not writing. Being happy takes some effort. We had our second counseling session last night so the relationship dynamic has shifted to another level. Things are being talked about and gone into, all of which is good . . . so this is the beginning of a long haul and commitment to save what was once a sinking ship, which is not the same as being on some great sailing voyage . . . although The Universe would beg to differ, I'm sure.

Money gets tighter, taking the fun out of some things, but bringing to the forefront the need to stop settling for, and create a different paradigm for abundance. When the tight, grooving, family unit thing is happening, all is right with our world . . . and *that* is worth saving. You could say we've signed up for The Universe's dance class, and our first two lessons have revealed just how different our styles and preferences really are. Me? I'm happy to crank the music and get my freak on, but that's not what the class is teaching. These new steps - which involve syncing up with a partner - are difficult and awkward, mostly due to, um . . . *differences of opinion . . .* as to who gets to lead.

———

Subject: re: hey
Date: Wed, 19 Apr 2006 7:49 AM
From: Lisa
To: Mark

aww . . . hang in there.

hug.

———

Subject: Hey
Date: Tue, 9 May 2006 3:59 AM
From: Lisa
To: Mark

How are you?

Things here are very busy. I had 20 coaching sessions last week, a record! Today I'll be at a coaching conference all day. Should be fun. Started really dating. It's fun though I hate it on some level. Zac is good. Miss you.

seven

Subject: ??
Date: Thu, 1 Jun 2006 5:31 AM
From: Lisa
To: Mark

Hey, how are you?

Lis

———

Subject: re: ??
Date: Thu, 1 Jun 2006 5:56 AM
From: Mark
To: Lisa

I know, I know. I'm here, but experiencing burnout and exhaustion these last two weeks. Household tensions rise and fall, therapy has been good, the band plays on, and I've begun my book. I owe you a way long letter . . .

I have not left you.

———

Subject: Hey you
Date: Thu, 1 Jun 2006 7:28 AM
From: Lisa
To: Mark

I have been writing, too. Zac is graduating next week from 8th grade, I graduate tomorrow with my advanced coaching certification (!) which has taken a year to complete. Client work is so good and I launched my new website. Did you see it?

I finally began dating again and have been seeing someone for the past month. The Anti-Jon: Outgoing, social, open, young (38), fun, sexy and not afraid to use it. LOL It has been an inner and outer exploration of the part of me that had been sleeping for over a year (god, talk about too long). I'm having a blast and while I believe Riley is Mr. Right Now, I'm cool with that. The energy and creative flow that has resulted is well worth it, although I know for the long haul I will want to be with a more spiritually connected man. He will arrive when we're both ready and that might take awhile. In the meantime, allowing myself to experience a deep part of me that I have missed dearly feels right. *Ahhh.. . .*

I'll look forward to that long letter, my dear.

Hugs . . .
Lis

———

Subject: ancient cobblestones
Date: Sat, 3 Jun 2006 7:05 AM
From: Mark
To: Lisa

Driving home from a gig last night I came across a Christian radio station playing a sermon from some guy who talked non-stop for twenty minutes about how (I'm paraphrasing here) even the most fucked-up moments in our lives, no matter how long they last, are intentionally given to us to help

59

us out with growing towards our highest good. The point was to allow and accept the feelings of frustration, anger, emptiness, depression and fear, and at the same time remember that we are being watched over, cared for, and loved . . . that it's all *fine*, don't worry . . . be *happy*.

So I'm listening to this and it occurs to me that The Universe sent me a similar message a few days ago. The reason this all was getting through to me is because I'd been feeling really frustrated and bummed out while installing a custom home-office center in a two million-dollar home. I spent a lot of extra time tweaking and inventing ways of making problematic stuff work. I'll go out to the house this morning - day three - and try to finish, but it will be a long day, and there goes my Saturday, and oh no, I bid the job too low and *fuck*, I didn't know I had to do *that*, and *shit*, I have to go all the way downstairs and make another cut on the saw, and . . .

. . . . *thank you* . . . Thank you for the work. Thank you for the chance to improve my skills. Thank you for yet another opportunity to practice patience and mindfulness. Thank you for guiding me towards another chance to earn money *making something beautiful*, to build something with my hands that will live in someone's home long after I'm gone . . . to leave something of myself *in* something that others will often use.

Now why would I want to be upset and frustrated for such an opportunity?

Why should I worry that the messy, worn-down house I'm renting with my frustrated, complaining wife and Star Child daughter is a sign of failure or stagnation?

Why should I believe I may never see Italy, vacationing after a book tour, feeling the cool, ancient cobblestones under my bare feet, sitting in a plaza sipping strong coffee with a dear friend?

Mark

_____
Subject: re: ancient cobblestones
Date: Sat, 3 Jun 2006 10:15 AM
From: Lisa
To: Mark

Oh, Mark . . .

There will be a book, you will see Italy, and there is a dear friend who believes in you, sipping strong coffee in Chicago and dreaming of ancient cobblestones . . .

Lis

___

I read your email again, about shifting your perspective . . .

I have been reflecting a lot lately on this very thing: what is the reason for all the crap that shows up in our lives? It is all fertilizer for our growth. What we need is always available to us. Reach out and pluck it from the tree. I am doing that now, and while the fruit is very sweet there is a cost . . .

You resurfacing now is perfect. You are my mirror in so many ways and keep my perspective sharp. As I find myself spinning out in a place of momentary pleasure I need to be reeled back in and reminded of what it is my soul truly desires. You have been that reminder for more than half my life. I am grateful and bewildered by this, but always more hopeful, knowing that the Universe is showing me the truth and insisting that I pay attention.

I talked to Jimmy yesterday for the first time in probably a year. I felt so incredibly detached and amazed that he used to be my *husband*. There is a surreal feeling that washes over me and I wonder who I was then, what was my heart seeking? Only to be loved, I guess. And he did love me. When I pledged my vows to him they felt subtly false in my soul, but I intended to keep them. What a different life it would have been had I kept them, however being left at home with Zac while Jimmy drove rock stars around the country was hardly healthy for my marriage, and a big reason why I left.

Don't get me wrong, I'm grateful for every choice I have made, every risk I took, of every tear I shed in sorrow, frustration, joy, or relief. No regrets. And now, as I make my choices with so much more awareness, it's easier to take risks, yet harder to let go . . . *to surrender*. . . because sometimes I can see outcomes before they happen. Leaping into the void is harder to do when you see the bottom and can already sense the crunch of bone against cement. Ouch.

But life is sweet and always surprises us. The void can look ominous, yet hold great wonder on the way down . . . and if you get it right, you can spread your wings (or fire up your flying machine) and rise up before you do any damage.

Wishing you a glorious day.

Subject: Inspired
Date: Tue, 13 Jun 2006 8:45 PM
From: Lisa
To: Mark

Spent 5 hours in Riley's yard today writing, writing, writing about relationships - what I know about how they work and how to get it wrong. Twenty-five pages on a legal pad . . .

It may not all be good but it was great to just have it pour out for hours.

Subject: re: Inspired
Date: Wed, 14 Jun 2006 10:15 AM
From: Mark
To: Lisa

Excellent! Lucky you, having five hours to write, write, write. I keep my laptop in my truck and write a bit when I first arrive at a job site, or while waiting for Savannah when she's at the barn.

You keep popping into my head when I write: *Lisa would love this!*, or *What would Lisa think of this?* Your feedback and encouragement inspires me, and I'm certain I wouldn't be writing much at all if it weren't for you.

During our therapy session last night it was suggested that I do some separate, one-on-one work with my own issue of the need to feel connected to my life's purpose. I willingly admitted that it had been one of the most important issues in my life for years. One suggestion for working out this issue: *write!* So I chip away, writing a bit each day . . . even a paragraph, or a few lines. The paragraphs are piling up, the thoughts are random and all over the place. You would love some of this. I'll send you something one day.

Til then, let us assume this is all headed toward Italy.

Mark

Subject: re: Inspired
Date: Wed, 14 Jun 2006 12:48 PM
From: Lisa
To: Mark

Sounds like some things are coming together, even in small ways. I'd love to read what you've written. Send it. It's good that we inspire each other and each time you talk about the time limitations you have I have a new appreciation of my open time. Zac is in Tennessee at his dad's this week, so I'm here alone. I intend to use this time wisely and cherish it.

It almost makes sense that as I take on writing about having an Ideal Relationship, I am *not* experiencing my own. Being in the same place of self-discovery and yearning as the reader lets me write about the *possibility* of love in a way that relates to them. I can express the longing, the willingness to get clear, and the deep need to be true to yourself from a place of being there *now,* and not from a memory of having been there and figured it all out. Seems more organic this way.

All headed toward Italy? Well, of course it is.

L

_____

Subject: hey
Date: Thu, 15 Jun 2006 6:25 PM
From: Mark
To: Lisa

A glass of wine, making dinner . . . thinking of you. Two things:

Next movie: *The Family Stone.*

Writing assignment: Send me two paragraphs about meeting me in Italy.

_____

Subject: re: hey
Date: Fri, 16 Jun 2006 3:57 PM
From: Lisa
To: Mark

I've seen *The Family Stone* . . . it was fun.

Hmm, a writing assignment. OK . . .

I checked into the Hotel California Positano, alone. Its white stucco exterior gleamed in the sun and the view of the Amalfi coast took my breath away. In the distance, small islands dotted the azure sea, bringing to life the massive framed photo of Positano that has hung on my office wall for years. That photo has inspired me, carrying a promise that one day I would be standing at the edge of the sea in the land of my ancestral roots.

I was travel-weary, yet filled with nervous anticipation knowing my dear friend Mark would be joining me tomorrow. I smiled wryly at the name of the hotel, as California is the place where our friendship began decades ago . . .

It's a start. More later.

———
Subject: Hey
Date: Sun, 18 Jun 2006 2:43 PM
From: Lisa
To: Mark

Happy Father's Day :-)

———
Subject: Good mornin. . .
Date: Mon, 19 Jun 2006 8:57 AM
From: Lisa
To: Mark

Watched *Under The Tuscan Sun* and was further inspired, not just by the Italian landscape and sea, but by some of the major points in the story... like they built the tracks through the Alps before there was a train that could make the journey. They built it anyway. Eventually there was a train that could make the trip. Leaps of faith.

———
Subject: re: Good mornin. . .
Date: Mon, 19 Jun 2006 8:09 PM
From: Mark
To: Lisa

Finally read your Italy assignment. Nice start. I won't have time to add on to the story before I leave town tomorrow. Depends on the next 24 hours. Keep going, though . . .

———
Subject: welcome back
Date: Mon, 26 Jun 2006 9:04 AM
From: Lisa
To: Mark

Hope your trip was fun! Zac's gone for a week so lots of time to myself. Here is a little of what I have been writing (unedited). Started at the beginning when 21 year old me arrives in California and ended with you signing your band's album at the gig we met at a week later:

To Lisa . . . Welcome to California - you are loved. Mark

I still can't believe you wrote that. Nice beginning to our friendship :-)

———

Subject: re: welcome back
Date: Mon, 26 Jun 2006 11:44 AM
From: Mark
To: Lisa

I envy your freedom and space to write whatever and whenever. Lucky you.

I only have a few minutes, then work. Frustrating to not have the time to write you at length. Spread thin by responsibilities . . .

Mark

Subject: Hey
Date: Tue, 27 Jun 2006 6:59 AM
From: Mark
To: Lisa

Might be awhile before I can write you at length. . . issues here . . . mostly me looking for God, and where I fit in . . . found Him in the mountains this past weekend, and crave going back . . . soon.

"Emergency" session w/ therapist yesterday - just me - followed by three hours in the library, writing. Picked up *Bridges of Madison County*. . .

These pics were taken Saturday. The lake is a 15-minute walk from the perfect writer's cabin I stayed in.

off to work.

Mark

Subject: Hey
Date: Tue, 27 Jun 2006 8:45 AM
From: Lisa
To: Mark

Wow. Great photos. The one of you is haunting and beautiful. So are the mountains. I see God there.

As I have my own issues here that I deal with, writing to you feels like a safe place to fall. As I delve into the places that this writing is coming from I face all my insecurities and how they have molded me, how they have drenched me in doubt and affected my choices. I have gotten past some of that, though some remains to be dealt with.

I'm happy that you got to do a one-on-one session in therapy. The couple stuff can only go so far, and it's always a good idea for both people to dive in separately to understand themselves and not just who they are in the relationship. I hope it helps.

Lis

P.S. Great book, *Bridges. S*eems the stories that come up for us have Bridge in the title.

_____

Subject: re: Hey
Date: Thu, 29 Jun 2006 6:07 PM
From: Mark
To: Lisa

Thank you. It's exhausting to give the details of all I'm going through and dealing with out here, and it helps that I don't have to. You feel pretty solid to me, like an anchor to a world I left behind long ago.

The mountain trip reminded me of *home,* that clear, centered place inside of me. The whole God thing is my effort to be at peace with it all, knowing that all the hard work is FOR something, that I'm not really flailing about in some pointless endeavor. I just miss being *home.*

The food is good here, though . . .

_____

Subject: Heads up
Date: Thu, 29 Jun 2006 7:00 PM
From: Mark
To: Lisa

This whole Italy fantasy is fun, but keep in mind I'm about 15% jerk, give or take. I wonder sometimes if the image you have of me would come crashing down if you were exposed to the Me only Mariah sees. I'm hoping *that* version of me is only there because of how she and I relate to one another.

_____

Subject: Hey
Date: Fri, 30 Jun 2006 6:48 AM
From: Mark
To: Lisa

Feeling much improved today. Some *thing* is leaking into my mind, like I have a fresh appreciation for just letting go, especially all the versions of holding back and second-guessing I do about my relationship to work and family. I'm seeing how much and how often I hold back some part of myself, not wanting to get into something too deep because I'm not so sure how long I'm going to stay with it. Now I'm feeling like I want to be more present, to "show up" more, putting more of my heart into my dealings with . . . everything. I mean, why not? If I really trust and believe in God, that the Universe really is looking out for me and serving my highest good, then why (for example) withhold being a loving, caring husband while I'm *here?* If you and I are *destined* to meet up in Italy someday, nothing I do now will affect that outcome.

It's the *split* that's messing with me . . . having this life here, while sensing a possible future with you. These writings and letters, the fantasies and mutual support, the years and years of knowing each other . . . there's just no way I'm going to let you go. Even if I push the earthly, ego versions of *us* aside, I'm still left with a whole lotta heart, spirit, soul-growth, and Universe *permission*. It's too easy to make Mariah the Bad Guy, relating to her as though she were in the way, or something . . . that's not a healthy perspective. If I truly trust that any of my desires will manifest, there's no reason for me to hold back *anything* in the present moment.

I've been acting as though what I truly want won't find its way to me because I'm *here*. It's hard sometimes: Mariah is this, she's that; I'm going through this and that, and staying in touch with you on the sly equals maybe-not-meant-to-be, or that I have to make up my mind *soon* about what I should do.

. . . but no . . . I can look past my own desires and wants, and see there is something meaningful and substantial about knowing you and staying in touch with you. *Of course* Mariah feels threatened. That seems normal, but my heart tells me to treat her well and be present for my family, and make these times as good as I can make them. The mechanics of whether or not I end up in Italy with you, for example, are something I need not be concerned with. It's like having the Universe as my travel agent: *just set it up and tell me when it's time to get on the plane . . . I'll be there.*

So all through today I've been thinking about *perspective* . . . the story I tell myself about where I am and what I'm going through affects my behavior, and I think my suffering and efforting is due to a *flawed* perspective. I can take the exact same circumstances I've always been in, and see them in a different light, one that has me expressing more love, creativity and thankfulness *now*, and be optimistic about what the future holds.

Wanna bet that all the holding back I do in my life out here is precisely what's been hindering the experience of cool, ancient cobblestones?

Ciao.

Subject: re: Hey
Date: Fri, 30 Jun 2006 7:19 AM
From: Lisa
To: Mark

Wanna bet this is all a great idea but highly unlikely that it will happen this way?

I am going to digest this over coffee and write more about it shortly. . .

Wish the phone were an option today.

_____
Subject: re: Hey
Date: Fri, 30 Jun 2006 2:40 PM
From: Lisa
To: Mark

You're right, you can't make her the bad guy. This is more about you being true to yourself and living the life that feels right for you. From the very beginning you have had problems with your marriage. So much secrecy while writing or walking on the beach or talking to me creates an inauthenticity that breeds all this discontentment in you and distrust in her. You owe it to yourself, and to her, to be real. If this shift has created the possibility of a more loving dynamic and desire flows from there, great - but you have to feel it, you can't fake it. If a true and real love shows up now for her, then why stop ever? I have always supported you being present in your marriage, not just for the two of you but for your daughter, who is the reason you are still there and got married in the first place.

The Universe has supported us for a long time, and I trust that, yet it can have something else in mind now and I have to be open to that in both our lives. You are married, Mark. I am so very aware of that. And I am living my life over here. You're in it and I can't escape that if I wanted to, which I don't. A choice I make. I can have other relationships that show up with what I need, yet until someone comes along that matches *this* connection, I'm still free.

Your feeling that your current life is temporary - and therefore why engage? - is limiting, yes. And by *really* engaging in your marriage it may change everything. You may fall in love with her and never leave. Maybe not. And what about me? What if I fall in love with someone else while you are 'waiting' on the travel agent? Have you thought of that? I am engaged in my life over here. I'm free. You don't know what the future holds and I don't either. My trip to Italy may show up in a year or two. If your life is in the same place as it is now, only better and more loving, can you really get on that plane when the Universe books the ticket? Maybe that trip is one I go on alone or with someone else, who knows? I need to tell the truth, more to myself than to you.

I am at the prime of my life and I am living it out loud. In all the many words I have written you lately you have not responded to my life and to what I am doing over here. I think about your recent emails, your search for God and your life purpose. Mine are about writing our story, or pieces of it, the one that you started about cool, ancient cobblestones beneath my bare feet. It has hit me that you don't ask what's going on in my life lately. You don't reply to my words, you just send more of your process. Like the one the other day that said you are 15% jerk and would my impression of you come crashing down if I saw that side, that you hope it is only your reaction to how you two relate to one another. I hadn't seen that side of you because you have no reason to show it to me.

Now maybe I see him. It's all about you, your experience and desire and, yes, I'm part of that. I just need to know what comes up for you when I send all these words off. Where do they land?

All I know is that you don't want to let go of me.

_____

Subject: re: Hey
Date: Fri, 30 Jun 2006 6:00 PM
From: Mark
To: Lisa

OK, I think I'm done with the "be true to yourself" lessons. Write your book, have fun in Italy with whoever. I'll look for you on Oprah.

The Jerk

_____

Subject: Your day
Date: 17 Jul 2006 6:48 AM
From: Lisa
To: Mark

Mark,

You haven't replied to my emails and it makes me so sad. Even though we are both licking our wounds, we are still the same people who have been close for nearly 25 years and that counts for a lot, damn it. I couldn't let the day pass without wishing you Happy Birthday and a new year of joy and peace. Have a wonderful day, my friend.

Love,

Lis

———

Subject: re: Your day
Date: Mon, 17 Jul 2006 6:58 AM
From: Mark
To: Lisa

Thank you.

———

Subject: re: Your day
Date: Mon, 17 Jul 2006 7:48 AM
From: Lisa
To: Mark

You're welcome.

Mark, this has been a difficult couple weeks and I have written about it, talked about it, raged about it, cried about it. The disconnect from you has felt like a power outage. We take for granted sometimes how much juice is required to run the things that make our lives work.

I have let go of much since then, including Riley, who woke something up in me and didn't connect in the ways that really matter. We both knew it and said so out loud. This is a good thing. It was so clear once the source of my emotional and spiritual juice went on the blink that it was no longer okay to feed that part of me with the other piece missing.

I went to a wedding yesterday and saw the love in these young people, shining and beautiful, their emotion flowing, especially his. I felt the deepest longing for *that* in my life: Big Love. It was never my intention to close that door for us. My fear pushed that door from wide open to halfway so that, if your new intention to "show up" in your life changed *everything,* a frigid, cold wind would not come through and freeze me to the bone. In reality, the Universe knows more than me and I am willing to surrender, opening all my doors wide.

When you talked about our future as *possible* and that you would hold that inside for the Universe to see, my heart swelled. Then fear immediately gripped it and squeezed, hard. I wanted to believe you, yet everything else you said was about loving someone else first. *Now.* Someone you already have a life with. All my defenses came up. I went looking for ways to poke holes in your vision so just in case it didn't happen the way you described - if the next letter is about how you are loving and happy - I wouldn't be shattered. We wouldn't know what we could have until we had the chance to have it. When you said you were considering ending your marriage, and then went into therapy, I felt the Universe was making a move and perhaps

70

that chance would become more real. Then it felt far away again.

I can feel your shift back to embracing your commitment to your family, through your connection with God. I love that you are on the path to being happy in the life you already have. I want you to be happy. Today. Especially today, your birthday.

I will be writing. I know you will be, too. Our stories continue and I can't help but believe they will still intersect.

Lisa

_____
Subject: Hey
Date: Tue, 18 Jul 2006 5:59 AM
From: Mark
To: Lisa

It's the content of your fourth paragraph that has me writing you again . . .

After *finally* finding myself in a place where I knew I no longer had to struggle with my actions and emotions regarding all these years of feeling split between two lives - the one I had and the one I fantasized about - I surrendered it all to the Universe. For REAL. That decision made the whole world look and feel different. No more struggle, no more manipulating or tweaking the Life Force, and, gratefully, no more withholding love . . .

It changed everything, of course, and I discovered a much-needed resolution to the tensions in my relationship with my family. Being secretive about the reasons for being only half-present was the "virus" which perpetuated the low-grade "cold" that would never go away. It was ME who was sick, and with my commitment to be totally present for my family came the healing. Even my job felt different, and I knew I was on the right track.

When I wrote about this, only to have you "poke holes" in it, I immediately saw you as The Enemy. I couldn't believe your response, that you didn't *get it,* and there was no way I was going to let any more of your words into my head, undermining this new, beautiful path my heart was turning towards. So: Wham! Power outage.

Whatever you wrote after my "goodbye" never got read. I deleted it without opening it. A week or two ago, after finally calming down, I went to read it but it was gone, permanently, so I have no idea what was said.

Things are much better now, although not perfect, but I can't believe the difference in the quality of my family life. I've stopped being afraid of showing up.

Mark

_____
Subject: Hey
Date: Thu, 20 Jul 2006 5:51 AM
From: Mark
To: Lisa

Beginning late tomorrow afternoon, I am off to spend two nights - alone - at that little one-room cabin in the mountains near all those lakes. I'm intending to write, write, write, walk, write, nap, write, eat, write . . . you get the idea.

_____
Subject: re: Hey
Date: Fri, Jul 21 2006 9:10 AM
From: Lisa
To: Mark

Sounds wonderful. Zac is at his dad's this week so I have time alone, too.

Write your heart out this weekend. Enjoy.

_____
Subject: Hey
Date: Mon, Jul 24 2006 9:03 PM
From: Lisa
To: Mark

Just wanted to share that one of my clients came here today and brought me a small ceramic box from Amalfi filled with stones and sea glass from the Positano beach in Italy. Beautiful.

Did you write your heart out?

_____
Subject: Hey
Date: Tue, 25 Jul 2006 6:29 AM
From: Mark
To: Lisa

Nah. I was disappointed overall with any writing accomplishments. Got there @ 4:30pm Friday, set everything up as soon as I got there and went over all the misc. pieces of stuff I had, looking for a thread to pull me in. Nothing. Sat on the tiny front porch and wrote in my journal til dinner @ 7:30. Came back and wrote a paragraph or two before falling asleep.

After an 8 am breakfast I drove a mile down the road and spent the day swimming in one of the lakes after a two-mile hike. Brought the journal but wrote nothing. Gorgeous day. I often felt like I was in Greece, having found a secluded spot with massive boulders and stones protruding from the water. I swam and sunned til 2 or 3, hiked back and crashed at the cabin, slept til 6. Showered, wrote a bit til 7:30 dinner, wrote a bit more after, but no muse. Was up @ 6am on Sunday, wrote a bit more before packing to leave, breakfast at 8, on the road by 9, listening to Michael Meade discuss the difference between fantasy and imagination as I drove through the Sierras.

All in all very little writing, and what I wrote didn't come easy. Way too short a stay. Need at least a week to let the deep quiet and beauty of that place work on me. The hike and swim were the highlight and boy, how great it would have been to have you there. I was really missing the repartee . . . could have used it, frankly.

It's been over 100 degrees here for a week. Everybody's wiped out. The men's retreat in Mendocino is coming up and I may attend. Have way more to write, but have to go to work.

Ciao

———

Subject: Hey
Date: Tue, Jul 25 2006 7:09 AM
From: Lisa
To: Mark

Sorry it was disappointing.

Zac just left for Jimmy's for a week and I almost decided to get on a plane for San Francisco. My friend Amy was here two weeks ago and we had a blast and she wants me to visit, as does Mary. Feels like tempting fate or something. The airline miles are staring me in the face, saying *Go! Why not?* Then all the reasons flood in . . .

———

Subject: Hey
Date: Sun, 30 Jul 2006 1:00 PM
From: Mark
To: Lisa

The girls left for the barn at 10:30 this morning, and I stayed behind to watch the last hour of *Bridges of Madison County* . . .

Hard not to think about you and I while watching it: All the "what if" questions . . . the four days of free-falling into one another while the spouse and kids are away . . . the impulse to run off together . . . the torment of him leaving and her family returning to her . . . seeing him one last time, standing in the rain, their eyes meeting, looking, looking . . . she and her husband pull up behind Robert's truck and she sees him hang her medallion on his rear-view mirror: that's when my own tears came.

It's not healthy for me to perpetuate a fantasy about you and what may or may not happen if I leave my family for a new, different life. I've been living with this split - withholding some part of me from Mariah and secretly giving it to you - for years, and in the last few days the thought is creeping in that maybe it would be a good idea to pull in ALL my fantasies, re-capture those energies, and give them to *myself.* Independent of my relationship with others, what is it *I* need to improve my life? I feel like I've been trying to put something over on The Natural Order Of Things, sneaking in some goodies when It's not looking . . .

I've turned our friendship and mutual support into an introduction to a fictional story which takes place in the future. All the images I conjure up in that story are injuring my family in some way, and when I really drop into that thought - like right now - my heart just aches, and tears flow . . .

. . . and I cannot dismiss what I've created with you. There is a place for what my heart tells me about you, and there is no shame or guilt in it. God Himself is free to look in my heart right this instant and I know He would not shame or admonish me about what He would see there because the pure, ego-less truth of how I hold you in my heart deserves to be kept alive. The only conflicts and problems I experience are a result of messing with it, molding it into a different form for my own selfish pleasure. I know you *like* my creations, but the different images I show you are manipulations of something which has a simpler, truer beauty when left in its original form. I believe I can let go of the temptation to mess with it, knowing it will flower into a thing of unique beauty in its own time. I think if I separate The Real from The Fantasy all will turn out well. What's real - what has not changed since the day you and I first met at the Apollo gig - is that you are loved. By me.

M

_____

Subject: re: Hey
Date: Sun, 30 Jul 2006 4:07 PM
From: Lisa
To: Mark

A day of letting go . . .

I have been sitting here writing, trying to understand myself and how I have created walls that have held True Love distant and attracted temporary distractions instead, like Riley. I had dinner with him last week and just enjoyed the moment, setting aside the conversation we'd had weeks ago when we agreed that this isn't going anywhere. It was great to see him, share a wonderful dinner, drink ridiculously expensive wine, laugh heartily and go home with him. I allowed the goddess a last hurrah. On the drive home the next morning I knew that I was letting go of not only Riley, but also a belief that I could engage in a casual way ever again. He was so clearly a symbol of what wealth is and is not and I knew that all the $400 dinners in the world could not replace the richness of spirit of the man who could truly meet me. While I did not call in his money and status intentionally, when they showed up as the meat of who he is, I could not partake for long. I left hungry every time, feeling vulnerable and fragile. I have never been so clear about what matters.

I have not written you this week so as to not perpetuate the fantasy anymore. It feels like it has evaporated and I, too, hold the pure, undiluted love that connected us when we met. It's in a safe place and is quiet. I can hear that it is in you, too.

Riley stopped by just before I got your note. I had asked him to drop over a few things I had left at his place and I gave him the few of his that were here. The letting go of tangible things made the rest more real. I sighed with relief as he rode off on his motorcycle, forever the free-spirited bad boy who is not *The Guy*. I feel free and open.

Getting your letter now feels like more letting go. More relief. More freedom. *Perfect.*

Tears flowed as I read your words, Mark. Robert and Francesca. Richard and Leslie . . . great lovers to feel such affinity to. We are honored with the distinction of life-long love amid obstacles. I have never wanted to be in the way of a happy life with your family all these years. I know with a clear heart that the issues you have faced in your marriage began long ago and had nothing to do with me. All that has come to pass is part of the bigger story.

Hugs,
Lis

eight

Subject: Hey
Date: Wed, 2 Aug 2006 5:08 PM
From: Mark
To: Lisa

I'll write more when I get some space to hang with you a bit. I'll be going to the men's retreat August 15 - 20. Auditioning w/ a new band Monday. trust u r well.

Mark

Subject: re: Hey
Date: Thu, 3 Aug 2006 6:37 AM
From: Lisa
To: Mark

Hey . . . that sounds cool. What musical genre?

Things are good here. Zac will be home tomorrow night. This weekend I'm going to a client's wedding up in Door County, WI. It will be nice to get away to somewhere beautiful for a couple days and meet some cool people. Women's Network luncheon today. Date tonight.

Subject: re: Hey
Date: Fri, 11 Aug 2006 7:08 PM
From: Mark
To: Lisa

Greetings, Earthling . . . local news from here . . .

Rock band audition cancelled. Haven't written a thing since I last wrote you. Plan on doing quite a bit during the retreat next week, including perhaps an ongoing letter to you while I'm there, if it's okay with you.

Reborn passion for music inside of me . . . dinner and conversation with a musician friend Wednesday night woke it up. Described to him the Dream Collage thing, reminding myself of its importance . . .

All fantasy aside, you are on my mind daily. Looking forward to writing you at length while at the retreat. I admit, in spite of previous declarations, that I run all kinds of little movies of you and I in my head. Seems normal, though.

Mark

_____

Subject: re: Hey
Date: Sat, 12 Aug 2006 9:07 AM
From: Lisa
To: Mark

Sorry to hear about the band. Not meant to be then. I hope other things are going well, getting better. Excited to hear you spark over the Dream Collage and music!

Lots new here, lots to say . . .

There is a new man. His name is Dave. Seems that clearing the path completely of the energy of unavailable men was the catalyst. All the pieces fell together that Sunday you sent your email to me, when Riley dropped by my stuff . . . the day that I completely let go. I sobbed for hours, surrendered. Got clear. Prayed. Released. *Changed.* Then got an email from Dave, someone I had met on Match.com. His letter was beautiful and open, inquisitive about my day and in it he asked what book I was engaged in, that he had been reading *The Five People You Meet in Heaven.* I had just started it after having it for months, the first of many signs.

He may well be *the guy.*

You have been on my mind a lot, for this man reminds me a great deal of you. Thirty minutes into our first date (cooking at my house) I looked over at him chopping veggies and thought of you. There was an energy that made me think that this is the closest I have felt to what I feel when I am with you. During a casual mention of the upcoming weekend I spontaneously asked him if he would like to go to the wedding in Door

County with me, and he instantly said *yes, I do*. Our third date was a 300-mile road trip to a wedding where I knew only the groom, and him only by phone. It was surreal, but beautiful, the most meaningful wedding I have ever attended. An amazing two days. On the way out of town a billboard read:

Live Deeper. Love Wider. Leave Bigger. The sum of it all . . .

There are stunning similarities between you and Dave. You have a similar build, both love music, to cook, to write, to dance. He is deep, spiritual and passionate . . . physical . . . does home remodeling for a living, and has a 13-year-old son who was conceived with a woman he was living with, then married when the baby was a few months old. He left after a year; she's remarried. He also has two grown sons from a first marriage. He believes in God. He believes in True Love, though it has eluded him. Like me, he has had several short-term relationships in the past decade with someone who was not the right fit. *This* feels right, he says. It does.

I've told him about you, our story, about the pure love that appeared when we met, that it will remain always in spite of the recent letting go. I told him about the similarities between the two of you and he gets it. You would like him. I am letting go of fear and allowing myself to be happy. To be loved. To trust.

The retreat sounds great. I look forward to hearing how the writing goes. And of course an ongoing letter to me is okay. I'll look forward to it.

hugs,
Lis

―――――
Subject: Hey
Date: Sun, 13 Aug 2006 7:58 AM
From: Mark
To: Lisa

OK, so . . .

I like Dave already, never mind that twinge of regret that he's available NOW and I'm not. If preliminary testing shows him to be The One, perhaps writing to you during the retreat is not such a good idea . . . or at least keep it less intimate. It will be spontaneous, but edited . . . hmmm . . . I see my fear coming through there. Tell you what: if whatever I write is genuine, coming from that place where there need not be any shame or guilt, I won't need to edit anything, and you'll know what to do with it. I do feel cautious, though, knowing your heart is soaring for The One Dave makes me want to back off a bit. Too soon to be truly happy for you . . .

I need to get over the impulse to have him whacked.

———

Subject: Hey
Date: Tue, 15 Aug 2006 7:42 AM
From: Mark
To: Lisa

Quick, give me your mailing address. I'll mail you whatever I write from Mendocino on my way home on Sunday.

———

Subject: re: Hey
Date: Thu, 24 Aug 2006 9:00 AM
From: Lisa
To: Mark

How was your retreat?

———

Subject: re: Hey
Date: Sat, 26 Aug 2006 6:38 AM
From: Mark
To: Lisa

The retreat was great. The only writing I did was journal stuff, and there wasn't much of that. Mostly I listened, and talked with a bunch of the guys during breaks and meals. I was asked to do bodywork for a spontaneous "healing pavilion" on one of the nights. Drummed a bit, but mostly listened, walked, and let my heart get opened way up. It was a lovely first week back at home . . . very different energy in the house . . . lots of listening going on, with good communication and sensitivity to spirit. We all got into the animal Medicine Cards for the first few days. I was full of nature and ancestor information, which I noticed made me really available to some of the deeper issues here at home. I was feeling fearless and willing, with clear insight . . .

But I can feel The World closing in on us again. Fortunately I can call up some of the retreat experiences and information to keep me from being swallowed up whole. Music and Nature is where I find my Self again.

The Medicine Cards had two strong messages for me when I came home: rely on and turn to Spirit more often, and . . . write! Nice support system, 'eh?

How art thou? Everything still groovy and yummy in Dave Land? I thought of sending you guys a case of wine for all the kitchen-connecting you seemed to be headed for . . .

Mark

Subject: re: Hey
Date: Sat, 25 Aug 2006 8:03 AM
From: Lisa
To: Mark

Glad the retreat was great and heart-opening. I'm happy to hear the energy at home was lovely and I hope The World doesn't swallow you up. Keeping nature and music close is a wonderful thing. Hopefully you can keep your heart open and flowing with love.

I am doing great. Busy last week with Zac's orientations for high school (!) and a minor surgery he had to remove a small bump on his head, a granuloma that is benign and only required a couple stitches. He starts school full-time tomorrow, marking the true end of summer. Back to the routine of schedules and homework. His 14th birthday is Thursday. I can't believe how the years have flown by and he has become such a young man. This summer really felt like the end of an era.

Dave Land is still groovy. We spent most of the weekend at his house and it was fun. He had his son Adam (13) this weekend and the boys hung out and ran around most of the time while we cooked and watched movies, running interference occasionally. We played a lot of Scrabble (my favorite game!) and Zac has become quite good at it. Dave's older sons were around a bit and I found myself adjusting to all the testosterone. Mostly it was a blast and I liked the activity. I found myself imagining what it would feel like to live with Dave and share *this* household. When I came home it seemed so much more quiet and calm here. Something to journal about - the blending of families and what it offers, and what it requires in terms of compromise.

The good news is that we talk freely about what we are feeling and I feel very comfortable expressing what's going on with me about that. He is very laid back about it all and listens to me with endearing amusement when I get in one of my 'spins'. I love that. Where he spins is about work, and I can see how The World can interrupt the flow of a lovely home when things like difficult customers put stress in the mix. He has more work than time at the moment and is struggling with keeping people happy and having enough help to get it all done. Add rain to the mix and he is pretty stressed out about the outdoor projects people want finished this week for Labor Day parties. I can see your life a little clearer, my friend.

This feels different than the 'dating' I have done for several years. More

80

serious. When I project merging our lives it makes me draw in a deep breath. Am I truly ready? I have had my own life with Zac for so long. Not a question I need to answer today but one I think about while the kitchen magic continues and all the amazing feelings keep growing.

Thanks for the wine thought. I like red.

Lis

_____

Subject: hey
Date: Thu, 7 Sep 2006 5:36 AM
From: Lisa
To: Mark

Hope all is well.

New development: A friend of mine out there has a production co. and she called yesterday about developing a 30 min. talk show for syndication starring . . . guess who? We brainstormed about it and she wants me to send all my media materials, and may have a crew shoot my next speaking engagement in October. This is big. The key is selling the concept and then, of course, me. If I come across great on camera they may go for it. Holy shit.

What happens when everything you want starts flowing to you? I'm not sure yet. So far, it is kind of freaking me out.

nine

Subject: Hey
Date: Thu, 22 Jul 2007 5:36 AM
From: Lisa
To: Mark

Ran across your email address and wanted to say hi! Happy birthday! Hoping you were celebrated and had a good day.

Would love to hear from you.

Lis

_____

Hi Mark,

I wanted to tell you that I shared my part of the Italy story (remember Italy?) with my writers group. It was a big hit with the women, especially Carolyn who was swooning in her cubicle at work, shooing away anyone who wanted to interrupt her while she read it. It was great to have positive feedback about my writing and of course there was much speculation about what had kept 'them' apart for so many years. I may go back to the story and start another chapter with where it all began, when we first met at your Apollo gig.

The cool thing is that Dave is also in this writer's group and he graciously endured their inquisition of me, then shared a story he wrote about me before we got married. It was a lovely thing.

Hoping all is well with you and yours and that you have a wonderful Christmas and all good things in the New Year. Today is my birthday and each year I reflect on all those who have brought me to who I am and you are always there. Glad we've reconnected, my friend. It was great talking with you at Thanksgiving after such a long time.

Lis

_____

I'm just discovering your email this morning. You've been on my mind. I knew you had a birthday, but didn't want to look stupid by getting the date wrong.

Anyway, good for you and your commitment to writing. I love that you're getting positive feedback on that Italy story. I'd like to have been a fly on the wall as your friends read it. Just hearing from you inspires me to write more. Are you writing it as fiction, based on a true story, or autobiography? I recently came across someone's comment about telling the truth as a good starting place for writers - especially writers who feel stuck or blocked - and the thought of you writing YOUR story feels right and good . . .

Random thought: Do you have a copy of Dan Millman's *The Life You Were Born To Live* ? I'm a 35/8, which means I'm here to work through issues of emotional honesty, independence, power, manifesting abundance, authority, and freedom through discipline and depth of experience.

What year were you born?

So, Life Coach . . . help me out here (again!) What's the first thing that comes to mind if you think of me in terms of "providing a valuable service in the world"? I'm having a hard time being objective about this.

I'll stay in touch. Got a New Years gig tonight and carpentry work is going well. Stay warm in snowy Chicago. Happy New Year to you and Dave.

Mark

Subject: re: hey
Date: Wed, 02 Jan 2008 8:26 AM
From: Lisa
To: Mark

Hi there . . . Happy New Year! Hope you had a great gig :-)

Ah, the Italy story. Fact or fiction? Only God knows for sure. It was written as fantasy and taking it further wasn't feeling like the right course. Starting at the beginning with what is real felt better, so I went there. I have attached it and when I presented it to the group there was a lukewarm response. The women who swooned at the Italy story weren't there, so I will be anxious to hear their feedback. To be honest, it was harder to write as lyrically about the truth. The fantasy just came so easily and going back 26 years is a stretch, too much like relaying facts. I've changed their names to Leslie & Michael to create more of a 'novel' approach vs. memoir, which feels better.

So your service to the world? Frankly, my friend, the first thing that comes to mind is writing. Writing about the path of the conscious man. Of his struggles with himself, with relationships, with the world as it is. 'Mr. Hang In There' but with the spiritual lessons learned along the way, with the beautiful crafting with words that you do about things like the crafting of a cabinet - remember that? When you wrote to me about that? Get out your journals and write the lessons from that day, that year, that decade. Write about now and where you are and who you are and what you know and what you don't know and want to find out. Just write.

Well, I better run. I am writing down my intentions for the new year, a year of new choices. No goals, only the choices I would need to make to create what I want. I am having my clients do this, too. So can you: what are the choices you can make in this new year to be, do, and have what you want? It all starts with choices.

Lis

_____
Subject: Hey
Date: Thu, 3 Jan 2008 6:21 AM
From: Mark
To: Lisa

SO . . . a 29/11, eh? Same as Savannah. In fact, I had Millman's book in my hand the day she was born. A doctor visit near the due date showed her to be breach, and the birthing team we preferred was available *now*. I opened Millman's book and looked up the info for that date. What I remember most - and convinced me we should birth the baby then and there - was that their energy field is way above the average. When inspired or excited about a creative project, they don't need as much sleep as most people. "Their attractiveness stems as much from a glowing energy field as from physical features."

We brought her into the world by c-section an hour later.

I have WAY more to chat about, but off to work. Thanks so much for responding to my life purpose question. I could write to you all day . . .

Mark

_____
Subject: re: hey
Date: Sat, 5 Jan 2008 12:01 PM
From: Mark
To: Lisa

OK . . . I just read the Michael and Leslie story you sent. Some thoughts:

It's really, really interesting to read your perspective on how we met. I remember talking to you and I remember the club and signing the record, but the thrill was reading your details about the orange I was peeling, the shaking of hands, the smile on my face as I signed your album . . .

It's clear that this story is wanting to be about the relationship between Leslie and Michael. The story bolts from her leaving Chicago right to the club in Walnut Creek, where it hangs out long enough to provide more

84

interesting details of what's happening to Leslie. It's in the club that the reader discovers she's self-conscious about her appearance and has a self-esteem issue. These details (to me) seem suddenly important because the pretty musician is presented as looking past any of that, and he sees something in her that Leslie doesn't see in herself . . . hence his kindness and interest in her. And I DEFINITELY want to know what happens next. *You are loved*, he signs. Loved by who? In what way? Even if I didn't know these two people I would read into their relationship that a special kind of spirituality is present and is likely to influence both their lives in a meaningful way.

Their interaction in the club shows Michael as kind-hearted and comfortable in his own skin, and there's something sweet in your description of him wanting to include Leslie in his life. Since in real life we know both of their lives will be affected and influenced by one another for years to come, I would encourage you to show the reader more of Leslie during her flight to California (doubts, fears, apprehension, excitement, rebirth . . . something that reflects more of her personal spirituality), so that when she sees the California ocean for the first time: *POW!* Something inside her *shifts* . . . something magical takes place at the sight, sound and feel of the ocean. This moment sets up the impact of her meeting Michael hours later.

The women who swooned over your Italy story will, I predict, be chomping at the bit to find out what happens next. If they dug the Italy story so much it's in part due to their wishing *they* were in Leslie's sandals. You might keep that in mind when fleshing out Leslie as she learns about herself, creates a new life, and eventually finds her way back to Chicago.

Hate to end here, but gotta move on to other things. I wasn't intending to send you a critique and then sign off. I'm enjoying the luxury of writing you while it's pouring down rain outside, but, with interruptions here, it's been two hours now. Shit. I'm just getting started . . .

More later. Be warm.

Mark

————
Subject: re: hey
Date: Sun, 6 Jan 2008 8:09 AM
From: Lisa
To: Mark

So, I love, love, love your feedback and you are absolutely right. I keep spinning this story in my head and I keep tripping on how I want to tell it. What is it *about?* Your questions are the perfect place to start. I'm glad you liked the detail. Funny thing: the crusty ex-cop writer in our group circled 'You are loved' on his feedback notes and said, "I just don't buy it. No one would say that after meeting someone for a few minutes." (grin) The truth is stranger than fiction, indeed.

Subject: Contest submission
Date: Mon, 7 Jan 2008 9:40 AM
From: Lisa
To: Mark

So I was thinking that I would look at writing competitions that would inspire me, set deadlines and possibly bring recognition and cash! I stumbled on this and it sounds like you, Nature Guy. It's only up to 1500 words. Not sure if an entry fee. But write fast if you are gonna do it! Deadline is January 11th.

Hope you got this in time.

L

P.S. Remember the book I contributed to, *A Day In The Life*? There was a review in Publisher's Weekly and it was good!

Subject: re: Contest submission
Date: Thu, 10 Jan 2008 11:00 PM
From: Mark
To: Lisa

Took the bait. Here's the story I'm submitting, "Rainy Day Man". This is a true story about an otherworldly experience I had while jogging in an intense rainstorm, then discussing the experience with the teacher from my psychology class. Hope you like it . . .

Mark

Subject: re: Contest submission
Date: Fri, 11 Jan 2008 4:53 AM
From: Lisa
To: Mark

I really like it! I was thrown a bit with the beginning in the teacher's office (knowing this is a *nature* writing contest) but then it became clear where you were going with it and the clarity of the day before was a great twist. Love the last page and a half!

Good Luck!

Subject: interesting story. . .
Date: Thu, 14 Feb 2008 8:40 AM
From: Mark
To: Lisa

Kick-started by your sending me that writing competition notice, I wrote
the attached little story for The Sun magazine on their topic "Porches".
The story centers on my childhood memories of playing on the front porch
of my best friend Frankie's house. When his family moved out of state
Frankie and I wrote to each other for a short time but soon lost touch, and I
haven't had contact with him or his family since. Frankie's mom and my
mom have been staying in touch via emails. Every few years my mom tells
me a bit of news about what they're up to, but I've still had no personal
contact with any of them . . . until yesterday . . .

I finished writing "Frankie's Front Porch" on Tuesday. Yesterday my mom
forwarded me a recent email she received from Frankie's mom which
contained the news that Frankie's dad was coming home after a lengthy
hospital stay involving, apparently, a drawn-out dialysis regime of many
weeks: he was coming home to die, with the help of hospice, and was very
much at peace with the whole thing.

That my mom would forward me that email was very unusual, but,
obviously, I was blown away by the timing: the day after I finish a story
about a family I've had no contact with in over forty years, I get an email
from the mother of that family telling of their sad news.

I wrote Frankie's mom immediately, sending her the story I wrote,
commenting on the timing of it all.

I got an email from her today, expressing gratitude and tears, and how
moving it was for her to read the story to her husband, now bedridden in
their living room. I'd told her in my email how many great memories had
come back to me in the writing of the story . . .

Finally, she said her three kids would be at the house tonight, and she was
going to ask Frankie - who knows nothing of the story - to read it aloud to
everyone before they begin discussing what to do in the coming weeks . . .

. . . oh man . . . I just had to share this with you . . .

_____
Subject: re: interesting story
Date: Tue, 19 Feb 2008 10:34 AM
From: Lisa

To: Mark

Incredible story! I love it. I hope it gets published . . .

I started cleaning out my office this weekend and uncovered years of my life. Swimming in a deep sea of memories, it was like finding hidden treasure. Wow. I can write my whole story from a day of cleaning the office. You were there, too, of course . . . letters, pictures, stories. There is a photo of you cooking in your little house in Niles when we hung out for the weekend and cooked and walked and talked endlessly. I distinctly remember the sound of the massive wind chimes outside the open front door.

Hug.

_____
Subject: radio show
Date: Wed, 20 Feb 2008 10:15 PM
From: Mark
To: Lisa

So I just finished listening (for the 2nd time) to the radio interview you did. I love how grounded you are while speaking . . . especially in contrast to the host. I got a kick out of the way she talked more and more about herself as the interview went on, and then once you were off the air she started another rap with "helpful" suggestions *using your information.* Sheesh . . . you'd be a much better anchor for that show.

_____
Subject: story
Date: Thu, 20 Mar 2008 6:14 AM
From: Lisa
To: Mark

Great talking with you yesterday! Here it is - rough, rough draft. Let me know what you think. Send me something of yours to read.

_____
Subject: re: story
Date: Sat, 22 Mar 2008 6:04 AM
From: Mark
To: Lisa

Send me your mailing address . . .

_____
Subject: hey
Date: Sun, 30 Mar 2008 5:55 AM
From: Lisa
To: Mark

Thanks for the editorial package! Wow. You nailed it in so many places (in a good way) and I really appreciate the time and thought you put into it. I will go through your notes and the ones from my writer's group and revise, explain, and flesh out parts that need it. A few of your "Try Agains" felt right on. I love your comments about whether it sounds like *me.*

I'll send you more as I write it, if you are willing to be my editor-at-large. You truly made me see the story in a different way - you always do.

_____

Subject: hey
Date: Mon, 31 Mar 2008 10:16 AM
From: Mark
To: Lisa

Hi there . . .

Got back late last night from a horse show down in the San Diego/Palm Springs area. We drove down last week Tuesday, had three days to settle in and make a camp (a money-saver, while everyone else does a hotel), then the event was Fri, Sat & Sun. Spring green down there in the desert area . . . very nice . . . and I had the luxury of sitting in a chair for two days, reading *Eat, Pray, Love.*

Well . . .

After sending off your edited manuscript, then leaving the next day for the horse show and jumping right in on the reading of "Eat . .", my head was swimming with a mix of: your story, writing, Italy, life choices, writing, envy (of Liz Gilbert's life), freedom, love, writing, and a rather significant interest in what your response would be to my editing comments. I'm relieved to hear that you took it the way I intended, and am flattered that you're genuinely interested in having me do some more. So, *sure*, keep it coming. It was really fun, actually. And I'll be happy to send you my stuff . . . when there is some. What little I've got going hasn't been transferred to the computer yet, but yeah, when it's there I'll send it along.

I'm resisting the temptation to spend the next two paragraphs with a quasi-journal entry about feeling a little depressed since driving home from the horse show. I'm pretty sure the reading of "Eat . ." put me in a contemplative mood. I was real quiet for the last few days of the show - having just finished the book - and felt calm, like after a two-hour meditation, unwilling to come out of my grounded place and interact with all these different personalities, you know? Being around all the horses and pitching in to help Savannah get through the event was very, very nourishing for me. There were several incidents where the two of us would walk together from one end of the grounds to the other, just hanging out and chatting as we walked, and Savannah would slip her arm into mine - almost unconsciously - and hold on to her dad as we made our way to wherever. Very sweet and spontaneous.

Something about being with her, horses, and having time to myself to relax and read put me in a great place. Then it ended with a whole other reality of Mariah and I packing up camp (with no small amount of bickering) and making the 8-hour drive home, me feeling alert but quiet, contemplating a life of peace, writing, and travel.

Aw, shit. See? Just couldn't keep myself from going there . . .

Anyway, I think that book was *working on me.* I kept coming back to you and your story, rooting for you to find your storyteller's voice, and especially flesh out your time with Alex The Canadian. There's a lot of *what-will-happen-next?* potential there.

Not having to be at work til later today, having the (messy) house to myself for a few hours and then finding your email is the perfect tonic for what ails me. I'm now remembering one of Liz Gilbert's male characters telling her at one point that a soul mate is not necessarily a lifetime partner thing. In my case I'm getting exactly what I've been asking for. My longings and desires for a richer life are directly connected to being where I am right now. The *future me* is pulling the *present-time me* through all of this sifting and sorting of feelings, intuitions and inspired moments. All is well, and I need only stay connected to what matters to me most and give those things my energy and attention, trusting that I'm on my way to a more joyful life.

So thank you for continuing to keep in touch and - whether you're aware of it or not - helping me to keep this writing thing alive. That whole process of editing your story was unmistakably stimulating. Even I was surprised by the energy and enthusiasm I experienced while doing it, so it's lovely to have you ask for more. I feel better knowing you see it as support and encouragement.

Til the next time . . .

Be well. Play nice. No biting.

Mark

_____
Subject: re: hey
Date: Thu, 3 Apr 2008 7:52 AM

From: Lisa
To: Mark

So very nice . . . thanks.

Lis

_____

Subject: re: hey
Date: Sun, 6 Apr 2008 6:59 AM
From: Mark
To: Lisa

In the midst of a steady influx of creativity and grace, several things at
once are going well. I really think a direct connection can be made
between where I'm at right now and your support. Thank you.

Mark

_____

Subject: hey
Date: Sun, 6 Apr 2008 9:22 AM
From: Lisa
To: Mark

You're welcome. I was just thinking of you this morning while watching
the movie *Into The Wild* - have you seen it? Wow. What a beautiful movie.
Moving and extraordinary. If you haven't seen it . . . you MUST!

Gotta go catch this first real day of Spring as temps inch towards 60
degrees and the sun is shining. Went to a house demolition sale yesterday
and we got a steal on over 200 retaining blocks for the front of the house.
We hauled them all home and are now starting the real work of building up
the flower beds in front. It will be nice. It felt *so good* to be outside
yesterday in the sun doing heavy lifting and *moving* after the long, dreary,
cold, snowy winter.

The gym just ain't the same.

_____

Subject: hey
Date: Tue, 24 Jun 2008 10:08 PM
From: Lisa
To: Mark

Hi Mark,

How are you? Any news? I'm busy coaching, Zac got his driver's permit

(!), and we're all enjoying summer. Hope all is well with you and yours.

Lis

Subject: hey
Date: Tue, 1 Jul 2008 12:37 AM
From: Mark
To: Lisa

Wrote to you from L.A. while on a Disneyland trip a few days ago. Did you get that?

Mark

Subject: re: hey
Date: Tue, 1 Jul 2008 4:15 AM
From: Lisa
To: Mark

No, it didn't come in. How are things?

Subject: re: hey
Date: Thu, 3 Jul 2008 7:07 AM
From: Mark
To: Lisa

Things are good. I found your email last Sunday while we were in L.A. doing Disneyland w/ Savannah and one of her girlfriends. I was up early Sunday morning and went to the hotel lobby to use the free internet. I logged in, and there was your letter. I was just finishing writing you with (harmless) news and updates when Mariah suddenly appeared at my side. Shit. She got a bit bent to discover I was writing you. I let her read what you'd written, and she left the room in a huff.

I signed off and joined her at a breakfast table. She wanted "answers" about how long you and I have been writing, why we've been writing, etc. Once I got to the part where you'd remarried she backed off. Within minutes she let the whole thing go. Apparently you didn't get that email for some reason.

Not writing much. Remodel work has been steady, and until recently was doing quite a bit of gigging with a couple of bands. This week has been quite physically demanding - a new kitchen job - which has me getting home late for dinner, then crashing in front of a movie before bed. Haven't heard from The Sun magazine yet about the front porch piece.

I think a lot about how I have interests in all these different areas - music, writing, carpentry, etc. . . and how I just don't have the discipline to leave any one of them alone long enough to really accomplish something with another. Mostly I notice I'm wanting to live well and happy *today*, being only *intermittently* inspired to stretch, and go beyond my norm. It's like I'm still tasting and sampling all this different life stuff, going from one to the other as my mood shifts. I'm trusting that some greater effort to *be* more and *do* more will come out of me someday. . .

Or not.

Hoo boy . . . I could really riff on this . . . this is the most writing I've done in a while. Feels good. But gotta head out for work. Write more when you can.

Hug.
Mark

———

Subject: hey
Date: Fri, 4 Jul 2008 10:44 AM
From: Mark
To: Lisa

Good morning . . .

I have about an hour to myself. After sending you that last message I was motivated to write more, not sure of *what* exactly, but something is wanting to be said. I thought I might as well just go with the impulse and see what comes out. An impulse, by the way, to say it to *you* . . .

Over the last few months I've had intuitions that you've lately been either unhappy or conflicted . . . or both. I'm not sure that I'm right, just wondering, because when you come into my mind my heart tells me you're troubled. Doubts, second thoughts . . . so I'm checking in with you - one of my dearest, longtime friends - to see how you are.

As I mentioned before, I'm being less hard on myself about what I'm capable of and what I actually accomplish. A few months back my therapist mirrored back to me that I'm "all about peace and ease", wanting to move through life with a sense of grace and effortlessness (you once playfully mocked me for that), working hard only when I needed to or felt like it; choosing beauty, relaxation and harmony over efforting, stress, and struggle. This, of course, has set up the volatile dynamic that I've so often complained about re: my marriage, since Mariah has such a willingness to be confrontational.

But I'm feeling just fine about wanting to do my life with a sense of peace and ease. It serves me especially well in areas of music and carpentry - lots of opportunities to create beauty there - and as I become more conscious of how much I *prefer* to be about peace and ease, it begins to spill over into things like cooking, which benefits my family. We've been having more dinners and get-togethers at our house, largely because I'm enjoying making these great dishes and creating good times for my mom and my sister's family.

One of the things that therapy helped with was for me to appreciate the value of wanting and creating beauty and ease as often as possible, and to just let Mariah - or whoever - go right on being upset or frustrated without it having anything to do with me. The bummer is that we don't sync up as often as we'd like, but, sorry, I don't share her 'glass-half-empty' perspective of . . . well . . . just about everything. I feel free of the spell I was under. I no longer make excuses, or blame other people or exterior circumstances for not being able to do what I want or to accomplish goals. My scale tips heavily towards how much in my life is going well and what I can be thankful for. All the various skills and interests I've acquired serve as a sort of 'All Access' pass to people and places I would never otherwise come in contact with, from kitchen remodels to gigs on the coast.

It's the *people*! I'm fascinated to see how they live, to hear their stories, to make music or beautiful kitchens with them. Wood, stone, horses, drums, cameras, food, music, nature. . . everywhere I go there are opportunities to enjoy my life, to connect with people . . . or take a break from it all and chill out with a long, hot shower at the gym after a good workout, popcorn and a movie at home with my family, hiding out in a coffee shop and writing, or letting everyone think I'm working in Oakland while spending the day in a Santa Cruz bookstore.

Here at home Mariah and I are making a conscious effort to communicate more effectively, without all the defensive posturing and bickering. It's been working pretty well - more patience with one another - but it hasn't affected the romantic aspect of our relationship one wit. That's mostly to do with me. All this therapy has yet to increase my attraction to her (that 'glass-half-empty' perspective is such a turnoff), but there's always opportunities to be kind, helpful and supportive.

Savannah is a total joy, and I just love being her dad. Your perspective on parenting Zac - "raising a man" - is something I think about with Savannah. She still - at fourteen and-a-half - crawls up in my lap or takes my hand when we're walking, and these days I'm more conscious of how those moments are influencing her future relationships with men. I make a mental note of this every time she's wanting contact with me. I sense, as she's about to enter high school, that these precious moments may come to

94

an end, but I tend to reject other people's predictions on this subject.

Ah, well . . . so this is what was wanting out.

Mark

___

Subject: Hey . . .
Date: Sat, 5 Jul 2008 2:21 PM
From: Lisa
To: Mark

Lots of thinking this weekend . . . so much to say, not the right time and space. You're instincts are right, I suppose. The blending of our households has been challenging and there is less kitchen dancing. We are building a pergola in the backyard which is great fun, hard work, and will be a nice addition for summer nights.

As always, reaching for perspective.

More soon.

Lis

ten

Subject: Life update. . .
Date: Tue, 9 Dec 2008 12:16 PM
From: Lisa

To: Mark

I came across an email you wrote me back in July, sensing that I was out of sorts, conflicted. I remember that I *was* in a frustrated place while adjusting to my new marriage. The day to day and the 'blended family' was really more difficult than I thought. There was more negotiation and less kitchen dancing.

So how am I now?

Well, still not much kitchen dancing. We have settled in. Things are mostly good, but sometimes not. The boys continue to challenge us as they wrestle with becoming men, each having a foot in both childhood and manhood. My stepson is with us every weekend, and he and Zac don't get along so well. I'm not writing as much as I want, but I am working with a coach on that. Dave's work is slow and money is tight, which makes for hard moments. We are working on better communication. He is more quiet and doesn't dig the big discussions that I love. Seems he did more in the beginning. We still enjoy each other in many ways, although I have made a shift to really plug into where I am in *me* and my place in the world, and not have so much attachment to where *we* are. I have fewer illusions about romance. Is this just what happens when you get married?

That makes me a little sad. And yet I guess I'm mostly happy.

I still think about my conversations with you. I wonder if there is such a thing as the blissful coexistence that allows for artist spirits to live and love, side by side . . . in a room, in a home, in the world.

I want to believe, yes.

Italy still beckons.

_____
Subject: re: Life update. . .
Date: Sat, 13 Dec 2008 7:56 AM
From: Mark
To: Lisa

Aw, Lis . . .

If I could, I'd wave my magic wand and *poof!,* I'd plop us both in front of a nice fire, two bottles of wine, and a comfortable couch. We need to talk my dear friend. A 'clearing session' . . . a weekend of books, music, walks, laughter, fine food and talk, talk, talk . . .

" . . . I have fewer illusions about romance. Is this just what happens when you get married?"

Yes.

. . . because, eventually, the 'Contact High' wears off, that buzz/glow thing at the front end of all relationships. It takes at least a good year of living with someone before all the goodies get transparent enough for the darker, hidden stuff to show through. We want to be loved and admired and thought of as special, so we agree to carry the projection our partner hangs on us:

HE: *You want a spiritual man who is earthy and funny and intimate and passionate and artsy and a good listener and great with kids and supportive of anything you're into? Okay, I'll be that for you, even though I may not* REALLY *have been that kind of guy all my life, but I bet I can keep up the facade long enough to keep you from leaving me or wanting to look elsewhere. I've never met a girl like you - your energy and beauty and how you combine the two and live* out loud *like that. I want to merge with you because you have qualities I wish I had, and to have someone like you be interested in me makes me feel special and valuable.*

SHE: *You want a goddess and a dirty little girl who will give you all the space you need to do whatever is important to you and likes to have a neat house and loves to drink wine and cook in the kitchen while listening to music and loves Nature and doesn't nag and is both independent of and devoted to you? Okay, I'll be that for you, even though it'll take a while for you to discover that the Goddess/dirty girl thing is how I manipulate men with my sexual energy. I like the part where you're proud of making good money because, as independent as I appear now, the time will come when I'll much prefer to have you support me and our kids. Chances are good that, after a few years, once we get more and more comfortable with one another and begin taking one another for granted, I'll gradually drop the Goddess thing altogether because I'll be so disappointed that you're not the man I thought you were, I'll lose all motivation to look hot just for you. I may even give it up for myself.*

Oh, yes, I've become quite cynical about marriage, but only because mine is the only marriage I've experienced. I highly recommend tuning in to your True Self - the version of you that you *intended* to come into the world with from the start - and not give a shit what others around you think. It's not coming from arrogance, but rather *truth.* We can be authentic and true to our Selves in the context of what feels like a restrictive or uninspired relationship. I mean, why not? May as well . . . YOU can dance and drink wine in the kitchen while you're cooking. It doesn't have to matter *more* to do it *with* someone. Run your own energy in whatever way makes you feel alive or happy. *Take better care of your Self.*

Shit happens, yes . . . but *cool* shit happens too.

oh man . . I'm just gettin' warmed up. More tomorrow.

You are loved.

Mark

Subject: re: Life update. . .
Date: Sat, 13 Dec 2008 7:56 AM
From: Lisa
To: Mark

Aw, Mark . . . keeping going . . .

You had me at "talk, talk, talk . . ."

Lis
ox

Subject: re: Life update. . .
Date: Sun, 14 Dec 2008 10:30 AM
From: Mark
To: Lisa

Good morning. Where was I? Ah, yes . . . spiritual musician, cynical about marriage, giving relationship advice to hot Life Coach . . .

SO . . .

Cool shit happens, too. Yes. Like last week, when Mariah and I went to a yoga retreat in Mexico . . .

She'd been talking about wanting this retreat for herself since last spring. I kept saying: GO! Then it got to be October, with a (now larger) deposit due. I'd been telling her to go to this thing every time she brought it up, but oh, the money, the time, what about Savannah, blah blah . . . Fine, don't go then.

The last possible day to turn in a deposit came and she was still torn. It finally came out that she was afraid that I might not be here when she got back. I was actually looking forward to a week of just Savannah and I while Mariah went for some much needed chill time, so the me-not-being-here thing was a little much, I thought. Whatever.

Then she made up her mind to go . . . right after she hit on the idea of taking me with her: *It could be the honeymoon we never had!*

Uh-huh.

Short story: We went. Mexico and the beach and the yoga and the food and the room and the people and the weather . . . it was awesome.

Not so awesome: The part where she expected this trip to be a re-kindling of romance and intimacy between us. It was lovely, but not romantic *for me.* The night before we left to come home we had a late-night talk about why there was so little romance in our relationship, a conversation we've had several times over the years. Feeling rested, healthy and grounded I had absolutely no problem telling her my truth: *Drop the negativity, take better care of yourself, and LIGHTEN UP about life - especially about the not-so-cool shit that happens - and* show *me the creative, sensual woman you keep claiming you are . . .*

Well . . . THIS time it got through. And together with her own insights and experiences during the retreat she's been quite committed to taking better care of herself and has immediately noticed a positive shift in her business. Better attitude . . . but still no romance. I can't (won't) fake feeling a genuine desire for her so we'll see. In the meantime it helped a lot to come home to that place in *me* where I can tell the truth about my needs and feelings and not feel defensive about it. Couples therapy, through the year, helped as well. By the time we did the retreat we'd developed much better communication skills, so there seemed (to me) to be a balanced give-and-take of getting our individual needs met while we were down there.

Before leaving for the trip she issued a quasi-warning to me that she was *expecting* me to be loving and attentive towards her while we were there, and that it wouldn't sit well with her if I got into my independent do-my-own-thing space. The impulse to get up at dawn and wander the beach before breakfast, just to have some quiet alone time with myself, was some kind of no-no . . . unless I did it with her.

I did get a moment alone and this poem about God came to me, almost in its entirety, while laying in a lounge chair on the beach, 80 degrees at 11 in the morning, watching the waves rolling in, crashing on some rocks. I didn't have anything to write with, so I just lay there, writing it in my head, and committed it to paper the next morning.

As for your last email . . . I could really *feel* you . . . looking around, taking stock of where you've landed, and thinking: *I thought it would be different.* This might be a good time to check out Ekhart Tolle's books, *The Power of Now* and *The New Earth.*

It's all ego. The depression, the sadness, the frustration, the disappointments are all ego. The True Self is being usurped by that thing in us that LIKES the drama and energy rush of out-of-control emotions. And by the way: It's temporary. All of it. The goodies AND the suckies. Our job is to pay attention because we planned way ahead of time to encounter it *all* during this life. It isn't happening TO us; it's happening FOR us.

_____

Subject: re: Life update. . .
Date: Mon, 15 Dec 2008 10:21 AM
From: Lisa
To: Mark

Love the poem. Beautiful.

I'm glad you got to Mexico. Fabulous place. Where? We went to Cancun for our honeymoon and then again in September for our first anniversary. It was spectacular. I loved my walks alone on the beach at dawn. I could live there on the beach, writing, coaching. Romance came easy for us in Mexico . . . but then we came home.

You're right. Ego does get in the way. I have been reading *A New Earth* for six months. Can't get through it all. The last time I picked it up and read a few pages I ended up writing in my journal how it may all be crap. Then a bird actually shit on the cover. LOL. So either I am resisting the 'Now' thing, or I'm smarter than the average New Age Bear.

I'm working with a new coach who specializes in personal branding and we are working on my 'next step'. It seems I have some things to clear out before I am ready.

Thanks for reminding me that it is all temporary. That's the truth. I'm so aware that the choices just keep coming and I keep making them.

All things are possible.

_____

Subject: See you on Oprah
Date: Thu, 26 Jan 2009 11:56 AM
From: Lisa
To: Mark

Remember when you said that?

Well, I won't be on the stage or anything but I have been asked to be an audience guest on an Oprah show about women and midlife hormones (some time ago I added my thoughts on bio-identical hormones to the Oprah website). It will feature Dr. Christiane Northrup, and Suzanne Somers will be talking about her book, *Ageless*. The taping is on Wednesday. Not sure when it will air. It's a step towards the day when I'm there talking about *my* book. It might help if I actually finish writing one. LOL

Things are better. Focusing on my gifts and sharing them where needed. Dancing with myself in the kitchen if the music moves me . . .

How are you?

Subject: re: See you on Oprah
Date: Sun, 29 Jan 2009 6:50 AM
From: Mark
To: Lisa

How am I? Uh, well . . . how's this:

I've started going to weekly therapy sessions on my own. At the beginning of January, while driving across the San Rafael bridge one day, something just clicked into place inside of me: *I want a better life.* So I called my therapist and asked for his help with this because I'm intending to divorce Mariah. I'm doing this without anger or blame, and am in therapy to make certain that I make this move for myself. All these years of secrecy, of sneaking off to take nature walks, see a movie, go to the gym, to a coffee shop to write? I'm done. It was our trip to Mexico when I just completely came alive and this whole other guy showed up: alive, masculine, sexy, eager to know new people, and so NOT compatible with Mariah. We're not a match, and I want to spend the rest of my years being fully alive. So here I go.

Mark

Subject: re: See you on Oprah
Date: Sun, 29 Jan 2009 7:29 AM
From: Lisa
To: Mark

Good for you. It is not good to spend the rest of your life with someone who is not a good match. Life is too short, and could be too sweet for that.

Over here we are working through our disillusions and time will tell which way I will go. What I do know for sure is that I will be fine no matter what.

So will you, my friend.

eleven

Subject: Happy Birthday
Date: Fri, 17 Jul 2009 1:08 PM
From: Lisa
To: Mark

Hope you are well. Lots new here. Some good, some not so . . . but it's life and life goes on. Hugs on your special day.

Lis

_____
Subject: re: Happy Birthday
Date: Tue, 21 Jul 2009 6:36 AM
From: Mark
To: Lisa

Well, hi there . . .

Thank you for the b'day greeting.

Your short, somewhat cryptic message about good and not-so-good changes sounds suspiciously like relationship turmoil. Hope I'm wrong. Being philosophical about sucky life stuff only takes me so far, like having to wait for the pukey carnival ride to end before you can get off. I can chant *this is good for me somehow, this is good for me somehow* all I want during the ride, but I still feel like shit until it comes to a complete stop.

What we need here is the tried-and-true, never-fails, bottle-of-wine-and-five-hours-of-talk thingy. I spent an hour of yesterday afternoon journaling about my weird, sucky week, and finished off what I was writing with wishing I was sitting next to the ocean with you, talking, talking, talking . . . . leaning against you, waiting for the source of the tears to make itself known. Swear to God, that's what I wrote . . .

Gotta get out the door to remodel a bathroom. More later. Way more.

Subject: re: Happy Birthday
Date: Tue, 21 Jul 2009 4:37 PM
From: Lisa
To: Mark

You suspect right. But it's all good. At the end of the day it's all unfolding the way it's supposed to. It usually does when we let it.

How's the end of October for that chat? I'll be in Northern California for a speaking engagement.

Subject: re: Happy Birthday
Date: Tue, 21 Jul 2009 5:49 PM
From: Mark
To: Lisa

YES! What dates you comin' out?

Subject: re: Happy Birthday
Date: Tue, 21 Jul 2009 7:13 PM
From: Lisa
To: Mark

I come on 10/22 to San Jose and have a couple of free days before my workshops on Sunday and Monday. I leave out of Sacramento on the 28th. Lots of friends and clients I'd like to see and not sure I will even get to hang out with everyone. Probably do something Saturday eve with the Marin girls.

I'll have to fit in a five-hour beach chat with you.

Subject: Get your ass out here
Date: Mon, 3 Aug 2009 2:29 AM
From: Mark
To: Lisa

I got your dates. That first Friday you're here (23rd) I'm doing a great gig in Napa with a pretty good blues band. Great vibe and scene. Try and make that one . . .

Hoping to make a beach walk/talk happen while you're here. Stay tuned. I know you have your own stuff to do, so let's keep in touch as to how we can do everything cool and fun and wonderful . . .

Taking the test for my contractor's license this Wednesday. Gigs Thursday nite and Saturday afternoon. Music stuff is VERY happening these days. New band forming with killer singer and rhythm section and three horns.

oooff. . . so much to chat about. Busy week coming up, so not likely to say much now. Just quickie stuff. *Brilliant and inspired*, but quick.

Hug.
Mark

_____
Subject: re: Get your ass out here
Date: Mon, 3 Aug 2009 7:15 AM
From: Lisa
To: Mark

I would love to hear you play! What are the odds of having Friday free before the gig?

Let's chat soon. Good luck on Wednesday!! I leave that day for Dallas for a Women's Network conference till Sunday.

_____
Subject: re: Get your ass out here
Date: Tue, 4 Aug 2009 6:30 AM
From: Mark
To: Lisa

Too soon to know what the day of the gig will offer up. More later.

_____
Subject: Off to see the Wizard
Date: Tue 11 Aug 2009 5:45 AM
From: Lisa
To: Mark

OK, so my conference in Dallas was unfreakinbelievable. Lots to tell but the coolest thing was coaching an amazing woman who hired me after a 15-minute intro session. She's an author and does workshops at - get this - *Wizard Academy* in Austin, TX. We met for coffee before we left Dallas and she invited me to come to her next workshop in December. They will put me up in the Engelbrecht mansion "dorm" for two nights. Sounds like Hogwarts for cool, creative grownups, right?

_____
Subject: re: Off to see the Wizard
Date: Fri, 14 Aug 2009 6:55 AM
From: Mark
To: Lisa

cool . . .

Subject: fun writing assignment. . . just cuz
Date: Sun, 23 Aug 2009 7:05 AM
From: Mark
To: Lisa

At the *moment* when you sit down to write give me three paragraphs on:

Right now, if I could wave my wand and have what I wanted, I would ask for:

. . . because . . .

Subject: Sure
Date: Mon, 24 Aug 2009 5:01 AM
From: Lisa
To: Mark

Assignment accepted. Hope you plan to do it, too.

Subject: re: fun writing assignment. . . just cuz
Date: Tue, 25 Aug 2009 7:58 PM
From: Lisa
To: Mark

Right now, if I could wave my wand and have what I wanted, I would ask for:

. . . my marriage to be complete.

The immediate thought that comes to mind is a complete marriage . . . with love and passion and commitment and joy . . . trust and truth and partnership and grace. A wonderful blend of interdependence and individual pursuit. A cooperative, in every sense of the word. Ironically, I've yearned for that *during* my marriage more often than when I was searching for The One.

So I say *Let's take some space.* And he leaves. And I thrive. And he struggles. He gets pissed off, cocky. Having space feels good for me even while riding the waves of sudden sadness that knock me down, then subside. Then he comes in all playful, golden brown and laughing. Melts me a little. Till I say stop. Till I say *leave.* Till next time . . .

So incomplete, with me unwilling to really say *I'm done. Completely done.* Yet my soul knows. It says that it is time to reclaim my life, my home, my body, my heart, my future. To reclaim all of me.

. . . because . . .

Limbo is too hard. Because I already know. And until I let go of my incomplete marriage I cannot begin to hope for my complete one.

Subject: re: fun writing assignment. . . just cuz
Date: Wed, 26 Aug 2009 6:14 AM
From: Mark
To: Lisa

Oh my . . .

Sure sounds familiar . . .

Subject: re: fun writing assignment. . . just cuz
Date: Wed, 26 Aug 2009 6:31 AM
From: Lisa
To: Mark

And what does your wand bring?

Subject: re: fun writing assignment. . . just cuz
Date: Wed, 26 Aug 2009 6:47 AM
From: Mark
To: Lisa

I need the space to hang out and write about it - which is not now - and I also want to really drop into it and go with where I'm at when I sit down to write; I'll have a different answer than whatever I could tell you now.

Good morning. : >)

Subject: re: fun writing assignment . . . just cuz
Date: Wed, 26 Aug 2009 6:59 AM
From: Lisa
To: Mark

Ah, I'll look forward to it.

Good morning to you. Have a wonderful day.

Subject: Wand waving
Date: Sat, 29 Aug 2009 10:03 AM

From: Mark
To: Lisa

I miss intimacy and desire . . .

It's taken a few years but I finally feel like I got a handle on how to enjoy the life I have, the centerpiece being: *earning money doing work I enjoy and feel a connection to*. I've been downright acerbic when moralizing my need - my *right* - to have my day job feel as though it were a form of creative self-expression, something I could feel the satisfaction of putting myself into. The Universe responded to my commitment and focus by unobtrusively matchmaking what I was internally yearning for with what was externally available to me, and gradually I found myself generating income through construction and music.

So what happens when I feel a great need for intimacy, but my partner does not remotely represent the object of my desire? My need is specific - I know what I want, and the *way* I want it - but my partner doesn't possess what I know will fulfill the level or quality of my desire. Now what? Do without? Make do? Settle for?

If I could wave my wand, I would ask for a partner I was attracted to, felt respect and admiration for, looked forward to seeing, and enjoyed being with. I've been so long without such a partner that I now seek these qualities in my work. I've become more focused and committed to the quality of my creativity, garnering a soul-satisfying pleasure in expressing myself as a musician and a builder. Music can be extremely sensual at times, touching the part of me that takes great pleasure in occupying *all* of my body, but obviously nothing comes close to the touch and feel of the skin, the hair, and the scent of a woman I like and admire. Any such opportunity to have sensual contact with a woman I'm attracted to is now a complicated matter because the *pursuit* of the opportunity carries with it a potentially calamitous chain of events. In fact, as long as I continue to remain with a partner who cannot fulfill a need I refuse to abandon, there will always be a tension-and-release dynamic in the relationship as the Universe match-makes what I'm internally yearning for with what is externally available to me.

So: The current strategy for coping with this issue in my life? *Fuck it. Let it go, and make choices on a moment-to-moment basis.* In the meantime, I'm becoming a better drummer and a better builder, leaving in my wake a whole bunch of inspired, beautiful things for others to enjoy. My time will come soon enough. I feel like the Universe has my back on this one.

_____
Subject: re: Wand waving
Date: Sat, 29 Aug 2009 5:45 PM

From: Lisa
To: Mark

Funny. Sexual attraction is one piece that still remains with me and Dave, yet desire is attached to so much *more* for me now. Spiritual connection. Conscious love-making. *That's* real desire for me. So, as I keep walking further away from my marriage I find it easier to walk away from what has become *going through the motions*.

I, too, am trusting that the Universe has my back on this one.

Always does.

Subject: Winechat. . .
Date: Wed, 2 Sep 2009 6:49 PM
From: Mark
To: Lisa

2007 Trader Joe's "Captain's Catch", while not a *sophisticated* red wine, it certainly is a notch above the two-buck Chuck (which I'm fine with, for drinking regularly while I'm cooking and pinching pennies).The first three sips are for flavor, texture, and palette. After the first glass it's all about getting a buzz on. The music on the kitchen speakers while making dinner gets the creative cooking juices flowing. It took a few years, but I *finally* flipped my resentment about being the resident food-nurturer into a Me Time thing: It's MY kitchen you want to be in when you want that fun, rock-the-house-while-making-food thing. Talk about *foreplay,* holy shit . . . the only thing missing is a woman I'm attracted to . . .

I digress . . .

Tonight it's a tri tip which has been sliced into several steaks, marinated in: light olive oil, lots of garlic, a lemon-garlic seasoning, and Dijon mustard. Sear the steaks in a hot cast-iron skillet and serve over rice with steamed broccoli.

Imagine enjoying this in a rented villa on the coast of Italy somewhere . . .

Which reminds me: *Thoughts become things,* and *Your beliefs create your reality.*

Let's eat!

(Feel those smooth, ancient cobblestones under your bare feet as you sit at an outdoor table under a Tuscan summer-night's sky?)

More wine?

Living moment-to-moment can be a powerful ally. Practice the *Be Here Now* thing from time to time. It's WAY better than being miserable . . .

_____
Subject: re: Winechat. . .
Date: Thu, 3 Sep 2009 5:08 AM
From: Lisa
To: Mark

Lovely recipe, full of flavor and *panache* . . . as I inhale the magnificent garlic wafting through the room my stomach growls in delightful anticipation. I swirl the wine in my glass as I slide my feet against the bare wood floor beneath them . . . oh, wait . . . that's green tea and I'm in my office. 5am is a bit early for wine, even for me.

Good morning.

I am practicing being in the now a lot lately and manifesting wonderful and powerful things by believing they are so. It's magical really, and misery has left the building. As I settle deeper (back) into my single life I am becoming more *me* every day. Zac is thriving as he takes a greater leap into manhood: bought his first car, starting his senior year and becoming a terrific young man.

Opportunities keep showing up like sparkling jewels in a meadow. All I have to do is look closely to notice that, while perhaps hidden, they are *already there*. More magic. Taking great care of myself . . . eating well . . . long walks on gorgeous days . . . writing . . . reading . . . music. Clearing out the crap from my soul, my being, my closets. I feel better than I have in . . . oh, I don't even know. I feel *that* good.

I got complete.

with me.

_____
Subject: re: Winechat. . .
Date: Thu, 3 Sep 2009 7:50 AM
From: Mark
To: Lisa

Good morning . . .

A day off, finally. Goofy, challenging past couple of weeks: truck got hit in a parking lot at a gig; wallet stolen; one job-related frustration after another. Today is free, tomorrow a GREAT gig in Napa. I'm sure I'll recover nicely.

I'll get back to you at length later this morning. Love the part where you're up at 5am.

Hug.

___

Subject: re: Winechat. . .
Date: Thu, 3 Sep 2009 7:59 AM
From: Lisa
To: Mark

Hey . . . nice to have a day off mid-week :-)

Any chance you can chat today for a bit? I have a break around noon your time.

___

Subject: re: Winechat. . .
Date: Thu, 3 Sep 2009 7:50 AM
From: Mark
To: Lisa

I don't think I'll be around for a phone call. I'll be heading out soon to run errands, tie up loose ends, and maybe see a movie. That's the thing about a spontaneous day off: what to do with my free time? Get things done? Do nothing? Or a little of both?

I'm very interested in hearing your story of going from married bliss to single bliss. Not likely to say it all in an email, I know, so the October reunion will be chatty I'm sure. But you seemed so *sure* this time, right? Eyes wide open, lessons learned, needs spelled out, smarter and wiser, blah blah blah. My own speculation is that there's a bunch of shit we don't want seen, and consciously or unconsciously we learn how to be crafty with denial and self-knowing. We get really good with hiding what we think others will disapprove of. It's much easier to keep wounds and issues hidden when you're not with someone 24/7 - the dating/get-to-know-each-other phase - and somewhere between our unexamined needs and our acquired skill of revealing only what we're comfortable revealing, well, obviously, if we had seen or been aware of some kind of deal-breaking quality in the other we never would have gotten involved. *Meant-to-be* and *soul lessons* aside, who wants to willingly endure a long-term, unfulfilling relationship? A key thing that's helped me endure mine is giving up expecting Mariah to provide me with something she can't offer.

Most of my core needs have to do with solitude, nature, creative self-expression, and physical beauty, things that ask little, if anything, of other people. It's been helpful not to have expectations of others or be dependent on them to fulfill a need I may have. And I no longer give a shit what others think of my priorities, of what matters to me, of what I value. Go ahead, judge me all you want (not you specifically). I've acquired a thick skin from years of being exposed to a woman who's been relentless in trying to get me to be the man she wants, instead of letting the man I AM be enough. Not enough intimacy in our relationship? Why do I not feel genuine desire for you? Well, adopting a glass-half-full attitude about life just might be a sexy, desirable thing.

But no . . . I'm told it's something in *my* past, or something *I'm* supposed to get over or let go of. *UGH!* It all sounds to me like excuses that keep her from doing the hard work of making changes she deeply wants for herself, while trying to convince me that she *is* sexy, passionate, and desirable.

The one key thing that's missing from my life is, like I said, being with a woman I'm attracted to. There was a long period of my life when that wasn't an issue, so it's not like I've lived my life without it. I've directed my passion into other areas. *Feeling* passionate is something that still comes around, but feeling passionate *with a woman* is something I've just let go of. I've turned into a borderline narcissist by doing the self-love thing - I like myself just fine, most of the time - and sometimes will drop into that melancholy place where I feel like I'm missing out on something special and grand. Eventually that feeling will pass, and at some point I'll put myself into a music or construction thing that turns me on - albeit differently - and life is good for a moment or two more.

But oh . . . 'the scent of a woman' . . .

_____
Subject:
Date: Thu, 3 Sep 2009 12:11 PM
From: Lisa
To: Mark

Nice rant . . .

Yes, lots to share about being sure and meant-to-be. I still believe Dave and I were meant to be. I was just wrong about the forever part. Feels a little like wanting Brazilian Cherry hardwood and settling for Pergo. Eventually, you just might want the real deal. I'd prefer to share the whole story with you while it's fresh, rather than dragging it with me to California like excess baggage and spending *that* time in *this* story. Let's spend our short time together chatting about *good stuff* going on.

So let me know if a call might be able to happen soon, 'k?

Till then, I hope your day off is wonderful.

Subject: Ok, so. . .
Date: Thu, 3 Sep 2009 3:10 PM
From: Lisa
To: Mark

So .ˑ. . you and I just had this great phone chat (very cool to talk with you) and I am going about the rest of my day, my last client session, etc. when I get a text from Dave that he is on his way over. Hmmm. When he appeared, it was an interesting feeling that came over me, a bemusement that I had just summed up my entire relationship with him in about 40 minutes. While talking to you, my dear friend, I came to stunning conclusions of clarity, making me realize that I really am *done*.

He was more captivated with me than ever. Of course I was more detached and relaxed than ever, but pleasant, making him more captivated, I guess. He ended up talking for 20 minutes. Had himself a glass of wine, and left with a bit of a buzz and a hard on, neither of which he came here expecting to leave with, I'm sure. Of course forgot whatever he stopped by for.

It all makes me grin. Not sure why. A wry, Cheshire cat-like grin.

what's up with *that*?

Subject: re: OK, so. . .
Date: Thu, 3 Sep 2009 5:46 PM
From: Mark
To: Lisa

You must be very satisfied with yourself. Deservedly so, I might add. You sounded very clear and grounded when describing where you're currently at with yourself these days, and the route you took to get here. I detect a bit of fucking with Dave's head, using your sexual power - *grounded* sexual power - and sending him on his merry way. Good for you. I totally support showing up for yourself, and letting the rest of the world try to keep up.

Superbabe has become impervious to the effects of Kryptonite . . .

Rave on.

Subject: re: OK, so
Date: Fri, 4 Sep 2009 4:46 PM
From: Lisa
To: Mark

Cute. And it does feel a little like that. Though the fucking with his head is not intentional. Energetically maybe, but not consciously. For some reason every time he comes over here the past few weeks he gets turned on just standing in the kitchen, talking with me. I do admit there is a certain power that comes from that, particularly on the heels of that icky place when our marriage was ending after feeling barely noticed by him.

Feeling good about yourself is a powerful thing, as we know.

~Superbabe

Subject: pieces...
Date: Mon, 7 Sep 2009 10:28 AM
From: Lisa
To: Mark

So I have been cleaning closets, etc. and in the past 24 hours have come across pieces of the past that took my breath . . .

First, in the back of a drawer I found a journal, all the pages blank except for a letter I wrote you on the plane ride back from California when I visited in 2000. Relived that one for a moment. Nice.

And then another piece . . .

I had a writing assignment from my coach to read my journals from my Janet Jackson tour journey. I pulled out the journals from 1989-1991 today. Out of the one from 1990 old pictures spilled out. One is of you with a glass of wine and a beard, taken in my little one-room basement apartment in 1983.

Subject: good morning
Date: Sat, 12 Sep 2009 6:12 AM
From: Lisa
To: Mark

How are things in your world? Enjoying this glorious Bay Area-like weather, coaching, taking walks and hanging with Zac. Life is good. Things with Dave are status quo as he settles into his sister's place, finally. It's all more real now that he has all his stuff in a new place. We are getting along nicely, and that feels good. Anger has left the building.

Getting excited about my events in California! I have 8 signed up already for the MidLife Women ROCK workshop, and the Rock Your Business event should be good, too. It's a benefit for the Women's Network Foundation. Can't believe it's only a month away :-)

_____

Subject: help me out here. . .
Date: Wed, 23 Sep 2009 7:15 AM
From: Mark
To: Lisa

Starting tomorrow, I'll have the house to myself til Sunday PM. I'll be working during the day, but will come home in the evenings and would love it if you'd send me random emails asking me questions or subjects to write about, catching me off guard, or making me think before I answer . . . a self-discovery exercise to get me to hang out with you and where I'm at in the moment. I have a gig on Friday night in SF and again on Saturday afternoon.

Feels right . . .

Thanks.

M

_____

Subject: re: help me out here. . .
Date: Wed, 23 Sep 2009 10:53 AM
From: Lisa
To: Mark

This notion has been running through my mind . . .

What if the right thing and the hard thing are the same?

Write about *that* . . .

_____

Subject: re: help me out here. . .
Date: Thu, 24 Sep 2009 8:11 PM
From: Mark
To: Lisa

Ooohh, *yum* . . . I'd be happy to write about that.

Just got home. Check your email around 11 or midnight. Gotta make food.

_____

Subject: help me out here. . . #1
Date: Fri, 25 Sep 2009 5:51 AM
From: Mark
To: Lisa

Started in on it late last night and ran out of gas. I'm working on it right now.

G'mornin.

_____

Subject: help me out here. . . #1 . . . is it morning yet? If so, get some tea . . .

Date: Fri 25 Sep 2009 6:51 AM
From: Mark
To: Lisa

(Started writing late last night. A glass of wine, a homemade pizza of roasted portabello mushroom slices and mild Italian sausage, mozzarella and fresh-grated Parmesan cheeses, steamed Swiss chard from the garden - picked by flashlight - with a splash of balsamic vinegar. Taking bites while typing . . .)

What if the right thing and the hard thing are the same?

Sometimes the right thing and the hard thing *are* the same, as when the hard thing to do involves hurting someone with a choice you must make, a choice that might be a step towards one's own personal growth at the expense of doing harm or causing pain to another.

As for the right thing: Who decides that?

There's knowing inside of yourself what the Right Thing is, at which point you can rely and take action on your convictions. It presupposes a belief in an Inner Authority, some part of your deeper Self that you implicitly trust. You will listen to and follow through with the information coming from someplace deep inside of you because - and only when - you've realized the answers to many of your complex problems are right there inside of YOU. This is an excellent belief to hold about one's self because it marks the beginnings of trusting one's own information. The trick is how to keep from doubting yourself: *If the answer came from inside of me it must be right, yes?* There's only one way to find out: Follow your own advice, and see what comes of it.

(next morning . . .)

"Self-improvement is masturbation", says the Brad Pitt character in *Fight Club*. He spits the line out, suggesting that people who want to "improve" themselves are basically narcissists. But later in the movie he does the coolest thing: He goes into a liquor store, pulls out a gun and drags the clerk out the back door, puts the gun to the guy's head and screams at him:

"WHAT DID YOU ALWAYS WANT TO BE WHEN YOU GREW UP?!"

The terrified guy is scared shitless and confused; he hems, haws, stammers, ". . . huh? Wha-? . . uh . . . "

Pitt repeats the question, knocking the guy to his knees, cocking the trigger on the gun, pushing it hard against the guy's temple: "What did you always want to BE?!!?"

"A veterinarian!", he finally answers, sobbing now.

"I'm coming back here in three months, and if you're not enrolled in veterinary school I'm gonna blow your fucking head off", says Pitt, then lets the guy go.

I'm paraphrasing, of course, but I am fascinated by that scene. I think it's because I lack the kind of inner authority that would motivate me to follow through with what I KNOW to be the right thing for myself. I can handle my own 'liquor store existence', but the discipline required to enroll in veterinary school - my lifelong dream or passion - seems too hard a choice, involving changes that take me out of my comfort zone. The *right thing* and the *hardest thing* are one in the same . . .

And now I'm wondering: What metaphoric gun would I have to put to my *own* head to get me to enroll in my own "veterinary school"?

The closest I've come to this is with music: I've had to learn to endure Mariah's protests about how often I'm out playing music - my core passion - and just accept the tension and separation it causes when we can't agree on how much and when. Or, when I have a need for alone time, to just be away from her for a while, there's typically a tense negotiation about getting each other's needs met. If wanting to take care of myself creates hardship or discomfort for another, well . . . sometimes the hardest thing and the right thing are the same.

And so I ask you: *What's the metaphoric gun you use on yourself to move past your own comfort zones?*

Subject: help me out here. . . #1 . . . is it morning yet? If so, get some tea . . .

Date: Fri, 25 Sep 2009 12:15 PM
From: Lisa
To: Mark

What to say. . . the obvious answer is that your need for the nurturing you seek, your passion for music, and being an artist all lie diametrically opposed to who you share your life with, therefore creating hardship. Therein lies the rub, right? If the nurturing you sought was found in her arms, would there be a hard thing at all?

Ah. It comes down to being willing to disappoint another to be true to ourselves. I appreciate your truth about not being willing to do the hard thing that is outside your comfort zone. Many folks won't.

I love the liquor store metaphor. I will give much thought about my gun.

Second assignment:
And now I'm wondering: What metaphoric gun would I have to put to my own head to get me to enroll in my own veterinary school?

Answer, please.

You so set yourself up.

_____
Subject: Hi
Date: Fri, 25 Sep 2009 9:15 PM
From: Mark
To: Lisa

Hey there . . . This comes to you from a band gig at the South San Francisco Conference Center, a retirement party. Free internet access in the lobby . . .

Won't be home til late. Haven't even started playing yet. Speeches and more speeches . . . May not get the time to follow up on metaphoric gun project, but I'm digging on the places it's taking me . . .

I'll be leaving the house tomorrow morning around 10 for another S.F. gig, so won't be around much. Sunday I'm planning on going to a horse event in the Sierra foothills, leaving the house at 6am to do the sunrise drive thing and have breakfast somewhere cool before hanging out with all kinds of horses, especially the Friesians. Time to go back in. More to come.

_____
Subject: got a gun?
Date: Sat, 26 Sep 2009 6:15 AM
From: Lisa
To: Mark

Good morning.

_____
Subject: re: got a gun?

Date: Sat, 26 Sep 2009 8:55 AM
From: Mark
To: Lisa

Mornin' . . .

It's almost 9am here. Gotta gear up to head out the door soon for the gig in
S.F. with the smokin' hot horn band.

I've been mulling over the metaphoric gun thing . . . That's a tough one . . .
How 'bout you?

_____
Subject: re: got a gun?
Date: Sun, 27 Sep 2009 3:58 PM
From: Mark
To: Lisa

Drove 2 1/2 hours to pet a couple of huge, beautiful horses and look at
some art, then drove 2 1/2 hours back home. Hot, sweaty and hungry now.
Still no gun.

_____
Subject: re: got a gun?
Date: Sun, 27 Sep 2009 4:35 PM
From: Lisa
To: Mark

Cool. No gun here either. Hmmm . . .

_____
Subject: re: got a gun?
Date: Sun, 27 Sep 2009 6:41 PM
From: Mark
To: Lisa

Hmmm . . . Maybe we're cool with where we're at.

. . . or not . . .

_____
Subject: I think I got a gun...
Date: Sun, 27 Sep 2009 7:02 PM
From: Mark
To: Lisa

Ok, ok . . . here we go . . .

Not sure of what the gun would be, but I think my style is to be playing
around with it in careless manner, then have it go off accidentally . . . or:

118

"accidentally", you know? I would *unconsciously* shoot myself, and then deal with the life changes that would come with recovering from the wound . . . then use the event as ground zero for moving towards the desired change.

So the "gun" would have to be an *event* that triggers the change . . . I think.

What say you?

———

Subject: re: holy shit
Date: Mon, 28 Sep 2009 5:17 AM
From: Lisa
To: Mark

Oh my God. Zac got in a bad accident last night and I believe in every prayer I have ever uttered . . .

A drunk chick hit him and flipped her SUV after hitting him nearly head on. Zac will be fine, thank God. Car is probably totaled, though. He is so upset. I hope this accident becomes a "gun" for the chick who hit him.

So, absolutely, events as a "gun" work for me. A huge one was my post-9/11 job layoff. Thinking about the ones that ended my marriages are trickier - that's the gun I am looking for. No big events to point to . . .

Instead, *turning* points.

———

Subject: re: I think I got a gun. . .
Date: Wed, 30 Sep 2009 2:33 PM
From: Lisa
To: Mark

Ah, so I have really pondered this: Are there really, truly *unconscious* acts?

By making changes as a sort of damage control, does that feel as empowering as a true *choice*? I am thinking: not. Yet that approach certainly gets you off the hook for any detractors, upset feelings or naysayers about your choices - *I didn't mean for the gun to go off! Look at all this blood. It really hurts, what should I do now?*- thereby alleviating true responsibility for making a *conscious* choice that may wound someone else, intentionally or not.

All this assumes that you are the one with the gun. For our poor wannabe veterinarian it is not by his own hand that the gun will go off, but rather

119

someone else is forcing him to own his life.

Or . . . someone can have a gun to your head and be forcing your life all along, keeping you from the life you really want.

Subject: re: I think I got a gun. . .
Date: Wed, 30 Sep 2009 6:54 PM
From: Mark
To: Lisa

So *courage* is a good word to work with here. Not wanting to be at the mercy of the 'authentic life' bandits, your efforts would go into making choices which continued to propel you in the direction of the life you really want. Any *conscious* choice made that would take you off your path seems like it could still be made from a place of intention, of power. Difficult or bittersweet perhaps, but it would take some *courage* to chose the harder, more difficult road.

Imagine someone putting a gun to your head, insisting that you do what you have always wanted to do . . . and replying: *I AM!*

Subject: re: I think I got a gun. . .
Date: Wed, 30 Sep 2009 7:39 PM
From: Lisa
To: Mark

So, if that happened, would the "I AM!" bring about a reprieve from the shooter . . . or cock the trigger?

Subject: re: I think I got a gun. . .
Date: Thu, 1 Oct 2009 5:56 AM
From: Mark
To: Lisa

Depends on whether or not they believed you . . .

twelve

Subject: sunset

Date: Fri, 2 Oct 2009 7:24 PM
From: Mark
To: Lisa

Back deck, sunset . . . roasting Pasilla chilies in hot coals in preparation for
making the best chile rellenos you will ever eat (swear to God). Clear,
mild evening; corn stalks are turning brown after having picked all the
corn weeks ago. Saved the dried stalks for some sort of Halloween
decoration; picked a couple of eggplants; at least a dozen silver dollar-
sized tomatoes should be picked before they dry out and split; carrots still
coming up, and the strawberry plants are having their second go-round;
there's chard that should be picked and eaten, but it'll have to wait: won't
go with the chile relleno dinner tonight . . .

_____
Subject: sunset
Date: Sat, 3 Oct 2009 5:22 AM
From: Lisa
To: Mark

lovely image . . . it all sounds very tasty.

_____
Subject: sunset
Date: Sat, 3 Oct 2009 6:24 AM
From: Mark
To: Lisa

Yeah, just random stuff that rushed through my mind as I was unwinding
on a mellow Friday eve. I was about to go off on a tangent re: this house
and how we live in it . . . or OUT of it, really . . . but Mariah pulled up and
I went back to skinning roasted chilies . . .

_____
Subject: re: some day . . .
Date: Sat, 3 Oct 2009 5:55 PM
From: Lisa
To: Mark

Went to hear Marianne Williamson speak today. Oh my God, THAT is
what I aspire to.

Is Saturday the 24th open at all for you? I am pretty flexible that day/night.

_____
Subject: re: some day . . .
Date: Sun, 4 Oct 2009 11:45 PM
From: Mark
To: Lisa

Not Saturday night. There's a 50th birthday party for a good friend that evening . . . but the morning and afternoon is a maybe. Savannah has Horse Club in the morning til noon.

Thursday the 22nd I'll be free til 5 or 6. Friday the 23rd is the gig in Napa, which looks like the best day for a visit of any length.

———

Subject: re: some day . . .
Date: Mon, 5 Oct 2009 3:01 PM
From: Lisa
To: Mark

Sounds good. Thursday late afternoon still looks good for a drink.

———

Subject: ordinary life
Date: Mon, 5 Oct 2009 9:47 PM
From: Mark
To: Lisa

There's an ordinary-ness going on in my life these days . . . and I'm not sure how I feel about it.

What's ordinary is the routine; getting up before sunrise, making tea and sitting at the computer for an hour almost every single morning to read the online news, peruse Craigslist for carpentry and drum gigs, drums for sale, photography gig offers. Then I make lunch, dress for the work day, and drive off by 7 or 7:30, depending on the job in progress . . .

I may or may not pick up Savannah at the barn on the way home from work. If not, I'll hit the gym for an hour or two if there's time, then come home to do my drink-wine-make-dinner-play-music ritual. Weekdays we'll put on a movie after dinner while Savannah does homework in her room. Fridays and/or Saturdays - if we're home - they'll be a movie *during* dinner, with T.V. trays, and ALWAYS a massive bowl of popcorn at the halfway point of the movie.

So with the exception of gigs and horse events, that's how my days go, one after the other, months ticking by until one day it's October of 2009 and I STILL don't own a house, don't have a book draft written, or have yet to be seized by a creative project that has a magical hold on me and won't let go. I could point to a dozen things in my life that may sound unique, special or even mystical to someone else, but to me it's just my life . . . normal stuff that *should* be counted as blessings, but it feels more like I'm just living one day at a time . . .

There are peaks and valleys; Lisa's coming to town: *peak.* Horn band gigging in S.F.: *peak.* Fender-bender in a parking lot: *valley.* No work for two weeks: *valley* (sort of) . . . you get the idea.

And then there are the moments like when I'm standing on the back deck looking out at Mt. Diablo in the distance while roasting chiles over glowing mesquite coals; seventy acres of open grassy pasture just on the other side of my back fence . . . it's so goddamn peaceful and serene . . . and I *SO* don't care about how this rental house is falling apart around us, or that I don't have straight teeth, or that I'm not in the middle of a book tour, or deeply in love with a woman I adore. I come upon a moment of bliss and contentment, where striving and trying and efforting and wanting to be *more* seems like such a fucking waste of time and energy . . . where the secret of happiness is feeling contented NOW, in this moment, detached from trying to keep and hold onto the contentment . . . feeling good about just *being,* you know?

Well guess what? *It's not enough.* When the blissful moment passes I'll invariably want more than just 'moments of contentment'. What I want is for some kind of Brad Pitt-psycho to put a gun to my pathetic head and threaten to blow it off unless I can say out loud *what the fuck is it that I want my life to be about*!

I cannot give a truthful answer to that question in an email . . . uh-uh . . . no way. There's waxing philosophical to you about going deep and being all I can be . . . and then there's having someone willing to end my life if, in a matter of seconds, I can't name and shout out loud the thing that's buried deep inside of me, wanting out. I feel like I got a glimpse of that thing when I was in Mexico, nearly a year ago, swimming in the ocean and out of my mind with energy, passion, and a crazy lust for being alive, ecstatic in my body, and it having nothing to do with *being with someone* . . .

But I later longed to turn it loose and give it to a woman . . . just not the one I'm with.

_____

Subject: re: ordinary life
Date: Tue, 6 Oct 2009 4:35 AM
From: Lisa
To: Mark

You think I can get that gun through security?

Take the two weeks of no work and make it a *peak.* Do something unexpected with it. Work on what you would like to be doing if you didn't have a job.

(You can write a lot in two weeks . . . just a suggestion)

And then you'll see me.

Subject: Ugh! and then: Ah.
Date: Fri, 9 Oct 2009 6:53 PM
From: Mark
To: Lisa

I'm 3/4 of the way through watching *Prime*, a romantic comedy with Uma Thurman and Meryl Streep. It's interesting how there are these moments in the movie when it stops being a comedy and becomes a rather poignant commentary on the reality of relationships. Lying, deception, making up, unintentional hurt, "I don't think I can do this anymore", feeling so high and so certain that we have something special and then: not. Also, a very cool thing about having one's art recognized and appreciated . . . and rewarded.

What are we looking for anyway? To be loved and appreciated? Well, sure, but it's funny how we're rarely very specific about the *way* we want to be admired. We respond to flattery, compliments . . . but I notice that --

. . . ugh! Never mind . . . it's too big to WRITE about . . . Have you left for California yet?

I'm right on the edge of something I want to say but can't put my finger on it

. . . try again . . .

Watching this movie is reminding me of you and I. Not that we're the young couple in the story so much, but the relationship dynamics that keep popping up are like *filmed versions of stuff you and I have been talking about for years!* Watching this movie reminds me of that movie about the guy who wrote a book about the story of him and the girl he was best friends with . . .

. . . ugh . . . try again . . .

O.K. Watching this movie makes me think about you. And now I want to see you.

Ah. There we go. That wasn't so hard . . .

Subject: re: Ugh! and then: Ah.
Date: Fri, 9 Oct 2009 6:56 PM

From: Lisa
To: Mark

12 days.

_____

Subject: and then. . . .
Date: Fri, 9 Oct 2009 6:59 PM
From: Mark
To: Lisa

Went back in to watch some more of the movie, and this was the next line, spoken by Meryl Streep, giving relationship advice to her son:

"Sometimes you love and learn, and then you move on . . . and that's okay."

_____

Subject: re: and then. . . .
Date: Sat, 10 Oct 2009 6:49 AM
From: Lisa
To: Mark

really working on that right now

_____

Subject: hey
Date: Mon, 19 Oct 2009 6:04 PM
From: Lisa
To: Mark

I will give you a call when I get into San Jose and we can go from there. Looks like I will be free at 3 Thursday.

Can't believe it . . . I'll see you soon.

_____

Subject: Lisa is comin' to town
Date: Tue, 20 Oct 2009 8:48 PM
From: Mark
To: Lisa

How 'bout I pick you up at the airport and take you where you need to get to? Or are you getting a rental car?

Friday is open so far.

_____

Subject: re: Lisa is comin' to town
Date: Tue, 20 Oct 2009 11:41 PM

From: Lisa
To: Mark

I am getting a car at the San Jose airport then meeting a client in San Jose. I'll be free 2:30 or 3 until 6 when I have plans in Lafayette. 3:00 in downtown Lafayette, maybe?

Friday open from mid afternoon on (I will be in Marin for lunch) then planning on the gig Friday night.

_____
Subject: re: Lisa is comin' to town
Date:Wed, 21 Oct 2009 6:36 AM
From: Mark
To: Lisa

Downtown Lafayette from 3 to 6 might be tricky. We'll figure it out. Definitely up for a drink/chat.

_____
Subject: tomorrow
Date: Wed, 21 Oct 2009 7:34 PM
From: Mark
To: Lisa

Tomorrow at 3:30? Nice bar at the Cheesecake Factory . . .

_____
Subject: re: tomorrow
Date: Wed, 21 Oct 2009 8:58 PM
From: Lisa
To: Mark

OK, see you then.

_____
Subject:
Date: Thu, 22 Oct 2009 9:08 PM
From: Mark
To: Lisa

Are you getting your emails out here?

Things are already different . . . inside of me. Bless you.

M

_____
Subject: meet later
Date: Fri, 23, Oct 2009 5:32 AM
From: Mark

To: Lisa

When you're done in Marin for lunch, I'll be at the Napa library. See you there.

_____

Subject: re: meet later
Date: Mon, 26 Oct 2009 6:33 AM
From: Mark
To: Lisa

Lunch with me in Davis. Noon. 1/2 hour from your event. Cool college town vibe . . .

Good chance I'll be going to Tucson, AZ, tomorrow or the next day to do a kitchen for a client with a home down there . . . a two or three day job.

Desert road trip. Money. Time alone to write and process.

Perfect.

Thank you for everything . . .

M

_____

Subject: oh my God. . .
Date: Tue, 27 Oct 2009 9:25 AM
From: Mark
To: Lisa

Had a couple of hours to myself when I got home last night. Consulted the I Ching, in view of just having seen you, with new insights and inspiration. Out of 64 possible 'answers', these two came up as the response to: *Now what*? The first text carries more weight when there are two, but the information in both is combined to give the most complete answer. I use the *I Ching Workbook* by R.L.Wing:

#40 *LIBERATION* (or, in the original Chinese text, *Deliverance*):

Prepare yourself to forcefully dispense with a great adversary. This is done with careful planning and clever timing. This is a formidable enemy so you must be constantly alert. When you have removed this obstacle to your progress, everything that you attempt will succeed. When LIBERATION is complete, when the tensions of the storm have passed, your spirit will be refreshed and stimulated. The ground will be cleared for new growth, and the future will appear promising. And, once you finally dispense with emotional ruts or resentments from former times, you will have an excellent opportunity for personal advancement. Overall, you should feel increased energy and clarity in your dealings with the outside world.

. . . and . . .

#21 *REFORM* (or, in the original Chinese text, *Biting Through*):

Either an inferior person who is working against you or a situation that has developed at cross purposes to your life is interfering with the attainment of your aims. There is neither possibility of compromise nor hope that the problem will miraculously vanish. It cannot be rationalized or ignored, and you cannot maneuver around it. It is a tangible, real, and self-generating interference in your life, and must be severely reformed before it causes any permanent damage to you. Know what you want, know what makes you feel good about your Self, know what brings you into harmony with others. These are your guidelines and principles. Other factors that assume control of your behavior or your health or that create inner discord are the obstacles that must be overcome. Be firm, unemotional, gentle, and clear in annihilating them and thereby re-forming your Self and your environment.

. . . uh, pretty dead-on I'd say, huh? I can feel my back being got by, oh, I dunno . . . *the whole fucking Universe?*

thirteen

Subject: Hey
Date: Thu, 29 Oct 2009 5:26 AM
From: Lisa
To: Mark

Good morning from Chicago. I so miss California . . .

Feeling a little disoriented here, but good. Zac picked me up from the airport which was really cool. He's such a man now. Wow. Had a great evening with him catching up on the week. Got the CD from Kathy's channeling session with me and started listening while laying in bed last night. Oh my.

Boy, have those guides got our number.

<hr>

Subject: Hey rain man
Date: Fri, 30 Oct 2009 6:04 PM
From: Lisa
To: Mark

I got caught in a warm, driving rain today. I relished in it and ended up walking, drenched to the bone, feeling really alive. I remembered you wrote something about this once and I found it. I particularly like this:

It could be argued that at any given moment one's immediate environment is an outward physical representation of who we are inside; Our homes, our cars, our desk, our partners . . . They all reflect something of our inner selves. This would then be equally true for waterfalls, sunsets and wildflowers: We are *the serenity of that sunset; We* are *the energy of that waterfall; We* are *the multi-colored beauty of those wildflowers . . . and I am the passionate intensity of that driving rainstorm . . .*

Who's to say I'm not?

Love that.

I'm wondering if you took the kitchen job in Tucson. With any luck you got the solitude that grounds you, the money you needed, and time to write.

ciao
L

<hr>

Subject: Hillman & Meade
Date: Sun, 1 Nov 2009 8:54 AM
From: Lisa
To: Mark

Remember telling me the "acorn theory" that day in Napa? Well, today I sat at my desk and happened to glance at a stack of business cards lying to the right of my laptop that have been sitting there for a few weeks. "Self discovery & well being", the top one said amid drawings of oak leaves. It was from a woman I met at a Spirit of Leadership conference where I went to see Marianne Williamson.

I turned it over and there was the Acorn Theory from the *Soul's Code* by James Hillman comparing our life's destiny to the Oak tree imprinted in the tiny acorn.

This is on the heels of a long walk to my favorite nearby spot in nature about a mile and a half from my house. My walk takes me along the creek into my secret, hidden clearing of glorious trees facing a wide span where the creek branches out. I listened to Michael Meade there. I *got* it. Love it.

_____

Subject: twin flames
Date: Mon, 2 Nov 2009 8:25AM
From: Lisa
To: Mark

Had a session with Kathy the channel yesterday. The guides said to look up 'twin flames' or 'essence twins', as that is what they say we really are. OK, hmmm. It explains a few things.

I had this incredible realization that this connection between us is *ancient*. It just *is*. Being aware of it creates the perceived need to *do* something about it, though that is just a choice. A series of choices, really, independent and interdependent ones that will be made over time, based on where we are, who we are, and what we want. By surrendering to my trust in it all being perfect *already,* I feel nothing but calm certainty.

_____

Subject: re: Hillman & Meade
Date: Mon, 2 Nov 2009 11:15AM
From: Mark
To: Lisa

Holy shit. Listened to a 16-minute excerpt of Hillman describing the acorn theory - the choosing of our time to enter the world, including the place, the family, and the circumstances. Some time ago, when I was slamming story ideas into my laptop, I went into a much more detailed riff on this concept, told from Savannah's point of view before she was born, as a way of explaining why she chose us as parents.

Got back from the Tucson trip about 4 pm yesterday, then straight to a duet piano recital of Savannah's at 4:30.

Much to write you about. No library time on the trip after all, but a sidetracking series of events that began Saturday morning with a pre-sunrise walk through downtown Tucson, taking pictures as the city started to wake up, then engine problems in Parker, AZ that afternoon, leading to a 3-hour ordeal involving a cast of middle-of-nowhere characters helping me get back on the road.

more later . . .

_____

Subject: re: Hillman & Meade
Date: Mon, 2 Nov 2009 2:13 PM
From: Lisa
To: Mark

I remember that piece you wrote about Savannah coming into existence, *choosing* to come in. I'm glad you found your way out of Arizona and made it back for her recital.

_____

Subject: Acorns
Date: Tue, 3 Nov 2009 8:35 PM
From: Mark
To: Lisa

Rough night last night out here, ending with getting out of the house by 7:30 this morning and being gone all day. An early morning horse chore, the gym, then a 3-hour library visit to speed-read *The Soul's Code* in a secluded, private study room. Wrote in my journal for a while, but not an especially satisfying day, all in all. This is the beginning stages of separation I think, and I lean on the Acorn Theory concept to pull me through. Feels right, but Jesus . . . here come the holidays . . . *oooff*. . .

_____

Subject: re: Acorns
Date: Wed, 4 Nov 2009 6:18 AM
From: Lisa
To: Mark

I can hear your discontent. Take things moment by moment. Write. Trust. Take your time.

I had an incredible moment last night while talking to a girlfriend who has read the Italy story. I was saying how I've been writing pieces that seem like essays and I'm not sure how it will weave into a book. She reminded me that the beginning of Italy was a writing assignment from you to *write three paragraphs.* She said:

"Just write the conversation the two of you have been having for years."

Oh. Yes. Of course. All the emotions, wisdom and observations surfacing through our conversations.

So I simmered with that idea in a hot bath . . . wrote some . . . and then collapsed into bed with chills and a fever. I don't know if I have the flu, it came on so fast. I feel wrung out, but the fever is down today.

So, let's keep this conversation going.

Subject: Hey
Date: Wed, 4 Nov 2009 11:18 AM
From: Mark
To: Lisa

Just started writing you in another window. How you feeling this morning, uh, afternoon? You down with a bug? Canceled clients for the day?

_____

Subject: re: Hey
Date: Wed, 4 Nov 2009 11:22 AM
From: Lisa
To: Mark

I'm a little better. Having tea and soup. No clients til 4pm. Rest and reading. You having a better day today? Writing me a long, juicy email, I hope.

_____

Subject: part 1
Date: Wed, 4 Nov 2009 12:02 PM
From: Mark
To: Lisa

No work today, other than a meeting with a past client who uses me primarily for advanced handyman stuff. It's all there is for now so I'll take what I can get, but really . . . I could give a shit about work and earning a living today. Or yesterday.

I'm giving myself over to the Acorn Theory - MY Acorn Theory - and am following its pull. Money can be made later. What looks like irresponsible or erratic behavior on the outside sure feels different on the inside, and I've given myself total permission to go with it. Today it shows up as an afternoon at the library to write and read; so be it. Even I can detect the tone of anger in what I'm writing here, remnants of the messy confrontation at 2am Tuesday morning with Mariah. She came into the previously quiet living room where I was journaling and got in my face about her hurt feelings, the trip this weekend to drive my mom to a party (Mariah wants to come), and to let me know she can't sleep because of how upset she is about the way I've been treating her.

The part where she defiantly planted herself in my quiet space to get into a discussion about her hurt feelings - at 2 fucking a.m. - so totally pissed me off that I became the coldest dickhead she's ever seen, and I SO didn't care. Fast-forward to me jetting out of the house at 7:30 that morning to do what I *had* to do, so I could later do what I wanted to do. Still a bit jacked up from that tiff. When she came home around 9:30 last night I apologized for

132

treating her so badly, and said nothing else about it. We left it at that, and I went out again early this morning to walk the horse - rehab after a surgery - and will have dinner with a close music friend this evening.

Anyway . . .

It'll probably take the second email to tell you more about the desert trip, but there was an interesting glitch on the way back involving a 3-hour layover in the middle of nowhere - I think I mentioned this - and though I got home just fine, that truck issue changed my previous itinerary and route. It was all good in the end, but *what the hell was THAT about?,* you know? It made me slow down and take my sweet-ass time getting home. I did NOT want to head back yet. All this being in the middle of nowhere felt right at home to me.

Hmmm . . . interesting: *Being in the middle of nowhere feels like home . . .*

To be continued . . .

_____
Subject: re: part 1
Date: Wed, 4 Nov 2009 12:09 PM
From: Lisa
To: Mark

Hmmm . . . keep going.

And what is YOUR Acorn Theory?

_____
Subject: part 2
Date: Wed, 4 Nov 2009 1:23 PM
From: Mark
To: Lisa

I left off with being stuck in the middle of nowhere because of truck problems . . .

That 3-hour delay changed my intended itinerary and route, and slowed me down. This now meant I would drive through the most beautiful part of the southern California desert *in the dark.* Shit. Even at 10pm I could tell I was driving along the shore of the Colorado River just south of Lake Havasu City, AZ. It would have been awesome to be making that part of the drive in the early morning light.

I had eaten a large dinner of Mexican food before pulling out of Parker, AZ, (where the desert-white-trash-truck-repair fairies live), and by the time I was going through Lake Havasu City just a half-hour later I was getting too sleepy to drive on into a much-less populated part of the desert with iffy engine issues.

I pulled into a large parking lot serving some restaurants and a shopping center. Noisy as all get-out, so I installed earplugs and a windshield sun visor. Slept restlessly on and off for four hours, then got back on the road at 1:30am. Needles was the next town, just across the AZ/CA border, and I made a quick stop at a convenience store for a quart of whole milk (I had a 4-inch blackberry pie I'd bought after lunching at the Black Bear Cafe in Goodyear, AZ, knowing it would make an awesome breakfast sometime after sunrise, but: *must have milk!*). I was thinking about that pie now, because it was looking like the breakfast hour would come while I was still in the desert. To keep the milk cold I bungee-corded it to my lumber rack above the driver-side door and got back on the road, cutting through the 40-degree desert air at two in the morning at seventy miles per hour, a quart jug of milk strapped to my lumber rack like some weird, vitamin-enriched missile . . .
Drove for just over an hour into the California desert, and with a nearly-full moon high in the black sky I could see I was now driving through an incredible landscape . . . in the *dark*.

Pulled into a rest stop packed with massive semi trucks, full moon setting in the west. Slept on and off for three hours, essentially killing time until the first light of day appeared. When I sat up to check the sky for the fourth or fifth time the rims of the mountain peaks to the east were glowing in pinks and peaches, and it was back on the road.

At this point I'm where I most want to be: adventuring through the desert at dawn, time on my hands, and an excellent camera on the passenger seat.

And I did NOT want to go home. Not yet.

_____
Subject: re: part 2
Date: Wed, 4 Nov 2009 1:16 PM
From: Lisa
To: Mark

Ah . . . to have been in that passenger seat.

Thank God for the desert-white-trash-truck-repair fairies. Too funny. What an adventure . . .with your dairy hood ornament and all. Did you take your pictures? Please share.

_____
Subject: re: part 2
Date: Wed, 4 Nov 2009 1:57 PM
From: Mark

To: Lisa

I'm at different library now. I had to negotiate another hour of computer time at the first one, but that was it. Looks like I only get a half hour here, though. Bummer. I was on a roll. Had to come here to continue.

Pictures are on the home computer. Nothing special came out of any of the desert pics. I was driving most of the time. BUT . . . some great pics of my walk in downtown Tucson. I can send you those later.

_____
Subject: re: part 2
Date: Wed, 4 Nov 2009 2:05 PM
From: Lisa
To: Mark

Send what you want to. I love reading it.

I'm still thinking about my story. I decided that the best way to plug into The Conversation is to go back and read our emails over the years. Hey, did you write YOUR Acorn Theory yet?

_____
Subject: re: part 2
Date: Wed, 4 Nov 2009 3:10 PM
From: Mark
To: Lisa

MY Acorn Theory? It's the James Hillman version, where all the recurring themes of my past - especially the 'be alone' stuff - are all pointing to the needs of the deeper, True Self as it makes its way to total integration with the rest of me, pushing the ego aside and taking the wheel.

_____
Subject: re: part 2
Date: Wed, 4 Nov 2009 3:15 PM
From: Lisa
To: Mark

Yes. The Ego twists us in a knot till the True Self gets strangled, and getting out of its grip before it kills us brings us to take a deep breath and gasp. . . *THIS is who I am and want to be.*

_____
Subject: re: part 2
Date: Wed, 4 Nov 2009 3:29 PM
From: Mark
To: Lisa

No, no . . . the True Self NEVER gets *strangled*; that's all ego bullshit, taunting you to believe that the ego is in charge and is running the show. The True Self merely waits patiently for the ego to quiet down enough, as in meditation, so the Self can make its messages heard. The belief that the Self can be controlled or manipulated by the ego is erroneous.

I think it's more that we have so little experience of being in touch with the True Self that we get misaligned with the manipulations of the ego, and think what the ego wants is what the deeper Self wants. I don't think the ego can control the True Self; I think it *gets in the way* and fucks with us, but doesn't usurp the Self.

———
Subject: re: part 2
Date: Wed, 4 Nov 2009 3:36 PM
From: Lisa
To: Mark

OK, OK . . . I get it. I still have seen, especially with some clients, the Ego really getting down and dirty with the True Self; the *feeling* of being strangled by it is what I was getting at, especially those who are clueless about quieting down and have no tools for calling up the Self when the Ego is having its way. This is such a practice and I have really gotten clearer, this year, about allowing my True Self to drive the train.

So how can you tell what your True Self wants vs. what your ego wants?

———
Subject: re: part 2
Date: Wed, 4 Nov 2009 3:48 PM
From: Mark
To: Lisa

That's what the work is: What tools do you have at your disposal that help to hear the voice of the True self? Meditation? Journaling? Stimulating conversation with passionate others with large hands?

———

Subject: re: part 2
Date: Wed, 4 Nov 2009 3:50 PM
From: Lisa
To: Mark

Cute. ;-) All of the above.

And music.

———
Subject: Acorn
Date: Wed, 4 Nov 2009 4:01 PM

From: Mark
To: Lisa

The theory says that all the goofy, unexplainable behaviors from the early years of our life, up to the present, are aspects of the fully-integrated Self showing through as we grow older, because what we are here to do and be is already inside of us. These "things" that come out of us - things we have a compulsion to express in some way - can be thought of as signals or signs, showing us which way to go.

The 'alone thing' that's been with me all my life is connected in some way to the work I'm here to do. And I can see where writing would align with this. There's a big difference, I discovered, between being left alone to write, and *secluding* myself from as much outside distraction as possible.

Time's up . . . more later. I have to do the horse thing in about 10 minutes, then dinner with a buddy.

_____

Subject: re: Acorn
Date: Wed, 4 Nov 2009 5:02 PM
From: Lisa
To: Mark

My thoughts: I absolutely see that your being drawn to deep quiet is a being drawn *into* - the crab in the shell, Cancer Man - into nature, into your interior world and the aching need to *connect.* Connection has been a core desire throughout your life. So how do we connect? Communication, exactly.

You are right on when you talk of communicating, and in your acorn are the many ways you do that: through music (audibly), photography (visually), and writing, the true expression of your mind, soul, heart. Interesting that writing requires the ability to be still, quiet and alone to do it. You're not only OK with that, you *love* the solitude thing (which is much harder for gregarious me, by the way).

So write you must.

I'm still reading our emails. In one from 2003 you were wife bashing, wanting a divorce and struggling to find the writer in you.

You need a new story.

_____

Subject: new news, part 1
Date: Thu, 5 Nov 2009 4:27 PM
From: Mark

To: Lisa

I'm at the library again. Good thing you haven't sent me anything til now . . .

Mariah knows. I should say she *suspects* that I'm up to something with someone - all her senses and intuitions tell her I've got some secret thing going on. I've convinced her that she's wrong, but she *knows*. This afternoon she came over to the computer at home to look in on the trouble I was having downloading a picture I'd sent to myself from my phone and there was no way to hide the long list of past emails there. I had deleted everything you and I have written but if you had sent an email during that window of time it would have been quite messy. In fact, we had JUST finished having the 'why-aren't-we-having-sex' conversation again, which was very hard, and very uncomfortable.

SO . . .

Time for a break. A week. This (you and I staying in touch) was way, way close to coming to an end. Mariah and I had gone for a long walk and talk this morning, making room to get clear on some things. It's been so helpful to have you to write to these last couple of days, I couldn't bear to have her get in the middle of it.

_____
Subject: re: new news, part 1
Date: Thu, 5 Nov 2009 4:47 PM
From: Lisa
To: Mark

OK . . . digesting . . . keep going . . .

_____

Subject: re: new news, part 1
Date: Thu, 5 Nov 2009 4:52 PM
From: Mark
To: Lisa

Don't tweak. I need to create a temporary hole, a big space for a few days where you and I have been hanging out, long enough for Mariah to chill, and me to relax. This is not that 'disappear for a year' thing, OK? I'll check in from the library, but not from home.

Anyway, dinner with my buddy last night was excellent. I got to hear myself put words to a bunch of feelings and stirrings, and got quite clear on how to proceed from here. It's going to work out best if I can stay focused and use the free time available now to *really do some writing*, and not go for a walk on the beach or go to a movie or the gym or whatever.

Do NOT sink into sadness. I'm hot on the trail of something important, and there are many issues to address as I grow into this New Self. You are part of that journey, so please don't let your ego mind-fuck with you on this one. All will be well, and the Universe will see to the care and feeding of our acorns.

More later.

I'm not done with you . . .

Subject:
Date: Thu, 5 Nov 2009 8:28 PM
From: Mark
To: Lisa

Are you willing to stay on this ride and not beg to have someone let you off? Even I don't know what's around the bend, but if I'm to stay committed to this path I have to be willing to say 'yes' to the incongruities that pop up, and trust that it's all good, all part of the lesson plan. That being said:

This hiding thing sucks. The alternative is to just say fuck it, and start not caring what happens if I'm "discovered", and then allow the revealed secret to be the impetus that sets a nasty split-up in motion.

But I don't want that. I want to preserve what is golden and supportive and keep the glass-half-empty crowd away from my good thing.

So when I tell you there needs to be a one week break, and then write you again hours later, it's a sign of me following the muse, and going with the instinct to do what I have to do to keep what's important to me alive and breathing. I must tell you that I find an element of humor in the absurdity of my behavior. I like the notion that my Deeper Self is starting to take charge, telling my ego to fuck off and take a hike. The ego has left things in a messy chaos, but the Deeper Self is taking a certain satisfaction in having discovered where the ego has been hiding that missing page of flying machine assembly instructions.

I'm still very much here.

Subject: re:
Date: Fri, 6 Nov 2009 10:05 AM
From: Lisa
To: Mark

I'm here . . . there's much to say . . . it's surfacing.

more soon.

___

Subject: re:
Date: Fri, 6 Nov 2009 11:40 AM
From: Mark
To: Lisa

By all means, write and send it. Leaving tomorrow morning with my mom for the weekend.

___

Subject: re:
Date: Fri, 6 Nov 2009 4:54 PM
From: Lisa
To: Mark

Write it . . . or wanna talk?

___

Subject: re:
Date: Fri, 6 Nov 2009 4:57 PM
From: Mark
To: Lisa

Sure, call.

fourteen

Subject: re: winechat
Date: Sun, 8 Nov 2009 2:06 PM
From: Mark
To: Lisa

The beauty of winechat with you the other night was the spontaneity of it:

perfect time and place. I had so much fun cooking and eating while pouring glass after glass of wine, talking talking talking about whatever . . . yeah, it was supercharged and electric . . .

Some cool shit happened while driving my mom back to the Bay Area this morning. Both of my sisters called as we were driving, one on my cell phone, the other on my mom's. So there's this moment when we're all connected and chatting, telling one another the latest news, cell phones being passed back and forth, and everyone's voice is upbeat and optimistic, especially because older sis in Phoenix may very well join the rest of us for Christmas or New Years this year. It was so *cool!*

Anyway, there was one awkward moment in the Solvang hotel room with my mom, just after we'd checked in . . .

One bed.

Mom made a comment about the bed thing – "I booked the reservation thinking I would be here alone." - neatly acknowledging the elephant in the room. It wouldn't have been any big deal to call the front desk for a rollaway bed, but neither of us bothered with that. The tacit agreement seemed to be that we were cool enough with the arrangements that it would be a non-issue. Al though I admit I was silently grateful that the bed was a California King.

Still . . .

I'm going to sleep in the same bed with my mother tonight.

It was clear, judging from the size of the bed, there would be more than enough room for the both of us to sleep comfortably . . . especially if we slept on our sides, backs to one another, at the extreme edges of our respective sides.

Which is *exactly* how we slept.

Subject: re:
Date: Sun, 8 Nov 2009 2:27 PM
From: Lisa
To: Mark

Interesting, awkward moment. One of those that you would not have anticipated ever, yet benign. Lots of room to explore our cultural norms that make that an uncomfortable moment, where in some cultures people sleep piled up in one room for a lifetime.

OK, I found an email today that you sent me last December about HE/SHE. It was not happy, but it shifted something in me that led to being honest about how unhappy I was in my marriage. It's what maybe 70% of people in marriage feel sometimes and I am so glad to not be feeling *that* anymore.

Nice rant. You really hit the nail on the head with that one. So when you write, stop describing and start ranting.

_____

Subject: re:
Date: Sun, 8 Nov 2009 2:54 PM
From: Mark
To: Lisa

Well, well . . . Yeah, I remember that piece. That came so fast and easy and unedited. So now I can see that the key is to *be connected to the material.* There was zero effort put into that rant because I was so in touch with my own frustration and anger at the bullshit I was seeing, and the bullshit I had fallen for.

_____

Subject: Hey
Date: Tue, 10 Nov 2009 7:47 AM
From: Lisa
To: Mark

What are you up to?

_____

Subject: re: Hey
Date: Wed, 11 Nov 2009 1:47 PM
From: Mark
To: Lisa

What am I up to? Talking myself out of a bummer mood . . .

Oooff . . . sucky energy these days. Moon's waning, weather here is gray but not sure if it wants to rain or not, no work, house messy and funky, lawns need attention. Just got back from dropping Savannah at the barn. No enthusiasm for anything. Blah. This is why I dig being alone in the desert: Nothing and no one to remind me of have-to's and such, plus: quiet beauty.

Next door neighbor has a small job for me. Ugh, don't wanna . . . need to get my photo file of barn pics over to Shutterfly so I can start putting it together . . . uh, yeah, well, I guess so. The no work thing messes with me after a while. Updated the resume and answered two more ads late last night. Can't believe they don't see I'm perfect for the job. Something else trying to get my attention maybe?

I've given this advice to countless friends: The image of water flowing down a creek bed, flowing, flowing . . . then having its forward motion stopped because of an obstacle. No fault of the water that it can't move forward, so it just sits and 'collects' itself, waiting, waiting, staying in one place but *changing* as it stays in one place (more and more of itself gathering up, collecting, accumulating) . . . Looks like it's stopped, stuck . . . but the water has no opinion of this; it's just being itself, completely unaffected by 'outside opinion', or outward appearances. Not even upset or worried . . . doesn't care if it takes minutes or months to begin moving forward again. Waiting, waiting, gathering more and more of itself up, waiting . . . and then . . .

Spilling over, around, or past the obstacle. Maybe the obstacle gets blown out of the water's way because the obstacle can no longer take the pressure of trying to keep it held back, held down, then BOOM! . . . water everywhere! Water continuing on its way, initially much more forceful and FULL of itself from having waited patiently, gathering itself up as it waited. Actually, it didn't even think of itself as waiting. It was totally fine with where it was at, knowing it was a temporary situation all along because . . . *the water knows itself.*

The obstacle thought it was controlling the water's movement. The water let the obstacle believe whatever it wanted to believe.

. . . the water had other plans.

_____
Subject: re: Hey
Date: Wed, 11 Nov 2009 2:22 PM
From: Lisa
To: Mark

These rants about the *nature* of things as it relates to people are my favorite. Whatever gets you in this vibe, try to remember it and keep it coming. There is usually a sense of discontent that gets you started on your way to connecting with the *truth.*

Love it.

_____
Subject: good morning. . .
Date: Thu, 12 Nov 2009 5:34 AM
From: Lisa
To: Mark

Hope your day starts bright. Mine has. Watched the sun rise, frost sparkling on the grass. It will be cold soon. *Argh.* Since I'm intending this to be my last Chicago winter, I will not complain. Just enjoy it for what it is.

———

Subject: re: good morning. . .
Date: Thu, 12 Nov 2009 5:40 AM
From: Mark
To: Lisa

I haven't been to bed yet. Just finished a bunch of stuff on the Hangin' With Horses book. NOW I'm off to bed. Looks great. Not finished, but thought you'd dig what's there so far . . . check out the link.

Chick on.

———

Subject: re: Hangin' with Horses book
Date: Date: Thu, 12 Nov 2009 7:47 PM
From: Lisa
To: Mark

Very cool book you did! Nicely done. The pride you feel for Savannah was oozing off the pages in such a deep and sincere way. Let me know when there is more.

My own proud moment tonight . . . I went with Zac while he and two other students were awarded for speaking on behalf of the school district to the IL Board Of Education. The kids talked about their success in programs that are at risk of losing funding. Zac spoke eloquently about his achievements in the Culinary & Hospitality program. I told him I was blown away by his confidence, saying that I can only imagine what he will be like when he is my age. His reply: "Are you kidding me? I'll be freakin' Tony Robbins."

My son the rock star.

———

Subject: re: Hangin' with Horses book
Date: Thu, 12 Nov 2009 7:58 PM
From: Mark
To: Lisa

Ha! Great stuff.

———

Subject: Tuscan chicken for dinner. . .
Date: Thu, 12 Nov 2009 9:03 PM
From: Mark

To: Lisa

Interesting moment while walking the horse . . .

Dawned on me that the photo book represents my effort to start making a place for myself in the larger world. Comes down to it, most of us want to be appreciated for *something*, but obviously we won't get far if we don't have something to offer.

Hence the email traffic, the two of us showing one another and sharing with one another our latest installment of writing, photo book project, or interaction with someone in which a shiny, gold-star moment happened: *See me? I'm doing good, yes? Check this out . . .*

Subject: re: email traffic
Date: Sat, 14 Nov 2009 8:08 PM
From: Lisa
To: Mark

I sat down a couple of times to write in reply to your email about *wanting to be seen.* I finally opened it earlier this evening, clicking it to fill the screen, to *breathe*, like a nice Cabernet.

Dave came by today. It was the first time I'd seen him since my trip to California. He patched the crack downstairs and took a couple more things before claiming his truck was too full for the few more boxes left. He'll be back. Seeing him doesn't upset me but one thing is clear:

He really doesn't *see me.*

Taking me right back to your email . . . I agree that much of the self-expression displayed as an artist is about wanting to be seen. Regardless of the medium, there is a deep need and desire to connect with another by evoking emotion through viewing the painting, the dance, hearing the music, reading the words - striking an emotional chord that makes them feel alive or understood. Very validating for the viewer or reader or listener - and for the artist. Our upbringings *do* factor in as artists, and of course, the most successful ones have had plenty of shit in their gardens to help them grow. As have we. *Fertilizer.*

Here's the thing, though, about us: I agree that our email traffic, as you call it, asks for each of us to be seen - validated - for what we have to say, which is in essence who we are. *I'm doing good, yes?* I felt a shiny bright-star moment in sharing my evening about Zac with you. I can share these with anyone and get some positive reinforcement, as can you about your Hangin' with Horses book, but there is something different about sharing it

145

with *each other*. Being seen by one another carries more weight. We hold up mirrors for one another that reflect us in our brightest light, reflections of how *we want to be seen.*

If our writing is a reflection of who we really are, then we have shown up most honestly with one another for most of our adult lives. Radical acceptance. Trust. Truth. We create a poetic exchange just sharing the day-to-day experiences of our lives. We don't do that with just anyone.

_____
Subject: mirroring. . .
Date: Sun, 15 Nov 2009 2:49 PM
From: Mark
To: Lisa

The 'holding up the mirror' part . . .

Others can claim they hold up a mirror for you, helping you to see yourself, by giving you feedback about whatever it is you present to them. In fact, most of the time, various people serve that function for us on a quite unconscious level: they're just telling us what they *think*, in some organic, spontaneous way . . .

But different people see different things. Some see what they *want* to see (being in denial serves them somehow), or maybe . . . they . . . don't . . . *really* . . . see you. Their feedback doesn't connect with where you're at with yourself . Maybe *you* are in denial about something. The point is:

When you mirror back to me something about myself that helps me feel more whole, or helps me connect with something inside that I haven't been able to name or put my finger on . . . THAT kind of mirroring has a stronger effect in part because of a unique, long-developed *spiritual* bond that cannot be named. It's a kinship born of old-soul compassion for another old soul. Your information about me carries more weight, in part, because *you know how I would ultimately like to see myself.* Getting feedback from someone who likes me is not the same as getting feedback from someone who *sees* me.

_____
Subject: re: mirroring. . .
Date: Sun, 15 Nov 2009 5:07 PM
From: Lisa
To: Mark

Yeah, that spiritual bond is part of it. I agree that there is something about the reflection of someone who really sees us. That is never more apparent than when with someone who *doesn't*. I really felt that last night when Dave was here.

146

So, I stumbled upon the last 20 minutes of the movie *Carolina* today. I remember the first time I saw it after you told me to get it and that it would remind me of us. I loved the scene where she goes to the book signing and he was reciting a part of their story that we had witnessed, musing about the everyday magic of his interaction with this woman he loves, who was blissfully unaware of anything but their deep friendship. It was a shame that she had to leave before he knew she was there. Oh, well. That's the nature of stories . . . they are best when unexpected things occur that surprise us. At least they had a happy ending.

Feeling pensive today. As the weeks go by I notice the memory of my time in California keeps fading. Like herbs hung in the kitchen to dry, I can still get a nice *whiff* as I walk by but the color is losing its vibrancy.

It would be easy to slip back into my life here, let my plans to move back to California float above me and not really take root in reality. Yet, as cold winds begin to blow, I am reminded that this is not where I want to call home. Your letters remind me of where home is.

Thank you for that.

———

Subject: re: mirroring. . .
Date: Sun, 15 Nov 2009 6:05 PM
From: Mark
To: Lisa

What's up currently is the quasi-dilemma of being mostly unemployed, and somehow not finding time to just be left alone for hours on end so I can write. There's always something that comes up. *harrumph*

Way more to come. Dinner time. Savannah and I. Roasted whole-grain mustard-coated pork loin, roasted garlic mash taters, roasted broccoli and cauliflower.

———

Subject: menu share
Date: Mon, 16 Nov 2009 6:00 AM
From: Lisa
To: Mark

Your dinner sounded lovely. I woke up really hungry so breakfast today: veggie scramble of eggs, spinach, tomato, avocado, broccoli and sweet onion with shredded cheddar. Delish!

You know, writing a couple hours at a time is way better than when you are working again and grabbing *moments* to write. Seize this time or you will be whining later about having wasted it. You know you will.

Remember that all the moments of your life add up to . . . your *life*. And if you have no work and you want to take this time to just write, then *take* it. Use your time for *that*. We don't find time or make time, nor are we given it. We use it. Use your time wisely *now*!

OK, I'm done.

_____
Subject: re: menu share
Date: Mon, 16 Nov 2009 6:00 AM
From: Mark
To: Lisa

Hey, wow, thanks for that. That was good. And good timing . . .

I'm having a hard time with the idea that I created this semi-unemployment so I could write. I have voices in my head guilt-tripping me that I should be WAY more proactive about job hunting. I do look around and submit resumes but my heart certainly is not in it. I keep thinking about hanging out in the library. I'll be heading there soon, after some lunch.

I'll check in with you later.

_____
Subject: re: menu share
Date: Mon, 16 Nov 2009 12:32 PM
From: Lisa
To: Mark

I have an interesting perspective about that not working thing that I could offer . . .

I so love libraries. My fave is in Oak Park. They hosted a book signing for me when *Purpose & Passion* came out. Tomorrow night I'll be there for a women's workshop on gratitude.

Talk with you later.

_____
Subject: re: menu share
Date: Mon, 16 Nov 2009 12:35 PM
From: Mark
To: Lisa

Well, I'm still here. Call if you like.

_____

Subject: re: menu share
Date: Mon, 16 Nov 2009 12:36 PM
From: Lisa
To: Mark

I am struggling with my own writing today. Maybe a walk will help. A call later would be better. Let's do that if we can.

___

Subject: re: menu share
Date: Mon, 16 Nov 2009 12:38 PM
From: Mark
To: Lisa

Cool. Later. Bye.

___

Subject: need some winechat?
Date: Mon, 16 Nov 2009 4:16 PM
From: Mark
To: Lisa

Just leaving the library. Quite unproductive. Heading home to drink and cook . . . and chat.

___

Subject: winechat
Date: Tue, 17 Nov 2009 6:13 AM
From: Lisa
To: Mark

Good morning. . .

I woke up thinking about the men I compared you to on our call last night. Kenny, Richard, Sting. Some of my faves. Interestingly enough, it is not that they are so attractive (which they are) but it's their ethereal, spiritual man thing I really dig. I lay there in bed thinking how I used to have a huge framed photo of Kenny's *High Adventure* album poster above my desk at Sound Genesis in 1983 (remember us manifesting that job for me with the crystal on the classified ad?) and how much I thought he looked like you. Now I have the book *Nights in Rodanthe* on my bedside table, Richard Gere grasping Diane Lane's face in his hands as they say goodbye. I love the picture and he really does resemble you. How a guy morphs from Kenny Loggins to Richard Gere is beyond me.

Ah, so I am wondering if your continued appeal to me is somehow connected to my attraction to these men who make me swoon a little in interviews where they show up as themselves with grace, spirit and smoldering sensuality.

149

Or do they make me swoon because they remind me of you?

fifteen

Subject: morningchat
Date: Wed, 18 Nov 2009 7:55 AM
From: Mark
To: Lisa

No work today. I drew up plans long ago for a computer desk to fit in the kitchen, so maybe starting in on that would be a good use of my time.

Filled out an app for . . . Home Depot . . . over the weekend, feeling a little bit desperate and defeated the whole time.

Problem remains: I have no clear vision of how I want this no-work thing to end up. Still have mixed feelings, so the Universe is getting a mixed message. Nothing solid for It to work with because *I'm* not solid. (sigh)

Subject: re: morningchat
Date: Wed, 18 Nov 2009 8:20 AM
From: Lisa
To: Mark

Yikes. Home Depot is not where you want to be. Can we talk about ideas for marketing your remodeling business? I have been down this road with Dave who works part time at Home Depot because he didn't have enough work and would not let my marketing/coaching expertise help him build his remodeling business. I like to think you are smarter than that.

———

Subject: quickie
Date: Wed, 18 Nov 2009 5:36 PM
From: Mark
To: Lisa

Short but sweet call. Thanks for your feedback . . . it inspires me.

———

Subject: In sync
Date: Sun, 22 Nov 2009 5:42 PM
From: Lisa
To: Mark

Up till 2am reading our emails. Interesting recurring themes: relationships, writing, Meade . . . nice memories came in.

Took a long walk today and I'm literally bopping and dancing down the street with *Love Story* by Taylor Swift blasting in my ears, oblivious to whether anyone passes by on the curvy road along the creek, when who drives up next to me? Zac. He says, "Mom, you are so embarrassing! I could have been one of my friends! You are like dancing in the street. You're such a freak." He will never let me live it down. :-)

So now he's gone out and I am back at my desk, writing. I dug out a compilation CD you sent me called September Songs, with the letter explaining why you included each song. It must have been '05. I haven't listened to it in a long time and out of the blue comes Marc Cohn's *True Companion*. It about knocked me out of the chair. *What?* In another September that's the song I wanted at my wedding . . . but Dave didn't agree, so it only made it on the dance mix CD . . .

Oh, and you have to find another song to associate with me, sweetheart because the sad James Taylor song you said could have been about me, *Like Everyone She Knows,* about the girl waiting by the window for True Love? That's a little tragic, even for me. Find me one where she's with the love of her life and they grow old together . . .

Ah, like *True Companion*, perhaps. LOL

———

Subject: even more stuff. . .
Date: Sun, 22 Nov 2009 7:17 PM
From: Lisa
To: Mark

OK, so there has been a lot to share today. . .

This afternoon on my hunt for your CD I found a stack of some of my old
ones in the closet that had been moved there to accommodate Dave's
collection. Among them were all-time classics like Billy Joel's *The Bridge*
and Loggins and Messina's *Mother Lode*. Oh man, what a blast I am
having! I am running my energy through it *all* today and it's fantastic! I'm
not even drinking wine because that would be too much.

My God, this CD is so incredible. Kenny just breaks my heart and lifts it
up at the same time and the music is so Apollo-ish in parts. Hey, can you
put the Apollo album on CD or mp3 easily? I would love to hear it again.
Today I wrote about meeting you for the first time at that gig. It feels good
to just keep going with what shows up. All the music really sparked some
things.

Ciao, for now.

_____
Subject:
Date: Mon, 23 Nov 2009 7:58 AM
From: Mark
To: Lisa

Almost no alone time yesterday, and not much today. School vacation,
everybody home, projects, distractions . . . and no job. *Oooff*. Rough. Keep
on soaring. I'll catch up.

_____
Subject: re:
Date: Mon, 23 Nov 2009 9:04 AM
From: Lisa
To: Mark

I *know* you will. You have all the manual pages now, remember. I'll keep
sending reports. . . Sunny skies now, but I'm sure to hit a storm here in a
while. Having you in the tower keeping an eye on me makes me feel safe.

_____
Subject: Get some tea . . .
Date: Mon, 23 Nov 2009 5:27 PM
From: Mark
To: Lisa

It isn't that marriage sucks, it's that I suck at marriage. All the evidence of what kind of marriage I was in for was there on the day I got married, most notably the *lack* of typical, normal wedding day props: A best man, a bridesmaid, a family member, a cake, a first dance, a band or DJ, flowers, rice, champagne . . . none of that was at my wedding. There was a lawyer who could legally marry us, his wife and their four year-old son, the lawyer's aunt, and my three month-old daughter, who was the reason for the marriage even taking place.

The one and only picture we have from that day was taken shortly after the ceremony. It shows my new wife and I standing shoulder-to-shoulder, smiling, holding our recently-born daughter between us. My wife and I are wearing smiles that seem to say: *We're cool, we can do this. We'll be alright.* Our daughter wears an expression that reflects a much more honest assessment of what that day was about. She looks . . . concerned, confused. She's looking back at you, saying: *Don't fall for their bullshit, folks. He didn't really want to marry her, and she didn't want to be left alone. They can smile all they want, but the marriage of these two nitwits is a total sham. I'm only in it for the horses.*

The interpretation of the look on my daughter's face in that picture is a total projection on my part of course, but it's an accurate one, based on sixteen years of marriage having passed with me spending most of that time wanting out and my wife trying to keep me in. Caught in the middle is our daughter, who has endured her parents bullshit-ridden relationship the way you endure getting caught in a rainstorm without an umbrella: it's mostly unpleasant, you know you're gonna get wet, so you just put up with it because there's nothing you can do about it.

I could add here that, as fairly self-aware parents, we know our shortcomings and flaws may or may not create long-term psychological scars in our daughter, the effects of which may not show up as behavioral tics for several more years. But until someone can prove otherwise I think it's entirely possible she knew exactly what she was getting into when she *chose* us as parents. The expression on her three month-old face in that picture is possibly her future, fully-realized Self looking out through her brand-new eyes, confused and concerned about the road she's about to embark on. She can only grow into the person she came here to be *through* us, and those "behavioral tics" will just be facets of the core personality she's bringing into the world with her.

This doesn't let us off the hook as a dysfunctional couple. It just means that part of the reason for our dysfunction is due to our own histories of being disconnected from our destinies. The stuff inside of me that wants out has a way of creating, over and over again, situations and opportunities that give me yet another chance to get connected, to hear and understand the inner voice of a soul that *refuses* to go on living an inauthentic life of insincere love, constrained passion, and quasi-freedom.

Subject: re: Get some tea . . .
Date: Mon, 23 Nov 2009 6:07 PM
From: Lisa
To: Mark

I'm only in it for the horses. Love that.

This is inspired.

Subject: re: Get some tea . . .
Date: Mon, 23 Nov 2009 6:07 PM
From: Lisa
To: Mark

Some of yesterday's musings on this end . . .

WDRV is tuned in on the radio. Classic Rock . . . the soundtrack of our lives. Heart's *Magic Man* pulsates through the room on this Sunday morning and my inner rocker chick wakes up, remembering the spell that was cast when I was barely more than a child myself, only 21 years old, and Mark entered my life in 1982. He was playing in a mystical band called Apollo, complete with fiddle and flute, each ethereal note they played sent shivers down my spine. Being the drummer he was hidden behind the rest of the band, but somehow he stood out. I was mesmerized by him.

I can still remember his beautiful hands peeling an orange while he sat on the edge of the stage during their first break. He looked up as I nervously approached him and held my gaze with kind eyes as we exchanged hellos. I relaxed instantly. In seconds I was gushing about all the wonder and excitement of my recent move to California. He listened intently, smiling and nodding, asking questions, interested in every word and too soon the band needed to start again. He encouraged me to come back after the last set.

When the show came to a close I bought their album and stood in line waiting to talk with him again. When I reached him he took his time and shared a bit more about himself - where the band was playing next, where he lived. I was surprised when he offered his number, asking if I would like to come for tea sometime so we could continue our conversation. Tea? Uh, *sure,* I said. His unforgettable message scrawled on my album left a permanent mark on my soul:

To Lisa . . . Welcome to California - you are loved. Mark

Dorothy had landed in Oz and found her Wizard.

_____
Subject: re: Get some tea . . .
Date: Mon, 23 Nov 2009 6:26 PM
From: Mark
To: Lisa

Aww . . . sweet. Lovely.

_____
Subject: re: Get some tea . . .
Date: Mon, 23 Nov 2009 6:40 PM
From: Lisa
To: Mark

Dave called tonight. I hadn't talked to him since early last week. He goes into this whole thing about wanting to go back to Cancun. *What? No, I don't think I want to go with you to Cancun.* "But, we're friends," he said. "It would be fun!"

NO, it would not.

And wow, I don't think *we are really friends.* It hit me like a ton of bricks. I don't think we were ever really friends. True friendship. I know what that feels like. We did not have *that.*

_____
Subject: Library rap. . .
Date: Tue, 24 Nov 2009 11:10 AM
From: Mark
To: Lisa

Sunny and almost spring-like here. Clear, cloudless, big-time fall colors still going on. I'll bet it's lovely around the Davis campus right now . . .

Still no steady job. Considering a cooking gig now. The cabinet project and the writing have lifted my spirits a bit and in the back of my mind I'm noticing the relationship between my state of mind and the expectation that all will be well and work out fine. The last several days have not felt that way, so I think the key is to keep being productive and creative in some way.

I'm trying to get the cabinet thing wrapped up before company arrives on Thanksgiving, so we'll see what comes out of the rest of today.

ciao . . .

Subject: re: Library rap. . .
Date: Tue, 24 Nov 2009 12:30 PM
From: Lisa
To: Mark

I'm jealous of the Spring-like weather. Most of the leaves are all gone now and it's gloomy today, in the 40's. Might snow on Thursday. Argh. I have been on calls most of the day and have a couple more. I can feel the inspired place I've been in coming through in my coaching. Feels good.

I'm free after 3 your time. Winechat?

Subject: re: Library rap. . .
Date: Tue, 24 Nov 2009 1:58 PM
From: Mark
To: Lisa

Yeah, winechat tonight. I have the house to myself from 2:30 til 10.

Subject: 100 gratitudes
Date: Thu, 26 Nov 2009 8:11 AM
From: Lisa
To: Mark

I write them every year. You're on my list. Have a great Thanksgiving.

Subject: sigh . . .
Date: Sat, 28 Nov 2009 6:59 AM
From: Mark
To: Lisa

Very little alone time these days. Not gonna get it til next week . . .

Subject: re: sigh . . .
Date: Sat, 28 Nov 2009 7:59 AM
From: Lisa
To: Mark

Dave was here yesterday to hang the drywall in the basement. Boy, he really revealed more of his emotions about our split. It felt good somehow to have him show up with his feelings, finally apologizing for being such an ass sometimes. It doesn't change that I am done being married to him. It just made me a little sad. He mentioned you, asking if I had seen you while I was in California. I said that I had. That was it.

Subject: good news
Date: Sat, 28 Nov 2009 6:13 PM
From: Mark
To: Lisa

Off to a gig after taking a shower and loading drums. Finally! Music!
Also, got a solid job offer today for a kitchen remodel company, starting
Monday. Finally! Cash flow!

_____

Subject: re: good news
Date: Sat, 28 Nov 2009 6:38 PM
From: Lisa
To: Mark

Great news about music and money! Go get your groove on and have a fab
night.

_____

Subject: Hey
Date: Sun, 29 Nov 2009 1:33 AM
From: Lisa
To: Mark

Writing while a John Mayer concert plays on TV, recorded at the Beacon
Theater in NYC. I remember being there in 1990 to meet up with Jimmy
(who was on the road with another band) at the end of my 3-month
overseas leg of the Janet Jackson tour. I had just arrived from Japan and
missed him at the Beacon so I had to get myself to his hotel in New Jersey.
The vivid memory is of being in the pouring rain with all my gear, trying
for an hour to get a cab driver to take me through the tunnel, eventually
convincing one to do it for 100 bucks.

_____

Subject: a great writing book
Date: Sun, 29 Nov 2009 12:29 PM
From: Lisa
To: Mark

Hey, at the library picking up books on writing and actually wrote from the
prompts in an awesome book by Natalie Goldberg, *Old Friend From Far
Away: The Practice of Writing Memoir*. Yeah, the title nudged me. First
assignment I randomly opened to towards the end of the book said to go
back and call out to your younger self, who had a victory or defeat, and
write to them for 10 minutes . . .

_____

Subject: 10 minutes with a younger me. . .
Date: Sun, 29 Nov 2009 1:57 PM
From: Mark

To: Lisa

Notes from me to my twelve year-old self, summer of '67in Southern California . . .

I see the baseball thing is going well. There will be an awards night at the end of the season and with all the league's coaches and players there you're gonna be awarded Most Valuable Player. All the coaches from all the teams voted, having noticed how you can pretty much do it all: pitch, hit, catch. Congratulations in advance . . .

It's cool the way Dad was one of the coaches for the team. I'm sorry to say, though, that this personal attention and interest in you is coming to an end in a few years. You'll be moving to the San Francisco area next summer and that's when things will begin to unravel. Soon after you're all settled into the new home there will be some talk about the family moving to Florida when Dad's company wants to transfer him there, but he'll go by himself when he and mom divorce. Yup, divorce. But you won't know the truth about *why* they divorced til after he dies in a St. Petersburg hospital. Sorry, yeah, that's coming too, but not for another twelve years. I know, I know. . . it seems so weird to think about that when things feel so good now, right?

So look . . . pay close attention to what's going on in the house with your mom and dad because the way they interact with you and your sisters is going to matter when he finally leaves for Florida. Once he's gone you'll be the only male in a house with three women.

Enjoy this time while you can.

———
Subject: 10 minutes with a younger me. . .
Date: Sun, 29 Nov 2009 7:00 PM
From: Lisa
To: Mark

Here's mine:

There you are, Lisa, landing in San Francisco, scared shitless and more excited than you've ever been. Walking from the plane in your black polyester suit, teetering on strappy high-heeled sandals, a fedora perched on your head, you're carrying a large picnic basket filled with assorted fragile treasures, launching headlong into your new life in California.

You're adorable.

Only twenty-one, such a baby, and yet an ancient soul. The very best part of us. Both brave and a little too stupid to stop yourself, you venture out into the world to see it, feel it, be part of it. You've had an uncanny ability to strike out on your own from the time you were a little girl. Yet you are not without fear. That's part of your charm. You can be quite the scaredy cat when it comes to silly things like bugs and unexpected noises in the night. You're nervous with driving too fast and terrified of heights. No, you are not fearless by nature, so striking out on your own so young is more remarkable, more brave.

I smile when I think of you, young Lisa. You with your big dreams, dreams too big to fit in a picnic basket . . . peeking out from beneath a great hat. You have moxie and verve.

I still wear fedoras just for you.

sixteen

Subject: hey. . .
Date: Tue, 1 Dec 2009 5:02 PM
From: Mark
To: Lisa

Just home from my day, ending with a Mexican food dinner for Savannah and I . . .

First day of the new job was okay. Lots of high-end custom work with this kitchen job. Have to let go of the low-money thing. The guy who delivered my materials to the job said he used to be a bodyguard for the Beach Boys. He looked to be in his early 60's, big hands, no hair . . . interesting guy.

Subject: beginning of the day . . .
Date: Wed, 2 Dec 2009 7:28 AM
From: Lisa
To: Mark

I leave for Austin tomorrow to stay at the Wizard Academy. Glad to hear you got some work.

Subject: hey. . .

Date: Wed, 2 Dec 2009 5:02 PM
From: Lisa
To: Mark

You around?

Subject: re: hey. . . yourself
Date: Wed, 2 Dec 2009 8:50 PM
From: Mark
To: Lisa

Yeah, I'm here . . . fucking marriage . . . what is it with . . . *ugh*, forget it.
Not worth it.

In other news . . .

My Hangin' With Horses book came in the mail just an hour ago, and man
is it beautiful! It really came out great. Inspires me to make a bunch more,
on different subjects, different themes.

Finished watching *Benjamin Button* late last night. Really got swept away
with the lines Pitt writes to his daughter in a voice-over towards the end of
the movie, about it never being too late to be whoever you want to be, that
there are no rules, and to live a life you're proud of. And if you're not . . .
have the strength to start over. It was nearly one in the morning when I
finished transcribing the actual words into a journal I'm keeping for
Savannah, and it popped into my head that it sounded like something I
would want to say to her as I headed out to start over myself.

I was working on a kitchen today, listening to a radio interview about how
so many people are looking for PURPOSE in their lives. Hard times are
here for a lot of people, and many are trying to make sense of what's
happening, what they're supposed to do with themselves now. Like me,
working a job that pays a survival-level wage and having so many things
feeling a little off, or wrong. So I write a few notes on the back of an
elevation drawing to remind me to write about it . . . and then go back to
my nail gun.

Subject: re: hey. . . yourself
Date: Thurs, 3 Dec 2009 4:42 AM
From: Lisa
To: Mark

Ah, Benjamin Button . . . I wish I had more time now to reply. It really is
never too late, Mark.

On my way out soon to the airport - off to see the Wizard. I'll write more there if I have time. I'm really excited to be getting out of Dodge!

_____
Subject: oh, man. . .
Date: Thu, 3 Dec 2009 6:03 PM
From: Lisa
To: Mark

Greetings from Wizard Academy. What an incredible place. I've had a great hike, chatted with another guest and now I have the kitchen to myself. I'm getting ready to cook. The only thing missing is my favorite Wizard, and warm weather (it might snow tomorrow). Here are pix of the place.

_____
Subject: re: oh, man. . .
Date: Thu, 3 Dec 2009 8:05 PM
From: Mark
To: Lisa

Nice. Love the kitchen. Looks yummy. Yeah, I could dig on being there now.

_____
Subject: good. . . ok, great . . . morning
Date: Fri, 4 Dec 2009 5:44 AM
From: Lisa
To: Mark

Greetings. I have decided to share as I go, hoping you can get inspired by proxy :-)

Long talks with wine flowing till midnight. The last two standing were me and another of my clients who came down from Colorado for this. Haven't seen her in a year and a half after meeting in Dallas. Now I'm off for a very early morning sunrise hike. Woke up at 4:30 and was wide awake so making the most of my time here. Spent a little time reading the guest journal in my room. I will write in it before I leave tomorrow. Looking forward to the program today!

More later . . .

_____
Subject: good. . . ok, great . . . morning
Date: Fri, 4 Dec 2009 6:09 AM
From: Mark
To: Lisa

Mornin' . . . Welcome back from your hike. Cold out there, yes? I made us some tea . . .

Subject: a cold, sunny morning
Date: Sat, 5 Dec 2009 7:09 AM
From: Lisa
To: Mark

Hey there . . . I leave Hogwarts today :-(But I'm happy that I am off to do my workshop with these cool women. There will be eight attendees. You had a gig last night, right? Good one? Hope so.

OK, so today's walk was really cold but sun coming up was beautiful (see pix). I really hope to come back again to this place. The visit feels too short. The groundskeeper was so cute when he saw me on my walks. We met when I arrived and he asked where I was from so each morning he would see me and say, "Hey there Chicago, is it cold enough for you?" Really sweet man. He walked and talked a bit this morning with me. Told me I look like Sandra Bullock :-)

Subject: good. . . ok, great . . . morning
Date: Sat, 5 Dec 2009 9:38 AM
From: Mark
To: Lisa

Well now . . .

Sorry I missed out on being able to contact you more during your Hogwarts stay. Left early yesterday morning for work then straight to the 7pm gig, home at midnight.

Even from here I can feel how your Hogwarts stay was too short. It was short for me as well because I thought we'd be writing more about your stay, how it was going, and some good winechat exchanges. The new job has forced me into a schedule I have no affection for. I'm sure you had much to share. I feel like I missed out on something by not being able to hang with you more during your stay . . .

In just the few days I was with this new company I felt something really wrong about it: a bad feeling, a depression, actually, that would not go away. It was so odd that I did not want to be there. Maybe it was the combined influences of picky customers, high-end performance expectations of the company, and low pay. It may not of been any one thing, but I've been looking forward to being done with this job since the end of the first day.

Eventually it dawned on me: this remodeling company can get all the cheap labor they want since the current economy is in the toilet, and even with my specialty skills in finish work and refacing there's no incentive for them to pay me what I'm worth. They'll just wait for someone else to knock on their door should I choose to move on. It sure looks like this company has very little interest in taking good care of quality workers, other than giving them steady work. No gas, medical, vacation, overtime, phone, vehicle . . . nothing.

So . . . that sinking feeling and depression I've been feeling from day one seems to have been a precognition of what goes on behind the curtain. These ass wipes have no intention of helping me get out of Oz. They seem to be enamored of the wicked witch's business model: *Let's get a bunch of flying monkeys to do our dirty work!*

Yesterday ended on a high note: The gig I was not-so-much looking forward to ended up being a pretty good musical experience after all.

Today is about running Savannah around in prep for her Winter Ball: hair, makeup, pictures and dinner with friends, then the dance. Mariah will be gone all day today and tomorrow for a weekend seminar so I'm relishing the time with Savannah. Kinda cool to have her *dad* run her around for this, right?

‎———
Subject: chat?
Date: Sat, 5 Dec 2009 3:34 PM
From: Lisa
To: Mark

Hey. Settling in the airport hotel . . . happy to see a long email from you.

Ah . . . you're back.

‎———
Subject: it's me
Date: Sat, 5 Dec 2009 7:00 PM
From: Lisa
To: Mark

Hope the festivities are fun. Please send some pix. I would love to see her on her big night out. I'll bet she looks beautiful.

Not feeling the writing thing tonight. I have allowed distractions to come in and actually welcomed them as the words just aren't there.

Even a call from Dave, who thought I was returning tonight. Talk about a truly Pergo moment:

Hi Dave. Brazilian Cherrywood isn't available for Hogwarts debriefing tonight so, sure, I will share my trip highlights with you since you asked and I'm alone and bored in an airport hotel with nothing going on since there are no muses showing up for me tonight, literally or figuratively. Hey, thanks for calling.

I moved from Hogwarts to La Quinta. Pergo seems appropriate. LOL

_____
Subject: heading home
Date: Sun, 6 Dec 2009 5:05 AM
From: Lisa
To: Mark

Mornin'.

Hope your night ended on a good note and Savannah had fun. I hung out in my mediocre room at the airport hotel and watched Saturday Night Live then fell asleep. I have a few hours before heading to the airport so I will get some breakfast and try writing again.

_____
Subject: Fight Club and pix
Date: Sun, 6 Dec 2009 9:20 AM
From: Mark
To: Lisa

I'm guessing you're home by the time you get this. I didn't get much hang time at the computer yesterday, and then everybody home after the dance.

Rented and watched *Fight Club* again, still intrigued by the scene where Pitt's character threatens to shoot Raymond, the convenience store owner, if he doesn't go back to pursuing the dream he once had of becoming a veterinarian. Pitt lets him live once he's satisfied that Raymond has been sufficiently scared into returning to vet school. Fascinating . . .

My take on this scene is that Raymond was one lucky fuck. Not so much because his life was spared, but because he was put back in touch with a dream he'd abandoned when someone appeared in his life who, perhaps for the first time, was going to motivate him to see that dream realized: Head blown off, or "too much school"? We never see Raymond again, but we assume he began filling out community college enrollment papers the next day.

There are two things about that scene that appeal to me . . .

The first is that, after over an hour of watching Pitt's character establish himself as crazy, dangerous, and unpredictable, I expect something bad is about to happen when he enters the convenience store with a gun. When it turns out that his intention all along was to scare Raymond into making a better life for himself I can't help but admire the Pitt character for rescuing Raymond from a life of soul-draining mediocrity. I watch that scene and I think: *I wish that would happen to me.*

The other thing has to do with magic, angels, and divine intervention . . .

Even if I believed there were no such thing as God or some sort of divine intelligence of which I am a microscopic portion, I would still feel compelled to do the Divine Intervention math regarding a dream I'd abandoned and the appearance of someone who reconnects me with that dream.

I can imagine Raymond sitting behind the convenience store counter on a slow night, doing a crossword puzzle or watching re-runs on a six-inch TV. Enter a man, brandishing a gun, who has come not to rob Raymond but to "inspire" him to get back to the business of dream manifestation. Where did this guy come from? What seemingly unrelated chain of events took place that brought these two together? Raymond's life will never be the same. Lucky fuck.

I see a bit of myself in Raymond. It's that quality of "settling for", of one day finding myself at a level of comfort and ease where life feels non-threatening, demands little of me, and I live as though I've been let off the hook from any responsibility to change, grow, or improve my station in life. I got used to the autopilot life of running my own metaphorical convenience store and I've convinced myself that I'm doing fine.

I've had my own version of giving up on ever becoming a veterinarian. Those golden moments of making contact with my heart's desire would lose their shine when the day-to-day reality of effort and sacrifice gradually became "too much school". I too have "dropped out" and fallen back on my *existing* skills and abilities to earn a living. Discipline and self-control turned into aimlessness and cruise-control, and at some point I began to feel proud of being able to make the best of whatever it was that life served up. I would eat whatever was put on my plate without complaining.

But it turns out that I'm a pretty good cook myself. What happened to me that I gave up on nourishing myself in better and more creative ways?

———

Subject: me again
Date: Sun, 6 Dec 2009 11:28 AM
From: Lisa

To: Mark

Hey there . . . greetings from 30,000 ft. Got your email.

Glad to have something to read. I'll be back with comments . . .

_____
Subject: ugh . . . bummer ahead . . .
Date: Sun, 6 Dec 2009 11:37 AM
From: Mark
To: Lisa

I'm experiencing the pointlessness of life right now . . .

Things feel bleak. There's a list of contributing factors that bring me to this
place. It isn't that there's any one thing that makes me feel this way, it's
more like . . . well . . . in general, I'm unhappy with the place I find myself.

Whoa. Stop. Try again. *Puke it out. Don't think . . .*

I'm right on the edge of wanting to whine about the quality of the life I
have. I did this to me, I brought myself here, and I cannot seem to grab
onto some better aspect of myself to pull me up and out of my hole. This
whole rap about the "deeper self", the true Me that lies under the surface of
the me I'm currently showing up as . . . it's not working. I am not inspired
to make changes. This deeper Self? *I don't hear his voice.* I'm not coming
up with intuitions or ideas that point at something better and more
fulfilling. I've said yes to a job that felt *wrong* from day one, and knowing
I can walk away only makes sense if I have something better to move on
to. But there is nothing better to move on to, not yet anyway.

ugh . . . Where is inspiration?

_____
Subject: ugh . . . bummer ahead . . .
Date: Sun, 6 Dec 2009 11:42 AM
From: Lisa
To: Mark

It's right HERE! Wake up and see there is a gun to your head *right now*. I
am happy to be holding it and I swear to Almighty God I will pull the
fucking trigger.

Wake up and see that you have had your motivator show up, goddamn it,
and she's right here and she's getting pissed. I mean it, Mark.

You sat before me, looked in my eyes and told me about seeing a different
life, a different story, a different choice. It kills me to hear you talk like

166

this and I mean it when I say I have the trigger cocked. I've been put on this path with you, whether I like it or not. I was starting to really like it . . . so find your way back to *that guy*. Sign up for school!

Sorry if I am making your mood worse; I really don't mean to. I only want to shake you up and help you see that this is your gunpoint moment if you want it to be. You can be the Lucky Fuck. And you don't have to feel like your life is about to end, but if you really need to feel like that I'm sure we can create a story where you can. You have chosen safe, and safe doesn't give you the edginess of gunpoint.

Subject: please read
Date: Sun, 6 Dec 2009 12:38 PM
From: Lisa
To: Mark

I know that I came across as harsh.

I may have put too much value on the time we spent talking and dreaming about the lives we envision and my power to truly motivate you. God knows you are motivating *me*. I have to admit when I read your email it made me sad that it dismissed any kind of inspired place you were in during our conversations since our visit in October. *Ouch.* I hate that for you.

For a guy who says he wants someone to put a gun to his head and force him to choose, you act more like someone who's walking through landmines: *If I stay in a safe place and walk very carefully I won't get hurt.*

And you won't get where you want to go either.

Subject: re: please read
Date: Sun, 6 Dec 2009 1:36 PM
From: Mark
To: Lisa

Hi. I've read your messages. I'm fine with it all. Jesus, my skin is thicker than you give me credit for. Interesting, though, to see the tone in your messages change in the time I was gone. Wow.

I'm having a hard time turning off the voices in my head, nagging me about low pay, disorderly house, so little alone time now that I have this job that I don't enjoy but don't have anything else in the wings either . . .

I could have just as easily written all my pity shit in my journal but it wouldn't come out the same, if at all. I just need to put words to the feelings and get them out of my body. Then I can look at what's laying there - the mess I've made - and decide what to do about it. At the very least it helps me get re-oriented towards something more nourishing. Gotta puke it out first. I KNOW it wasn't pretty. Jesus . . . I'm beating myself up about it all just fine, thankyouverymuch . . . but message received. Thanks.

_____

Subject: your mail
Date: Sun, 6 Dec 2009 2:27 PM
From: Lisa
To: Mark

Hey . . .

The tone and thick skin thing:

My shift was interesting. For some reason, in the insulation that an airplane creates, it felt like I was hearing my own words very loudly and they sounded so harsh. My intention was to give you what you said you wanted. I know you have thicker skin now and I have to keep reminding you that you called in someone to put a gun to your head. I'm that person and I am ready to get tough, baby.

_____

Subject: your mail
Date: Sun, 6 Dec 2009 2:38 PM
From: Mark
To: Lisa

Wouldn't want it any other way.

Thank you.

seventeen

Subject: happy Tuesday
Date: Tue, 8 Dec 2009 5:16 AM
From: Lisa
To: Mark

Woke up to a blanket of snow outside. It's really pretty, yet I am not ready for all the snow and cold. Argh.

It's Fun Client Tuesday here - three weekly fun folks joyfully getting their shit together with my assistance. They are all very smart and funny! I love Tuesdays.

Make the most of your day. Get in your groove. Remember that email you sent a couple years ago about making a built-in cabinet, creating something beautiful and lasting, and how you can't get pissed off doing that?

Pretend this job is fine Cherrywood and get into it. See that the better job with good money is coming soon. This gig will end, a better one will come, and you'll write in the gaps. You'll see. ox

_____
Subject: re: happy Tuesday
Date: Tue, 8 Dec 2009 6:11 AM
From: Mark
To: Lisa

Yeah, gotta watch where the mind goes, especially when I'm in a funk. Thoughts become things, blah, blah . . .

Felt great after talking with you, so thanks. Good energy in the house when the girls came back from the barn. Walked through a cool neighborhood while Savannah had a math tutor appointment: cold, clear, Xmas lights, good to move around, everybody upbeat for the rest of the night. Nice change from the norm.

Became aware that I've been disconnected from that *knowing* feeling that something better is coming, that all will be well. I have memories of being really optimistic, expecting things to get better. Lost that feeling over the last week or two. Had to stop by the Rock Star clinic to get vaccinated against the What's-The-Point? virus. Thanks again, doc . . .

Love the sound of your day ahead. Rock on.

_____
Subject: re: happy Tuesday

Date: Tue, 8 Dec 2009 11:31 AM
From: Lisa
To: Mark

Wow, what a great coaching day so far! I'm putting guns to heads all across the USA. Lots of "community college enrollment" going on! LOL Whew! I love my job. Now if I can make *myself* sit and write after all that.

Hey, and about that vaccination . . . you need to stop back in at the clinic frequently for boosters to stay immune. Doctor's orders. Something better is coming.

~Dr. Rock Star

_____
Subject: winechat?
Date: Tue, 8 Dec 2009 6:30 PM
From: Mark
To: Lisa

Home now . . . got a half hour if you wanna chat . . .

_____
Subject: Today's workout
Date: Wed, 9 Dec 2009 7:41 AM
From: Lisa
To: Mark

Today's workout was the removal of 2 inches of heavy, wet slush from my very long driveway before the temp goes down to 4 degrees tonight with a 20-below wind chill and it turns to a sheet of ice that will not thaw till March. Of course the snow blower does not blow slush so this was accomplished with a shovel. It is a balmy 32 now with a 15-degree wind chill which was, of course, blowing hard and whipping around my head as I cussed out loud to the gods to . . .

GET ME THE HELL OUT OF HERE!

California here I come.

_____
Subject: Waa . .
Date: Thu, 10 Dec 2009 7:05 PM
From: Mark
To: Lisa

I have just a few minutes. Savannah home soon, dinner (fish tacos) to prepare.

Long day yesterday. Off to work early then to gig in S.F. at the end of my day. Trying to watch my mental state to make sure I stay open to something better waiting around the corner. I do NOT want to work for this company.

I was up til 2 am, writing about the weirdness of knowing a divorce is coming while still being here. At some point I dropped into the quiet of the house and thought: *YES! Solitude!* What a luxury to be able to keep bizarre hours and write at whatever time the muse is working . . .

_____
Subject: re: Waa . . .
Date: Thu, 10 Dec 2009 7:14 PM
From: Lisa
To: Mark

I hear you about the work thing. Hang in, you'll be finished soon. Ready to talk about *you* becoming a coach on our next chat? It's a cool Plan B.

_____
Subject: winechat?
Date: Fri, 11 Dec 2009 4:07 PM
From: Lisa
To: Mark

Got wine? Got time?

_____
Subject: re: winechat?
Date: Sat, 12 Dec 2009 6:47 AM
From: Mark
To: Lisa

Got neither. Home at 8pm, bath, dinner, movie, bed.

Worked late to help move the job along, wanting the homeowners to have a functional kitchen by the weekend.

Came home at 8 and headed for the tub since dinner wasn't ready. I'm enjoying hot water, quiet, and down time in the tub when Mariah comes in, has a seat, and hangs out, chatting, chatting, chatting til I think: *the hell with it*, and cut my tub time short just to put an end to the chatter (ten more minutes - *just ten more minutes* - and I'd have been out) *ugh* . . .

How are you?

_____
Subject: re: winechat?
Date: Sat, 12 Dec 2009 7:23 AM

From: Lisa
To: Mark

I'm *great* . . .

It's quiet and I have been sitting here reading a wonderful book called *Write From The Heart*. The author has just talked about the need for solitude, especially for writers. He writes beautifully about being in the forest alone with his thoughts and legal pads. His description read like it could have been one of your journal entries. I sat and listened to the silence in my house while Zac was sleeping. *Ahh.*

Curled up on the couch in my jammies, I wrote in my journal about looking forward to a place of my own. It has been twenty years since I have been the sole occupant of my home. I lived alone for ten years prior to moving from SF to Tennessee with Jimmy. I've missed it sometimes. Living alone may bring some loneliness perhaps, but I will always have the chance to connect with those I love and invite them in to share my world.

So it will be interesting to reclaim a world in which no one else's stuff . . . energy . . . habits . . . voice . . . friends . . . or *attitude* come in to pierce my bubble at unexpected moments. Much like your story of your bath, I guess. I can hardly imagine plopping into someone's bath time uninvited. That seems incredibly uncool to me, particularly since you are someone who loves his space and solitude.

Subject: Overflowing life!
Date: Sat, 12 Dec 2009 3:30 PM
From: Lisa
To: Mark

My dream collage is coming along beautifully. It may cover the whole wall. Many dreams.

But I have collected so much fabulous stuff for my collage that is takes up all of my dining room table and there is still more in the folder :-/

Subject: re: Overflowing life!
Date: Sun, 13 Dec 2009 7:38 AM
From: Mark
To: Lisa

Simplify. Look for repetitive themes, and distill them down to saying only and exactly what you want to manifest.

Subject: Good Monday morning
Date: Mon, 14 Dec 2009 5:24 AM
From: Lisa
To: Mark

Thanks. Another week begins, a busy one for me, with some open time to finish my collage. It's very wordy right now but I will edit through the week to have it on the wall by my birthday on Saturday :-)

I can't believe Christmas is next week. I've still got to do some more shopping and wrapping, then on to the groovy new year. It all seems to be happening quickly and I have moments that grab me by the arm and say:

"Hey, what do you think you're doing? Do you think you can just up and change your life like that?"

Yes, I think I can.

"Well, you better be *sure*."

Yeah, I know.

So I take a breath and think about what makes me feel sure. *What do I really want?* When I answer, all paths still lead back to California. The Universe keeps confirming, too, that it will all be fine.

I overheard Zac talking to a friend, saying he was excited to be going to Tennessee after Christmas to check out the school down there and his Dad's place where he might live. He's the same kid who's resisting leaving this house, this life with me.

So, how about you? Are you done with that job or do you still have to finish?

_____
Subject: re: Good Monday morning
Date: Mon, 14 Dec 2009 5:29 AM
From: Mark
To: Lisa

Job not done. More to do. Very dark time here. Nothing upbeat or positive to report. Getting worse. Flying machine broken, repairs required.

_____
Subject: re: Good Monday morning
Date: Mon, 14 Dec 2009 5:32 AM
From: Lisa
To: Mark

173

Oh, sorry. :-(

Mechanical crew available for assistance when needed. I'm here sending thoughts of better days.

Subject: Sweet dreams and flying machines
Date: Mon, 14 Dec 2009 7:01 AM
From: Lisa
To: Mark

You know, my friend, James Taylor's flying machine grounded early and often. But oh, how he soared. Remember *Fire & Rain*? Go watch the video on YouTube . . .

Your pages are all there. Have faith.

Subject: re: Sweet dreams and flying machines
Date: Mon, 14 Dec 2009 6:27 PM
From: Mark
To: Lisa

Aw, Lis . . . you're the best. That was good.

Mood lifted somewhat. Got over a huge hurdle at the job site which feels like a big rock in my path has been pushed aside. As I climbed into the truck to leave it felt like the biggest source of my depression had a lot to do with working for this disorganized company (ooh, it was BAD this morning . . . really, *really* depressed). Now that the hardest, most time-consuming part is behind me I feel lighter, which helps my sanity.

Speaking of sanity, give me a call if you're there. I have at least a half hour.

Subject: New writing assignment
Date: Tue, 15 Dec 2009 5:37 AM
From: Lisa
To: Mark

My book coach is published in the next edition of *The Six-Word Memoir* with her entry: "It All Changed In An Instant".

Your life. Six words. What are yours?

Subject: re: New writing assignment
Date: Tue, 15 Dec 2009 5:41 AM

From: Mark
To: Lisa

"Only In It For the Passion"

_____
Subject: re: New writing assignment
Date: Tue, 15 Dec 2009 5:42 AM
From: Lisa
To: Mark

Oh! One for you: "He Hung in There Long Enough" LOL

"And She Lived Happily Ever After" Not original enough, I know. I'll keep thinking.

_____
Subject: re: New writing assignment
Date: Tue, 15 Dec 2009 5:45 AM
From: Lisa
To: Mark

No wait! . . .

"I Just Have a Lot To Say" the sequel to:

"She Talks A Lot, Doesn't She?"

_____
Subject: re: New writing assignment
Date: Tue, 15 Dec 2009 6:04 AM
From: Mark
To: Lisa

"No Thanks, I'd Rather Be Happy"

_____
Subject: re: New writing assignment
Date: Tue, 15 Dec 2009 6:07 AM
From: Lisa
To: Mark

"The Universe Has The First Move". This is my fave so far. Or, "You Want Me to Do *What*?"

_____
Subject: re: New writing assignment
Date: Tue, 15 Dec 2009 6:09 PM
From: Mark
To: Lisa

Better today. A victory: job's done and they want me to do windows at another house tomorrow.

DSL dropped out this morning so I couldn't get back to you. Love the six-word memoir game. LOVED "You Want Me To Do *What?*" . . . Picked up wine and chicken at Trader Joe's, then here at the library to return books. Savannah and I tonight. She's in a good space. She's clear to start riding her horse again, and boy has she been in a good mood. Gotta keep the horse thing alive.

_____
Subject: woo-woo week
Date: Wed, 16 Dec 2009 4:49 PM
From: Lisa
To: Mark

That was fun, wasn't it? Great news, all around. All good.

Lots of woo-woo this week: psychic night at Dad's tomorrow with tarot cards (still can't believe he's doing this for all of us!) and then a session on Saturday with Kathy (her b'day gift to me).

They should be able to see me glow from space by the weekend LOL

How are you?

_____
Subject: How am I?
Date: Wed, 16 Dec 2009 5:55 PM
From: Mark
To: Lisa

call and find out . . .

_____
Subject:
Date: Thu, 17 Dec 2009 6:00 AM
From: Lisa
To: Mark

I have a couple calls this morning then free much of the day. I want to finish the collage today. In other news, Zac left for school today in a suit to do a mock trial in his law class. OMG he is such a man now. wow. He looked so handsome. I stood at the window watching him get into his car and drive away. I was so incredibly proud. He is going to do great stuff in his life. He leaves on the 26th to go to his dad's for a few days and check out the school down there. I have so many feelings around him landing in Tennessee. Whew.

To my Dad's tonight for psychic night.

___

Subject: re:
Date: Fri, 18 Dec 2009 5:25 AM
From: Mark
To: Lisa

mornin' . . . home way late last night, then computer down all night.

How was psychic night?

___

Subject: Psychic night
Date: Fri, 18 Dec 2009 5:36 AM
From: Lisa
To: Mark

Another enlightening reading! Very interesting. More so even for the fam because they don't do stuff like this all the time like I do :-)

My reading was good. Again, the big career thing. She asked if I spoke to large groups. She saw a lot of travel . . . a lot of money (!) . . . my divorce . . . the move to California . . . Zac trying to figure out what he wants to do.

Oh, and there's a friend far away who could be a romantic interest . . .

She was good.

___

Subject: you there?
Date: Sat, 19 Dec 2009 10:48 AM
From: Mark
To: Lisa

You there? I'm at the library, writing to you on another page . . . Oh! Happy Birthday, by the way . . .

___

Subject: re: you there?
Date: Sat, 19 Dec 2009 11:03 AM
From: Lisa
To: Mark

Thanks :-) I just got home from breakfast with my family. Stayed at my sister's last night. I tried to leave at midnight but then they broke out the limoncello they brought back from Italy!

So, I just came across one of your 15 page journal letters from like 6 years ago. I haven't read it yet.

Subject: ugh . . .
Date: Sat, 19 Dec 2009 11:23 AM
From: Mark
To: Lisa

At the library for two reasons: our DSL is down again, and I had to get out
of the house after another head-butting session with Mariah. This time it
was a holdover from last night when I announced I had quit my job.
You've heard me rave for weeks about how awful it's been working for
this kitchen remodeling company, right? The low pay, the disorganization,
the abundance of design mistakes and the lack of support for the workers .
. . This company has no heart. So what is your first instinctive reaction to
hear me say I quit that job? I'm guessing it's something along the lines of
good for you, something better will come along, right? Well . . .

I was home by 9pm last night after a good gig, free of that miserable job
and optimistic about finding something better. I was very, very tired from
three weeks of mental and physical difficulty. After a late dinner Mariah
asked about the job. When I told her I'd given my notice the first words out
of her mouth were: "You QUIT? But we need the MONEY!"

Bang! Instant descent into depression, futility, and utter exasperation for
not being supported or understood. Not one word of encouragement. The
rest of the evening - and up to just an hour ago - was spent head-butting,
arguing, and defending our points of view. Later, when I was soaking in
the tub trying to find some peace from . . . everything . . . she came into the
bathroom, picking up the argument where she'd left off . . .

Ugh.

No surprises, I know, but I mention this whole thing for a reason: It just
keeps getting easier and easier to justify the need for us to separate . . .
even for her. When the end does finally come I doubt she'll remember how
awful that night became, or her half of the responsibility for creating it and
the dozens of others like it.

Yada-yada . . . this was all a total downer, but serving the Greater Good, if
you ask me.

Also: Heartbreaking to have Savannah witness this mess.

‾‾‾‾
Subject: re: ugh . . .
Date: Sat, 19 Dec 2009 11:33 AM
From: Lisa
To: Mark

Good for you, in lots of ways. Yes, the job had to go. You do need to follow up with something behind it, of course, and you will. But it had to go. I get that. As for Mariah, it sounds like she may be hanging by threads that are not holding too well. You're right that this split will be best for her, too. It can't feel good for her either, to be at odds the way you two seem to be so much of the time.

Regarding Savannah witnessing the mess, when the end finally does come she will likely have a sense of relief from the discord she has lived with for a long time.

I read that letter I found yesterday that you sent me in the fall of 2005. It begins with Bruce Cockburn lyrics, *Isn't It Hard to Be The Strong One?* Remember it? You had disappeared for months and you were catching me up on everything. You could have written it this morning. It's uncanny the way your words mimic things you have said to me so recently . . . looking for the right company to work with, trying to write, fighting with your wife. And this, which jumped from the page:

So anyway, as you can see I've spent most of 2005 trying to make contact with the "eventual me".

It seems to me that you are finally so close to making contact with the "eventual" you.

And to God you wrote: *How long do I have to go on feeling like some great life is right around the corner? It that YOU inspiring me to keep going or is that some part of me that can't let go of a false self-image? I'm so DONE with the struggle and the waiting . . . hello?!? HELLO?!!?*

You can let go of the rope and let go of the struggle. You're *so close.* Closer than ever.

––––––
Subject: A miracle. . .
Date: Sat, 19 Dec 2009 8:53 PM
From: Mark
To: Lisa

. . . a much-needed miracle . . .

Tonight, in the kitchen making dinner, completely and totally withdrawn from Mariah who was putting up tree lights in the other room and carrying on like all was fine and well, I was paid, um . . . a *visit* . . .

I'd been in the kitchen for hours, focusing on nothing but making food, a welcome diversion from having spent the day feeling very, very down and despondent, but just letting it all be when: *Wham!* A burst of light behind my eyes, knocking me to my knees, and a sensation of floating in a limitless sky . . . I *saw* what this struggle was all about, why it's happening. Everything just came together so perfectly and beautifully. I was on my knees, sobbing, holding a dish towel to my mouth to keep my moaning from being heard over the stove fan and the Christmas music in the other room . . .

In this moment I was *shown* that I'm . . . well . . . being *called*. I'm SUPPOSED to leave. It's fine. Nothing to worry about. I've been fretting and efforting my way through this time, guilt-ridden, as though years of conflict and not getting along didn't justify the impulse to leave.

I just sobbed and sobbed. It just was so *right*! And so incredibly sad that, for all the genuine love I feel for the family I've helped create, it's time to move on from this marriage. It's like God came to the door, saying: "Okay dude, time to go. C'mon. Train's leaving". And I cried to know that they will have a very hard time believing me, cried to know that I no longer have to figure anything out or work something through or *hang in there*. In ten minutes all of my gloom and despair just went away.

My depression, misgivings, doubts, fears, uncertainty were all there because I couldn't see what the outcome would be, and I was trying my best to figure it out and make sense all the different thoughts and scenarios.

But this moment in the kitchen was . . . well . . . a whole-body *epiphany*, revealing that the certainty and instinct I've felt for years was absolutely correct: *there is a happier and more honest life I'm supposed to be living, and I will never get to live it if I continue saying 'yes' to a toxic, inauthentic marriage.* Which, by the way, my daughter has also been subjected to.

I can let go now. I'm home.

———

Subject: re: A miracle. . .
Date: Sun, 20 Dec 2009 6:44 AM
From: Lisa
To: Mark

Aww, Mark. That's beautiful. How incredible that you were feeling *that* while I was reading your past Self writing to God several years ago, saying you were so done with "the struggle and the waiting". The struggle and efforting has been about *resisting* that call for years. In another part of the letter you ask God to show you the path you are to take to stop the efforting to hang in there. You finally found your way to the train station and the train has *arrived*. Yes, they're waiting. Yet know that when you board that train you are not ever *leaving* Savannah, for she has a pass to ride *with* you. What a good thing it could be for her to see her father be all that he can be.

Your miracle has really struck something in me about being *home* . . .

As I feel called to come home to California I have a similar desire to help those I love in my family to understand, particularly Zac. Having been on *my* train a while, I have less struggle around it and feel comfortable surrendering to the call, yet the feelings of how my answering that call affects others is no less uncomfortable. But I know they'll adjust, it will all work out, and they will answer their own call one day and understand even more. If they don't, then that is *their* struggle to handle. We are all eventually called to something. There is a destiny waiting to be fulfilled for each of us. Trust this. Faith is the track that the train rides on. Hugs and love to you, my friend.

_____
Subject: re: A miracle. . .
Date: Sun, 20 Dec 2009 8:48 AM
From: Mark
To: Lisa

Man . . . I so love having you in my life . . .

_____
Subject: next movie choice
Date: Sun, 20 Dec 2009 8:48 AM
From: Lisa
To: Mark

If you haven't seen *Julie & Julia* get it.

The beautiful love story between Paul & Julia . . . the writing scenes of Julie at her laptop through the window. . . I just love the promise of how following one's dream can begin with a simple step like writing a blog or taking a cooking class . . . and how that leads to bestselling books.

_____
Subject: re: next movie choice
Date: Sun, 20 Dec 2009 11:42 AM
From: Mark
To: Lisa

Seen it. Loved it.

give a call. home alone.

Subject: Happy Monday
Date: Mon, 21 Dec 2009 8:42 PM
From: Mark
To: Lisa

Interesting breakthrough today: Went to pick up my final (only) check from *that company* and had a chat with the owner, who wanted to know why I was leaving so soon. Turned into a half-hour pow-wow about the inefficiency of his company (he's bleeding money, he admitted) and he offered me more money to stay, but not enough to make me say yes right then and there. "I'll think about it", I said. It may turn into me helping him get his company running more efficiently. He's nearly clueless about what's actually taking place in the trenches - the time and resources being wasted there - so we'll see.

Subject: re: Happy Monday
Date: Mon, 21 Dec 2009 10:17 PM
From: Lisa
To: Mark

Dave took me to see *Avatar* tonight to celebrate my birthday. Wow. It was amazing. You have to see it. Then we went for sushi and after came back here to have the wine he brought. He was so sweet, really putting on his best all around. Brought a beautiful *To My Wife* birthday card complete with a lovely note he wrote inside. I enjoyed the sweetness of it all and was a little taken aback by the romance. So I really tried for a minute to drop in to see if there is *any chance?*

Nope. There is a bit of attraction but not *connection.*

I'm just done. Mostly I knew for sure when we sat at the sushi bar and I kept the conversation going, asking all the questions. He didn't really engage in asking what I was up to, what I was thinking. He was focused on the outside me, not the inside me.

(sigh)

He knows that I'm really done. I knew he wanted to stay tonight, but I didn't offer and he didn't ask. Yesterday he was upset that he couldn't find his wedding ring because he wanted to put it on. He looked for two hours and couldn't find it. "We are still married till we have the talk that says we're officially divorced," he said. That kind of freaked me out since I thought we had pretty much decided we were done when we didn't get back together or do anything to work it out for six months. I was relieved when he didn't have that ring on tonight. God must have hid it pretty well.

Subject: re: Happy Monday
Date: Tue, 22 Dec 2009 6:48 AM
From: Mark
To: Lisa

Wow. The ring energy . . . check this out . . .

About 5:30 your time on Sunday Mariah realized I wasn't wearing my
ring. We were at Savannah's Christmas piano recital and I was looking at
the cuts and scrapes on my hands when Mariah noticed the missing ring.
When we came home to get ready for a Xmas party she retrieved the ring
from the top of my dusty desk - where it had been for a month - and
ceremoniously put it back on my finger before going to the party. I just let
it be, thinking: *As if it makes a difference or changes anything.*

So it was 6 or 6:30 your time when The Ring out here was "found".

_____

Subject: re: Happy Monday
Date: Tue, 22 Dec 2009 7:08 AM
From: Lisa
To: Mark

That was just about when he was looking for his, Sunday evening around
dinner time. He had taken it off and left it on his nightstand when we
separated in June. It devastated me at the time even though I was the one
who asked for the separation. I had put it in a shallow box with things from
his dresser when I packed his stuff. He said he knew it was in that box and
had put it somewhere safe when he moved in with his sister. Real safe,
apparently.

Mariah hadn't noticed you weren't wearing it for a *month*?

By the way, after my phone conversation with Dave about his ring, I really
wanted to talk with you about it. I know I have to say difficult things to
him soon and I know that my seriously adverse reaction to the thought of
him wearing his wedding ring is pretty powerful. Tears still come even
writing about it. When you get a free chance alone to talk, let me know, 'k?

_____

Subject: re: Happy Monday
Date: Tue, 22 Dec 2009 7:15 AM
From: Mark
To: Lisa

Of course. Heading out the door for horse duty. Time to chat around noon.

I'll be back here at 9, my time.

———
Subject: re: Happy Monday
Date: Tue, 22 Dec 2009 9:36 AM
From: Mark
To: Lisa

here now . . . You there?

I pulled out *Bridge Across Forever* and opened the book to a passage that basically says if you don't believe in marriage and live it honestly, get unmarried fast . . .

Amen.

eighteen

Subject: hey there
Date: Sun, 27 Dec 2009 10:00 AM
From: Lisa
To: Mark

What's up?

———
Subject: re: hey there
Date: Sun, 27 Dec 2009 3:03 PM
From: Mark
To: Lisa

I know, I know . . .

Just got the house to myself for the first time in days. My older sister and her family were here for the holidays which was fantastic and consumed all my time . . . not to mention Christmas shopping, get-togethers, and a few new head-bashing sessions with Mariah.

The gap between us gets wider, and I own up to my full 50% responsibility for 100% of our problems.

So I'm currently giving my precious free time to myself, to write. And just to be clear: I'm not going away or dropping out; I'm writing my ass off . . .

Gotta go.

_____

Subject: re: hey there
Date: Sun, 27 Dec 2009 3:29 PM
From: Lisa
To: Mark

Nice to hear it all. Let's talk soon. A lot to tell.

_____

Subject: re: hey there
Date: Mon, 28 Dec 2009 10:39 AM
From: Mark
To: Lisa

Savannah's home on vacation for the next seven days, and Mariah will be around more, too. I've got some side job stuff going on through the week, so probably not much chance of a phone chat. Emails are fine.

My worst enemy these days is my own head. Wow, I just can't seem to keep from feeling small, like I've made huge mistakes somewhere when I'm around friends or family who seem to have it so much more together than me: nice homes, harmonious relationships, and steady work that provides the means to afford it all. I'm so not that, and Acorn Theory feels like thin ice. I'm working on becoming my own support system, in part to keep from having you or anyone else always play cheerleader to my depressions. I don't doubt my potential, but I am being worn down by the daily efforts of enduring my own dark thoughts.

I'll spare you any more sob stories about how unbalanced and ungrounded I've been feeling. It's a lot, and it's best that I just keep trying to find my own voice to guide me and pull me through. Would love to get a newsy email from you saying what's going on out there, since a phonechat is unlikely.

ciao

_____

Subject: re: hey there
Date: Mon, 28 Dec 2009 11:17 AM
From: Lisa

To: Mark

Nice to hear that you don't want to burden me with your funk, and want to be your own cheerleader, yet I hope you still feel free to share the highs and lows. A big part of your problem, my friend, is you think too damn much.

I will work on the newsy email.

Subject: newsy email
Date: Mon, 28 Dec 2009 6:34 PM
From: Lisa
To: Mark

So what's going on with me? Let's see . . .

Zac is in Tennessee, left on Saturday and back on Wednesday. I have a light client week. I'm enjoying the time alone, feeling reflective mostly. The Muse is MIA lately (hmm, you have been, too . . . a coincidence?) The holiday was nice, though not particularly memorable. I was a little melancholy not being with Dave, having spent the past few years with him during the holidays. He called frequently, feeling the same, and came by on Saturday for a while. He is being so sweet. I couldn't have the Big Talk and instead enjoyed hanging inside during the blizzard we had, cooking and watching a movie. I saw a glimpse of Who I Thought He Was and it confused me for a moment, then it passed.

It is an interesting time for me emotionally.

I am feeling an inner stillness. With Zac gone I am imagining what it would feel like to have him be far away most all the time. It feels foreign and unnerving. I actually like when he is away for a few days, knowing he will be back. Soon it will be different. He likes being there, where he is temporarily the center of attention. He says that he wants to move down to his Dad's, though who knows what he will feel in 6 months. It is all real and yet . . . not. I keep hoping that I did the best I could for him, that I gave him all the tools he needs to make the right choices. I did the best I knew how and still retain my identity, my life. There were certainly things I could have done better, yet I know our journey has been exactly as it's meant to be. I can hardly believe that he will be going off to college soon, and I will be leaving this place, too. It's time. I walk around my house and imagine where I will be living next winter. The weather has been harsher than usual this year already with lots of snow and very cold. We are expecting below-zero temps again later this week. Brrrrrr

I hate it.

So I snuggle under the cotton knitted throw I bought myself for my birthday last week and dream of warmer days in warmer places. I read and drink tea. I am finishing *Tuesdays with Morrie* tonight. I just love that book. Tomorrow I will start Mitch Albom's new one, *Have a Little Faith.* I asked for it for Christmas and my sister had already bought it to take with her to Italy last month. She gave me her copy that traveled in her backpack through all the Basilicas, churches and the Vatican - ancient places of God for a book about faith. My favorite gift this year.

Speaking of Italy, I have been emailing with my Italian second cousin in Recco at the coast near Portifino. My sister saw her in Italy and has given me her email. *Buon Natale*, I sent her. *Merry Christmas*, she sent back. Very sweet. I have an open invitation to stay with them when I visit Italy.

Off to make some tea . . . ciao.

Subject: your turn
Date: Tue, 29 Dec 2009 10:48 AM
From: Lisa
To: Mark

So, Zac has called to inform me that he is staying in Tennessee till Saturday night. His Dad is home on Thurs-Sat so more time with him, etc. That gives me all this free time by myself till then. One more session today and only a few sessions booked for tomorrow. After Zac's call I immediately got an email from Travelocity for a $198 last-minute airfare to Oakland. Book Now! it said. Ha. The Universe is funny (don't worry, I'm not coming). I know I should be excited about all this space to myself as we cross into the New Year. But I'm not. I feel a little sad.

I need inspiration. If you read my last email, you'll know that.

Please inspire me . . . *a muse* me.

Subject: re: your turn
Date: Tue, 29 Dec 2009 5:51 PM
From: Mark
To: Lisa

Aww, c'mon now . . . . you can do this. All this space to yourself means you're being given a big chunk of time to do what you want, right? You're getting a taste of what it's like to spend time with All Of Who You Are. Who's in there wanting out? Is she someplace else, having left you behind? I doubt it.

I'm doing side job projects this week and am making an effort to be more disciplined there as well. It's another big lesson in getting out of my head, moving projects and work responsibilities along without all the mental chatter about how I'd rather be somewhere else doing something fun or entertaining.

Subject: re: your turn
Date: Tue, 29 Dec 2009 6:13 PM
From: Lisa
To: Mark

Thanks for the boost. I'll let it sink in. (smile)

Subject: hey
Date: Wed, 30 Dec 2009 7:26 PM
From: Lisa
To: Mark

A better day today. Contemplating the past year . . . the past decade . . .

Hey, I wanted to ask you about the Course in Miracles. I have not done the course though I have been exposed to a lot of it in Marianne Williamson's books. I think I remember you did the course years ago. What was your experience? Do you suggest the commitment to the year of lessons? I had a client who is nearly through who said it is kicking her ass but changing her life.

Thoughts?

Subject: course in miracles
Date: Thu, 31 Dec 2009 12:50 PM
From: Mark
To: Lisa

I've had that book since I've known you. I go in and out of it, depending on where I'm at and what I'm going through. Got turned on to it by a therapist. I did spend some time trying to do the daily practices -- one lesson for each day of a year - but didn't last long. There are parts of the book that speak to me, but on the whole I lean more on Jane Roberts's *The Nature Of Personal Reality,* even to this day. The "Course" book is deep, but it doesn't inspire. Not me, anyway. It lives on top of my desk, in a stack with the *I Ching Workbook* and *The Urantia Book.*

Subject: !
Date: Thu, 31 Dec 2009 2:28 PM
From: Lisa

To: Mark

Thanks for the Course info. I got the book and will look through. Not feeling the whole daily lesson thing yet. We'll see. Just got back from a mani/pedi outing with my friend Michele. Fun. She and her husband are going out downtown tonight, with their friend Jim. They invited me to join on a blind-ish date (I met him once) but I declined. Not in the mood for the whole big New Years Eve deal or the guy, though he does have a house in California somewhere LOL. Dave is stopping by later to "wish me a Happy New Year". The lesser of two evils, I think.

I am back in my groove and feeling good going into the new year, new decade. Lots has shifted and moved forward for me in 10 years. I'm blessed all around. I know it.

Happy, happy New Year, my dear friend. Great things ahead in 2010 and beyond. Many good things.

Love and hugs,
Lis

nineteen

Subject:
Date: Sat, 2 Jan 2010 8:22 AM
From: Lisa
To: Mark

Zac comes home tonight and I can't wait to see him, though I'm not looking forward to going to the airport in this frigid, bitter cold. Wind temps are -15 to -20 below zero. I so hate it. Dave was here last night. He stopped by to bring snow blower oil and stayed for a movie. We fell asleep on the couch and he asked if he could stay instead of going out in this cold. Weird, but not. Not a big deal, but not igniting any feelings of wanting him here again. Kind of good at this point to be annoyed by him by the time he left this morning. Back to more of the reality of who we were when we were together than his recent best-behavior routine. Glad to be by myself again.

———

Subject: re:
Date: Sat, 2 Jan 2010 8:35 AM
From: Mark
To: Lisa

Hey, Course In Miracles . . . Pulled mine out last night when I went to bed. Interesting: I didn't realize I had underlined and highlighted so much of the first 60 pages. The stuff I underlined reminds me that it was a time of being quite sincere about connecting with God, His plan for me, and my willingness to keep that connection active and alive. This means I have a journal or two where I was writing about that stuff regularly during that time.

Zac coming home must feel good. It'll be interesting to hear his stories of his time away . . .

House waking up here. May not get back to you til later.

_____
Subject: re:
Date: Sat, 2 Jan 2010 9:14 AM
From: Lisa
To: Mark

Yes, can't wait to see Zac. I hope he hasn't been too spoiled and redneck-ified!

Yikes

_____
Subject: hey
Date: Sun, 3 Jan 2010 7:42 AM
From: Mark
To: Lisa

Mornin' . . .

Sounds very cold and forbidding out there. I picture you holed up in your room with a big ol' cup of tea, blanket draped over you, sitting at your desk with your laptop.

Hope all is well with Zac being home and Dave popping in and out. The situation with Dave sounds awkward . . . but manageable. Keep me posted.

_____
Subject: re: hey
Date: Sun, 3 Jan 2010 7:58 AM
From: Lisa
To: Mark

Hey . . .

I just sat at my desk and that is exactly how I look. It is *so* cold here, but brilliant sun which makes it tolerable. I have to get out today as I have been holed up since Friday except for the airport to get Zac. I need fresh food and to move around outside in the sun, even if it's freezing cold (-15 wind chill right now.)

I am clear that hanging out with Dave is not what I want. You're right, it was awkward, yet comfortable. Sure, it's someone to watch movies with, cook, laugh. But when it got deeper, it got weird. I believe we had a nice holiday run of sweet time and now I'm really moving on, so ready for all the newness of the coming year. Good to have Zac home, though he went out to see his friends nearly immediately. They came back and we had fun talking about his trip, him imitating Jimmy and cracking us up with his Southern experience. Imagine Dane Cook at 17, that's Zac.

Hoping this week brings us a winechat or teachat . . . any chat opportunity will do. Feels like a long time.

_____

Subject: I have shared "Reality Cafe" with you – please review!
Date: Sun, 3 Jan 2010 12:36 PM
From: Lisa
To: Mark

Got your Google Doc. I like the working title of your story.

I'm back from my excursion across the tundra. It was great to be out in the sunshine and breathe fresh (albeit very cold) air. The house is stocked with good food, a freshly brewed Wild Sweet Orange is by my side, the shawl I bought in Sausalito during my visit is draped around my shoulders and I'm cozy. Zac is at work and the house is quiet.

I pulled a Rune stone this morning, asking: *what do I need to know?* I plunged my hand into the leather bag asking to be given a message that reflects how I am to live my life. I pulled GATEWAY. Ah, of course . . . *the frontier between Heaven and the mundane.* Nodding, I read about the contemplation and non-action required before stepping across the threshold of the Future. I am told to look back at the past, bless it all, release it all. *Let go.* I know this is right where I am. I know, in part, it means Dave. I know that waking up here alone this morning, greeted by the magnificent sun, is exactly, precisely where I need and want to be.

_____

Subject: re: hey
Date: Sun, 3 Jan 2010 3:50 PM

From: Mark
To: Lisa

This is great. Makes me miss the Rune stones. I was way into them before
I lost one. Never replaced the set. Now I go to the I Ching . . . which
would be really helpful now. *Oooff* . . . bad head space today.

_____
Subject: Good mornin'
Date: Mon, 4 Jan 2010 5:29 AM
From: Lisa
To: Mark

It is a whopping 9 degrees this morning but no sunshine. Can't have it all. I
am in a great mood and excited about what this new week of the New Year
will bring. I know, gag me. LOL Seriously, everything we want awaits.

Our call last night had to end so quick and I felt like there was so much
more to say. If you can pick it up again I am free most of the day.

I really hate it for you that you are in this spin that drills you down into a
dark place sometimes. I have seen you happy and inspired and I've seen
you overwhelmed and frustrated. Happy is better. So if I was heavy
handed and pushy on the phone, hey, I didn't mean to be yet I am not
entirely sorry. I want to help you get where you want to go, get through
where you are now, and see you feel good about it all. It's what I do, and I
realize that most of the people closest to me don't want anything to do with
Coach Lisa, yet you are not necessarily one of them. Just tell me if you are.

So if you were annoyed tell me to pipe down and we'll talk. If you aren't
then this was just another reminder that someone isn't giving up on you
and that you are loved.

Lis

_____
Subject: re: Hey
Date: Mon, 4 Jan 2010 10:47 AM
From: Mark
To: Lisa

No, no, not at all. In fact, here comes the email I was just writing you . . .
you'll see . . .

Time is short these days. Sorry to have to end our call. Let's get into *your*
scene when we start talking next time.

Got the 3rd degree from Mariah this morning, an interrogation about my plans for work while trying to get me to sign on full-time with that awful remodeling company, blah-blah . . . These kinds of exchanges are futile, so I drop out, wrap my half-eaten breakfast, and go out the door to walk the horse just to get away from the tension and the dark energy in the house. Nothing new here, except to say it just adds fuel to the divorce fire.

Interesting though: I was on the computer at 4:30 this morning, transferring more of my story from paper to computer. The dialogue I was entering was Kevin telling Cody why he had to get away from his crazy wife. Ha!

So, again, the healthiest thing for me to do is give my time and attention to the story. Back to it . . .

_____
Subject: re: Hey
Date: Mon, 4 Jan 2010 10:59 AM
From: Lisa
To: Mark

Good to know :-)

About Mariah and her tripping on where you are right now - she is not crazy. This is her way to cope. She wants you to take the sucky job because that will help pay the bills. She doesn't see that it will suck the soul out of you, and if she does she may not truly care. Since she's not so happy, why should you get to be? Not having much love or fun with you must not feel so great. You can't blame her for wanting things to be "normal" again - you out making money working a regular job with a big focus on Savannah and family stuff.

Harping at you about getting a job is what she truly feels is important to talk about. Please try to stop judging her for feeling that way and calling it "crazy". She isn't wrong, she's just not who you want to share your life with. It is much more compassionate to separate without malice and not because one of you is right and one is crazy. Kevin's wife can be crazy, but it doesn't sound like yours is.

I understand her. I have *been* her. I became pretty miserable in my marriage to Dave and ended it when I couldn't stand being the nagging, complaining, frustrated woman I had become. Sometimes once the situation is over and the healing begins you can feel good about the person you once felt great fondness for. I'm starting to feel that for Dave. That could also happen for the two of you. It's important that you see where she's coming from and not make her wrong for how she feels.

_____
Subject:

193

Date: Mon, 4 Jan 2010 11:22 AM
From: Mark
To: Lisa

Excellent, well said.

Thanks for talking me down. Kevin, in fact, stops talking when he catches himself about to launch into a bitch session and reminds himself to stop demonizing his ex-wife.

Good advice.

Gotta pick the girls up after school and take them to the barn . . . followed by a walkchat with Mariah.

_____
Subject: re:
Date: Mon, 4 Jan 2010 11:34 AM
From: Lisa
To: Mark

Have fun with that. Catch ya later.

_____
Subject: here it is: another chunk of the story
Date: Tue, 5 Jan 2010 12:33 AM
From: Mark
To: Lisa

Here's a chunk of Chapter 1 . . .

_____
Subject: mornin'
Date: Tue, 5 Jan 2010 4:29 AM
From: Lisa
To: Mark

Yes. A wonderful beginning. Page 2 is brilliant. Love that the "paddock has no gate" and the whole horse metaphor. And that Cody looks like Sandra Bullock? Well, that's just fun. ;-) Keep going!

I have a radio interview today – check out the link on my website.

_____
Subject: re: mornin'
Date: Tue, 5 Jan 2010 12:30 PM
From: Mark
To: Lisa

HA! Love it! Will you be talking from your home, or in studio? Great energy in the picture of you, by the way . . .

The "paddock" bit was originally more like: *the problem wasn't with the horse, the problem was the way the horse was being treated* . . . which wasn't true, and didn't work. I was entering it into the computer last night - after a really grueling chat with Mariah - and came across that paddock thing. I realized it made Kevin look like a victim, so I rewrote it to make him more responsible for his situation.

Off to the barn. Got kicked in the knee by the horse yesterday. Limping today, but nothing broken. Ouch.

_____
Subject: re: mornin'
Date: Tue, 5 Jan 2010 1:07 PM
From: Lisa
To: Mark

Phone interview – station is in NY.

Great choice to revise that bit. The truth is the truth. I hope that, though grueling, some good things come from your chats.

Send more writing when you can. Open space for a call soon, please. It's a whopping 21 degrees here and I am in a wicked-good mood - good time to catch me to talk and not get beat up. LOL Ha!

_____
Subject: snowy morn
Date: Thu, 7 Jan 2010 6:13 AM
From: Lisa
To: Mark

Woke up to a couple inches of snow with 3-6" more on the way. It really is pretty. The attached picture is out my front window.

_____
Subject: re: snowy morn
Date: Thu, 7 Jan 2010 6:59 AM
From: Mark
To: Lisa

Love it . . . looks lovely. I'm always surprised how there's so much space between houses in the East and Midwest.

I'm in a much better mood. Got past the hardest, trickiest part of this carpentry job, which was a victory. Came out perfect. Then I came home to an empty house and started on dinner, playing music, wine, etc, singing, groovin', especially to a tune by The Mavericks.

Doin' good . . .

Nice chat with you last night, by the way.

_____
Subject: re: snowy morn
Date: Thu, 7 Jan 2010 3:23 PM
From: Lisa
To: Mark

So glad the thing looks perfect. Just back from court for the DUI case of the woman who hit Zac. Frustrating!!!! Oh well. It is what it is. Then to chiropractor with Zac who is released from treatment so now we can finally settle with the insurance company. I will be happy when this is all over.

_____
Subject: another snowy morn
Date: Fri, 8 Jan 2010 6:09 AM
From: Lisa
To: Mark

Another 5 inches has fallen and the temp is in the teens and headed to zero by this evening. Wind chills are already single digits. Best to get out and snow blow now while it's "warm". Brrrrr. I am so not into it this morning. Beam me up, Scotty and get me out of here! :-)

Off to the tundra . . . what's your day look like?

_____
Subject: re: another snowy morn
Date: Fri, 8 Jan 2010 4:29 PM
From: Mark
To: Lisa

DSL was down this morning, so I spent an hour transferring Chapter One into a document. Man, once I get going writing the story I really get sucked in.

And you need to get to it, darlin'. Want an assignment?

Your character works for a major rock star on tour; last night was the last show of the tour, in Paris, and everyone partied til dawn. Your character wakes up at noon, in bed, next to someone they don't remember meeting. OR . . .

Two paragraphs on the moment of arriving at your new California home.

_____
Subject: re: another snowy morn

Date: Fri, 8 Jan 2010 4:39 PM
From: Lisa
To: Mark

I'll pick door number two, Monty. The I'm-a-rocker-slut scenario doesn't quite work for me, though waking up at the end of a rock star's tour in New Jersey next to a redneck hillbilly? Now THAT I can write about from experience! But at least he married me. LOL

Thanks for the nudge. Your excitement about your story is enough to get me going! Send it over when you can. I am off to dinner in a few. I'll check back in when I get home.

_____
Subject: Reality Cafe
Date: Sat, 9 Jan 2010 1:01 AM
From: Mark
To: Lisa

Well, okay then . . . Have a blast.

One in the morning here. Just finished the enclosed piece . . .

_____
Subject: unsnowy morn!
Date: Sat, 9 Jan 2010 6:08 AM
From: Lisa
To: Mark

Ooh, something to snuggle back in bed with and read. Great way to start a great day - especially delighted to see there is no new snow! Off to get tea and my little laptop. Meet you under the covers.

_____
Subject: re: Reality Cafe
Date: Sat, 9 Jan 2010 8:25 AM
From: Mark
To: Lisa

give a call.

_____
Subject: hey
Date: Sat, 9 Jan 2010 5:18 PM
From: Lisa
To: Mark

I just saw *It's Complicated*. Very funny movie. I enjoyed it. Two things: Meryl Streep is wonderful and I want to be half as talented as her when I grow up, and Santa Barbara is definitely where I want to live when I make a lot of money, in the house that's in the movie. Great kitchen and garden.

Subject: mornin'
Date: Mon, 11 Jan 2010 5:46 AM
From: Lisa
To: Mark

How are you? Get any more writing done this weekend? I didn't, I though tried.

It was really, really cold. I got into a movie mode and curled up in a blanket with some old favorites. Did lots of cooking, reading and some cleaning. Hung out with Zac and we talked about the move to California. Lots on my mind about the move.

Subject: re: mornin'
Date: Mon, 11 Jan 2010 8:03 AM
From: Mark
To: Lisa

No writing. Worked Saturday, then straight to a gig. Sunday was barn, gym, then show at Yoshi's.

Playing hooky today. Laptop in the truck, and will hang out in the library. No time to hang here this morning. I'll check in from the library around 10am.

Attaching a pic of the Calico band from a gig in October. Tall guy is Bill - closest friend - as is Mitch, in the sunglasses. Love these guys.

Subject: good evening
Date: Tue, 12 Jan 2010 5:24 PM
From: Mark
To: Lisa

Just now getting home from a small job and an appointment for a new one. You there? I'm starting dinner . . . winechat?

Subject: awesome. . .
Date: Wed, 13 Jan 2010 10:13 AM
From: Lisa
To: Mark

The "Be A Rock Star" teleclass call I just facilitated was just awesome. Thanks for the prep help on the phone last night, it made all the difference. I'll send you the link to listen when I get it.

You good?

_____

Subject: re: awesome. . .
Date: Wed, 13 Jan 2010 4:05 PM
From: Mark
To: Lisa

Yeah, I'm good. Rough day yesterday, mentally and creatively. Mentally rough this morning . . .

I was in a downer mood, sitting in my truck at a Home Depot parking lot, writing in my journal about how I've spent a lot of dialogue in my story with Kevin expressing a need for solitude and reflection. Since he's *me*, I got a big hit that it was something I could use myself, so I cancelled my work appointment and headed for the ocean . . .

Good choice. Walked along the shoreline for hours, talking out loud, having imaginary conversations with various people as I walked; talked to God a bit; tried not to think about anything at all for moments at a time, just watching waves . . .

The beach walk grounded me, and helped me get to a more solid place. It's still fresh, so I've come to the library to write. I'm even considering dropping the fiction thing, and starting over. With so much dialogue to edit and economize, I keep getting stuck, trying too hard to make it believable that one guy would really say so much and talk so deeply to someone he hardly knew. Well, that is exactly something I would do, so instead of editing down the fictional guy I think I may just let it rip as the real-life guy. It would be easier to just lay out my beliefs, tell my story. Seemed like a good idea at the time.

I'm gonna let it soak in and see if it takes.

_____

Subject: re: awesome. . .
Date: Wed, 13 Jan 2010 4:37 PM
From: Lisa
To: Mark

Whatever gets it up and out of you sounds good to me. In the end you will know what feels right when you write it.

Love the beach vision. I am soooo envious! Sounds like a wonderful day. I must say it was downright balmy here at 36 degrees, sun shining, didn't have to bury myself in a hat, gloves and scarf on my face. Really nice. Had a session with Lorraine (therapist) today which went really well. I like her better than I thought. She is a big advocate of *plan the move to California and let Zac figure out what he wants . . . he will be fine*. If he decides not to move to his Dad's he can always come with me, though he isn't the least bit interested in that. I told her a bit about you today, too.

I shared the 10 minute version of the Story of Us and she was intrigued. She asked the right questions to gauge my intentions in moving out there and how much might involve you. I put it like this: the picture I have about living there has nature, the lifestyle, and opportunities in the foreground, in crystal focus. You are in the picture, but in the background with my other friends and a little out of focus. You are closer to the foreground than they are but in the background none the less. I felt satisfied with that image. She did, too. It felt good to talk about it with a neutral person. It's also good for her to have the whole picture as I navigate this journey.

I have been thinking so much about the move and my future that I don't want to lose track of who I am today. I see a lot of energy wrapped up in tomorrow and I have to remember that a lot of what happens *today* is good. I want to savor that. Like your splendid day at the beach. I need a day like that . . . out in nature by myself. I'll take a creek walk today between sessions.

Needing to get back to my story, I wrote something in my journal recently that I'll share. It was the morning after we talked. It seems all I can muster these days. The podcast of my teleseminar is on my site if you want to listen.

———
Subject: re: awesome
Date: Thu, 14 Jan 2010 5:56 PM
From: Mark
To: Lisa

listening now . . . go ahead and call me

———
Subject: Trusting the Universe
Date: Sun, 17 Jan 2010 5:12 AM
From: Lisa
To: Mark

Remember when I told you at the library in Napa last Fall that I was moving back to California and you said, "Hurry up!"? Well, the Universe must have been listening . . .

Yesterday my Mom found her dream townhouse in a really nice area near here and put in an offer. It's a low offer and it may not fly, but it has been on the market a long time. She has already worked out borrowing money from my Dad to float her till the time we sell ours. She's really excited.

I am thrown by this, reminding her that it's only *January* and we can't leave till at least June, which is much earlier than my plan of October. She wants to put the house on the market right away in case it doesn't sell for months. She's willing to risk having two places for awhile. This is all a Big Maybe right now till she negotiates her offer, but her and I have incredible housing karma. I have to believe that if it is meant for her, she will get it.

A lot is coming up for me . . . everything is getting very real. Most profoundly that I will really send Zac off to Tennessee and not see him for months at a time. I know this is what all parents face as their kids go to college so it's normal, yet for me to move so far in the opposite direction widens the gap. I feel incredibly responsible to go do something *really important* out there. I broke down into tears as I just wrote that, God's verification that I'm right. I think I'm ready.

It all comes down to walking my talk, doesn't it?

Thoughts, please?

––––––
Subject: Thoughts
Date: Sun, 17 Jan 2010 7:43 AM
From: Mark
To: Lisa

This is kind of how it goes when you're really sincere about making changes. It's a sign that for all the hoping, wishing, wondering, and debating with friends about which way to go, a time will come when you'll feel like you're completely on your own at choice time. It's also significant that the lives of others are being affected by the forces working on your behalf. Mom and Zac appear to be running a few better-life scenarios of their own . . . inspired by you, darlin'. One could only concur that you're living in some sort of *yes vortex*. This isn't luck. This is the Universe division of UPS delivering the ruby slippers you ordered awhile back. It's a C.O.D. agreement, by the way; no wonder it all feels "very real". You're not thinking of sending them back, are you?

I didn't think so. That slightly panicky feeling is normal; just pay no attention to that ego behind the curtain. Such a coward, messing with you like that. Put on your new slippers and click your heels together three times and say: *there's no place like home . . . there's no place like home.* You'll end up where you're supposed to be.

Savannah's Sweet Sixteen karaoke party here last night. HUGE hit, and big fun for all. House full of teenagers singing and dancing, colored lights everywhere. I had a blast cranking out nine different pizzas from the kitchen, keeping everybody fed. Nice change of energy: a house full of people having fun. Wow.

The rains are here. Gonna be a wet week ahead. Love it.

_____

Subject: re: Thoughts
Date: Sun, 17 Jan 2010 10:55 AM
From: Lisa
To: Mark

Wonderful insight . . . thank you. It feels good to be me.

_____

Subject: mornin
Date: Mon, 18 Jan 2010 6:51 AM
From: Mark
To: Lisa

Saw *The Book OF Eli* at the movies yesterday and got some writing inspiration: Kevin's gonna find out what's behind all those random visits from God he's been having since he was a teenager . . .

_____

Subject: re: mornin
Date: Mon, 18 Jan 2010 7:01 AM
From: Lisa
To: Mark

Ah, nice. I'll have to see it.

Free till 1pm. Errands to do and going with Mom to see the townhouse. No word yet on her counter offer. Looking straight up the mountain right now and the climb looks steep but I'll get there. I have some great ruby hiking boots.

_____

Subject: hey
Date: Mon, 18 Jan 2010 2:23 PM
From: Lisa
To: Mark

Just back from looking at the townhouse my Mom wants to buy.

I can totally see her living there. It couldn't be more perfect for her. So far one of the two owners (sisters) has said yes to her bid and the other is holding out. We'll see. I have a feeling she'll get it.

The Emerald City is looking ever nearer.

_____

Subject:
Date: Tue, 19 Jan 2010 8:36 AM
From: Mark
To: Lisa

I can hang with you here for a while - I'm at a Sacramento library - but by the end of this day I'll be out of contact for a few days. The shit has hit the fan. I spent last night up here with my buddy, Bill.

I was making dinner last night when Mariah came in to "talk" about my plans for finding work. Round and round with our familiar bickering style of communicating, which quickly turned into her saying, "I can never talk about things with you", yadda-yadda . . . This went on longer and louder until Savannah came into the kitchen and chimed in with, "Stop it!" - meaning ME! She was taking Mariah's side. . . I couldn't believe my ears . . . and that's when I snapped: I felt something inside of me cross over that line, the one where once I step over it, there's no going back.

All I could do was stand still and wait for a whole bunch of new gears, new feelings, new perspectives, to click into place. It took a bit to hold down my rage. Neither one of them were SEEING me, what I was about, contrary to Mariah's claims, and I had to tell her three times to get away from me and leave me alone. She eventually did. After processing what I had at the ready to get me through the night without packing anything up, my last words before going out the door were: "Dinner will be ready when the timer goes off." Got in the truck and drove two hours to Bill's, who fed me and hung out with me til 2am as I talked everything out. Been here at the library since 10am. Whew!

_____

Subject: re:
Date: Tue, 19 Jan 2010 1:34 PM
From: Lisa
To: Mark

Wow. How do you feel?

_____

Subject: re:
Date: Tue, 19 Jan 2010 1:44 PM
From: Mark
To: Lisa

I'm ok. Just in a holding pattern for now. Not even sure when I'll go back to the house, although Bill has offered me a couple of days work at his place, which means I would have to go home for some specialty tools . . .

Subject: re:
Date: Tue, 19 Jan 2010 1:48 PM
From: Lisa
To: Mark

That might be a good thing. The question is: when you crossed that line did that start something in motion that you are ready for? You wanna talk?

Subject: re:
Date: Tue, 19 Jan 2010 2:01 PM
From: Mark
To: Lisa

No need to talk. I did it all with Bill, so I'm off to a good start. And I really have no idea what I'm gonna do next. I came to the library to write, and haven't left the computer since I got here. I'm really just kind of killing time, floating, not wanting to go home yet . . .

So I'm gonna pull back from phone and emails for a bit. I don't even want to go near having to sneak around checking and writing emails from home as changes are happening. I'll check in from libraries from time to time, so after this current session I'll ask you not to send me any emails unless you hear from me first. You OK with that?

Subject: re:
Date: Tue, 19 Jan 2010 2:19 PM
From: Lisa
To: Mark

Sure. You need to do what you need to do. I am here sorting out all my stuff, too. Mom put in a counter offer and it looks like they will take it. Ruby slippers are paid for and not returnable. Keep in touch when you can. I'll know you're there . . . and I'll still be here.

Subject: re:
Date: Tue, 19 Jan 2010 2:26 PM
From: Mark
To: Lisa

Cool. Thanks. Later.

twenty

Subject:
Date: Fri, 26 Feb 2010 11:04 AM
From: Mark
To: Lisa

I have two things I want to apologize for. The first is for dropping out of
contact without an explanation, and the other is for the tone of the coming
letter, which I already instinctively know will be somewhat bleak. I
suspect you'll be glad to hear from me and maybe wish it were under rosier
conditions, but I'm writing to my friend Lisa right now because I can't
afford to put myself in therapy. That's not a joke. I really think I need
professional help because I'm getting to the end of my tolerance for
hanging in there. But this time, it has nothing to do with Mariah . . .

It's just me.

After staying at Bill's for two days I went back home to get my things and
move out. But when I got home - and after long, uncomfortable talks with
Mariah - I found that I couldn't bring myself to risk doing some kind of
permanent damage to my relationship with Savannah. The immensity of
putting all my shit into boxes (that I didn't have) and going out the door to
live . . . *wherever* . . . was unthinkable. I spent the next two days writing in
the last pages of a separate journal I've kept for Savannah since she was
born, finishing it, then falling into a heap of tears when I read out loud
what I wrote. Cathartic. Healing.

But look . . . there's more to that story, which ends with me staying and
things being somewhat easier by not having to hide my contact with you,
since there wasn't any. But where I'm at right now isn't about any of that . .
.

I essentially pleaded to get back my job with that remodeling company
because there was absolutely nothing else coming my way. This time
around I've kept my mouth shut and tried to be grateful for even having a
job, but there's still this feeling . . . like . . . I don't really *belong* there. I got
hired because they have more jobs than they can handle and my reface
skill is needed, except they want the jobs done a day or two faster, for half
the money.

Again, it's that square-peg-in-the-round-hole feeling: I just don't get why it is that I can't break through into a better job situation. And the therapy need has to do with a sense that maybe I rely too much on magical thinking: *things HAVE to improve because I'm talented and gifted and willing to work hard!*

Haven't written a thing since you last heard from me. Just journal writing. My instinct is to drop the Kevin story and move into Eat, Pray, Love-mode: tell the truth about what I know and what I think. Whatever. I haven't been inspired to even head off in *that* direction.

And finally, there's a peculiar thing happening with regard to making contact with high school friends that I haven't heard from for over thirty years . . .

The short story is that I found myself looking for old friends on Google soon after coming back home, and ending up on Classmates.com, which brought me back in contact with my closest friend in high school. We've been writing heartfelt emails to one another. That's where my writing is being kept alive, much as I was doing with you.

So: I'm keeping my family intact, and have let go of blaming my marriage for anything.

I find it disturbing and confidence-eroding that my work/earn-a-living situation has been so stagnant and unrewarding for so long, especially in view of the number of ads I've answered describing a need for a guy *just like me*. It's weird.

And I just cannot find anything to grab onto that would help me feel like this is all temporary, that the much-needed change I yearn for is on its way. Problem is, I've been living with that feeling for what feels like WAY past the due date.

Time's up. I won't see your response til this evening.

———
Subject: uh-oh. . .
Date: Fri, 26 Feb 2010 7:21 PM
From: Mark
To: Lisa

I've just read what I wrote to you, and I'm thinking maybe I may have misjudged where you're at with me these days, like, maybe not so glad to hear from me after the long silence and then, out of nowhere, turn to you for help and support.

... like maybe I broke something that can't be fixed.

I'm getting that 'uh-oh' feeling . . .

(sigh)

———
Subject: re: uh-oh. . .
Date: Fri, 26 Feb 2010 10:51 PM
From: Lisa
To: Mark

I've been staring at the blinking cursor for awhile now . . . what to say?
There is so much and yet I don't know where to start.

Yes, I was surprised to get your email today since I had gotten to the place
where I stopped looking for your name in my inbox. Such mixed feelings
for all these weeks. I have not stopped thinking of you, of course, that
happens almost daily; hearing a song, showing up in a dream, stumbling
upon one of the (many) pictures of you that keep cropping up around my
house, buried for years, now choosing to look back at me. And it seems
there is something I want to share with you all the time.

Your message was not a surprise. My intuition (and logic) told me that you
had chosen to stay. I knew why. You need to do what you need to do.
Hearing your resignation, I applaud your decision not to blame anymore.
It's clear that you're not happy and you say it's not about your marriage. I
hear that a big challenge is the work thing but you have to know that it's
all tied together. Your frustration and misery is still attached to your *life*
and not just your work. Could you have gone as far as you did and come
back home to it all being OK and groovy, except for getting work? Maybe
so, but not too likely.

I believe the work thing is not happening for a number of reasons: first,
your heart has not been in it to do that work. You had shifted your
intention, remember? Shifting it back could take a while. You told me
when I saw you in October all about how you really didn't want to do
carpentry. You've said many times, for months, that you want to write and
speak and play drums. The Universe supported that and gave you lots of
time to pursue those things. Second, you are not the cheap labor that is out
there, being a contractor (are you telling them you are licensed?) and you
could be perceived as being too experienced. Most of all, you talk about
someday speaking to groups of people who have read your book and your
energy may be holding out for *that*. Do you remember how powerful you
are? No? Yeah, well you are.

I'm not buying the poor me thing. Sorry. I had to say it.

Here's what I mean about that . . . Mark, you are talented and gifted and work hard and want to be in sync but do you really want that with a construction company? If you do, then get out there and find the top ten contractors you want to work for and hound them, go talk to them, show them your passion and get them to give you a shot. Manifest it, goddamn it! You can do that. You are that guy. . . *if you really want it.* I'm not sure I believe that's what you really want, and so that's why I think you don't get it.

Now a word about magical thinking . . . Yes, we like to talk about wand-waving and putting things into the Universe to "happen" and many times they do. Maybe not always like we imagined, but happen they do. The catch is that there is *always* action attached to creating that thing we want. The Universe sends the opportunities to act and we seize them. That's the way it works. Sometimes things come that sound good and then don't happen (and they aren't supposed to or they would). We have to convince the Universe of what we really want. And sometimes we have to look harder for those opportunities. Or pay closer attention. You know exactly what I mean. What the fuck do you *really* want?

OK. So figure that out and get back to me. Let's grab onto *that.*

In the meantime, I have a few more things to share, a bit of winechat as it were. Here goes . . .

You were right to get the uh-oh feeling. I was a bit taken aback by what you wrote to me after such a long hiatus . . . *Hey, can I get a little free therapy? No joke. There's a whole story about why I went away but this is not about that . . .* Not so much as a little "How are *you*?" Ouch.

I have wanted to write so many things and being shut out felt really bad. I have to be honest that I was upset with you. Not freaking-out-miserable upset, but upset, mostly because I have things going on that you have been supporting me with, too. And then *poof* no more. I missed ruby slipper emails. I missed winechat. I missed you. It didn't seem fair and the worst part was that I somehow expected it after the first week of not hearing from you. *He's gone.* And that really sucks. Especially this time after I asked you not to do that, please. Remember? I really didn't think you would.

There is a torn place in our fabric that needs mending, but the integrity of it is still whole. I take responsibility for my part in letting it be OK forever that you come and go at will and turn off the pager when you feel like it. It doesn't feel OK anymore. Not just like that. Your email tonight says that you see that. We're not easily broken.

(bottle of wine dangerously close to empty . . .)

About the writing . . . yes, the Kevin story will be harder to continue since your trajectory no longer follows his. You want to write about what you know and what you think, *your* Eat, Pray, Love? You better find the life you want first. She didn't write that *while* she was crying on her bathroom floor wondering how to leave her marriage.

One last thing . . .

I have given a lot of thought to how I would feel if you never leave and how that would impact my moving to California. It doesn't. I really didn't plan to move there for you, and I wouldn't want to *not* move there because of you either.

I'll be back.

L

_____
Subject: re: uh-oh. . .
Date: Sat, 27 Feb 2010 7:28 AM
From: Mark
To: Lisa

I feel the need to defend myself a little bit . . .

The tone of my email lacked warmth and sensitivity because of the conditions I wrote it under. I was at the library and had exactly one hour to communicate the need for help to the only person I was willing to turn to. With the amount of time that had gone by, and the sheer volume of events and stories that had happened in both our lives during that time, I took a big risk in bypassing the necessary courtesies you would expect for re-establishing contact and went straight for that solid, 'you-can-always-count-on-me' place I thought we shared. Under the circumstances of the moment -- very, very troubled and conflicted, unable to pull myself through or wait for it to pass -- I went from sitting in my truck, writing in my journal, to reaching out for help. And, because of reaching out through a library computer, I only had an hour to say whatever I was going to say. I was very much aware that I was blowing right past all the things I suspected you *needed* to hear in a first email from me after so much silence, and goddamn it, don't think for a second that I haven't missed you or thought of you or doubted my choice to drop out for a while because it felt right *for me* . . .

I understand feeling guarded, angry, indifferent, or taken advantage of -

upset - to have your next communication from me be one of *need*. On my end, the alternative was to not reach out at all - I'm pretty good at that - and get over myself, by myself. The letter that came out of me, when I re-read it now, missed its mark. It didn't convey what was happening to me when I was sitting in my truck an hour earlier, thinking I understood why people commit suicide. At some point you just want to put an end to your private little hell. Me? I chose to reach out to the only person I knew would say the thing or two I most needed to hear, whose feedback I could trust and respect. My friend Bill would have come at me from the Christian angle - no magical thinking allowed - and the therapist I would otherwise have turned to wouldn't be available RIGHT NOW.

So I can only thank you for including your support and feedback along with your need to let me know of your hurt and anger. It helped. And I apologize for not conveying an interest in *your story* of the past month(s). You'd be wrong in assuming that I don't care or am not interested . . .

Mark

Subject: re: uh-oh. . .
Date: Sat, 27 Feb 2010 7:59 AM
From: Lisa
To: Mark

I know, I know.

I didn't get that you were in *that* bad a place, a horrible place, one that doesn't get a do-over if you go over the edge. I hate to think of anyone getting even close, especially someone I care so much about. And you know I do. You know. That's why you come to me (that and my incredible insight and wisdom LOL)

I'm still here. I offered what I could last night after so long and so much between us. I am willing to be buddies and let go of thoughts of anything else. That's what has sustained us, so pour it all out and I will hold the container.

Just know that it was so good for me to let you know how I feel and to express that in my guarded (slightly wine-drenched) state.

You care, I know.

Subject: Hey
Date: Sun, 28 Feb 2010 6:20 AM
From: Mark
To: Lisa

Writing back to you now seems like something of a project: So much ground to cover, plus - as I was thinking when I got up an hour ago - I'd just be saying the same old shit. I was gone all day yesterday, running Savannah around, and the wee bit of (boring) journal writing I did was mostly about how you showed up for me. I even brought my writing 'kit' to try and re-start something, but *feh* . . . too pre-occupied with the sucky work thing, which continues tomorrow. *Ugh* . . .

I almost sent you the thread of writing I've been doing with my high school friend Randy, but . . . nah . . . nothing you haven't heard before . . .

Better that you let me know what you've been up to.

_____
Subject: re: Hey
Date: Sun, 28 Feb 2010 6:34 AM
From: Lisa
To: Mark

I'm curious, how did you write that I "showed up for you"? Did you really feel I was indifferent to your reaching out? I really didn't mean to sound that way and I wasn't angry. Hurt, yes, upset . . . but I have not been walking around pissed off at you. In fact, I had been sending a lot of my energy your way this whole time, feeling how lost you are. I knew it was easier for you to stay away from me. I could feel it.

_____
Subject: re: Hey
Date: Sun, 28 Feb 2010 7:31 AM
From: Mark
To: Lisa

Got a return email from Lisa . . . There's just no denying how much better I feel after turning to her for feedback and/or advice. I laid out some of the details of my conflicted mind, my confusion and frustration with this new job, and the continuing inability to get connected with satisfying, meaningful work. The gist of her feedback was to support myself as an artist since I've made it clear, time and again, that my heart is not in being a contractor. And so why would I be surprised at not feeling satisfied with construction work? And if I were to at least stay with it as a means of income, she reminds me that I have the ability - the power - to seek out a company that I would WANT to work with, and make myself known to them.

_____
Subject: re: Hey
Date: Sun, 28 Feb 2010 8:40 AM
From: Lisa

211

To: Mark

Lovely, thanks for sharing that.

I thought about not hearing from you a fair amount while you were gone. More than I wanted to. Your absence felt palpable at times, yet it opened space to focus my attention elsewhere. Like on my house.

That has been a central theme since Mom's offer on her townhouse was accepted. She is closing in a couple weeks and we're putting our house on the market. I have been interviewing realtors and cleaning closets. It all feels pretty surreal. I have moments of what feels like true grief for letting go of this home where I raised Zac. So many memories live here. It is a new chapter in so many ways for us. He's doing great and has Senior Fever, big time. He can't wait to be done and lots of energy is focused on prom, graduation and college.

We will be going down to Nashville soon to tour the campus and check out his new pad at his Dad's. There's an apartment above the garage so he will have his "own place". It's all very exciting. I will also be back to California to check out areas I want to live. Alameda island keeps coming up and I love the charming Victorians and cottages there. We'll see. The realtors here expect that our house will sell in 3-5 months, which feels soon. I am hoping that the timing works beautifully with Zac's graduation, etc. So I am putting my energy into it all unfolding well. I am in no rush. Besides, Zac would like to do his last summer as a camp counselor here till mid-August. If the house sells before we're ready to go there are options for us to stay with the fam.

Since you've been gone Dave has been around more. I've wondered if I manifested that purposely, but mostly it's because he is finishing the basement bath remodel he started before we separated and doing some other things that have to happen to sell the house. It's all getting done and aside from one intense evening of too much wine and too little sound judgment, we've really started to move on. We finally declared ourselves divorced and agreed to be friends. So that's feeling complete. He leaves tomorrow for Florida to work on his brother's place, so even more space between us occurs, which feels right. We're done, we know it, and life goes on.

On a personal front I have been focusing on taking care of myself by eating well, yoga, etc. I am itching to get outside to walk and the weather this week will be above freezing so I can get out and do that. I can't wait for Spring. I have been struggling this winter with all the snow and cold. I am so happy to leave it. I've hibernated a bit and keep moving through the house to clear out all that I can. I wrote a piece called 'Stuff of Life' about downsizing my home and upsizing my life. It's on my blog. I have been doing lots of kitchen dancing with my Self and I love that. I'm down nearly 10 lbs since fall and I feel good in my skin.

I'm feeling like I let myself down a bit by not continuing on my Rock Star workshop tour. The winter didn't feel like a good time to do it and thank God I didn't plan east coast dates since they have been slammed with blizzards. I haven't been writing enough either. My book seems to have taken a backseat to the move and I have to be okay with that or shut up and write. I try to journal and blog to replace it and hope some of that will weave into the story later. I have some journaling about you that I'll share if you'd like to read it. One day springs to mind when I was seeking the lesson for me in the silence.

Subject: mornin'
Date: Sun, 28 Feb 2010 9:33 AM
From: Mark
To: Lisa

I've been writing to Randy. Haven't seen or talked with him for some 35 years, so it pretty much reads like a Readers Digest version of my life story since high school. Kinda cool to relive the moment when I finished my first (and only) year at Berklee College of Music, called my mom, asking her for permission to fly to Nebraska where my girlfriend was, wanting to drive and camp our way back to California. Mom's response: "You're eighteen years old now, you don't need my permission. You can do whatever you want." I hung up the phone, feeling like I had just been handed the keys to the rest of my life. I walked out of the dorm, onto the street, and *WHAM!,* the whole world looked and felt different . . .

Sigh . . . I'll forward you the letter, if you're interested.

Subject: re: mornin'
Date: Sun, 28 Feb 2010 9:35 AM
From: Lisa
To: Mark

Forward it, by all means . . .

I've been typing up an entry from my journal that I wrote to you a couple weeks ago. It will give you a bit of insight into where my head (and heart and soul) were at during your absence. Here it is:

A cold, gray morning greets me as I begin another day. Will today be the day the I hear from you? I wonder, as I nestle under the covers and play out in my head the words of your last email: Cool. Thanks. Later. *You said*

213

you would be gone for a bit and check in from time to time. A month feels like a lot longer than a bit. I thought a week, maybe. I keep hoping that it doesn't stretch to months, which feels impossible, but we know that has happened in the past. Once you disappeared for over a year.

I go back to October in that cafe in Napa, telling you that my heart was wide open and that disappearing from me again was not an option. You promised not to do that and I trusted you wouldn't go away. That you couldn't. That you would not let someone else decide if you could or could not be in touch with me. And here we are. Weeks going by without a word. "I'll check in from time to time. . . Are you OK with that?" you asked a month ago, as if I had a choice. Yes, I really was OK. What doesn't feel OK is not to get even one email from you in all that time, even one that said: I am here. It is hard. Please know that I will be back.

It is silence that I can't bear. It goes way back for me, to a young girl who was always waiting for that call that didn't come.

I reach far back into my mind to ask what you really owe me. What do I expect and have a right to? I come up empty-handed. My mind can't comment as there is no logical expression of our "contract" because there isn't one. My heart feels left behind, a remnant of Daddy stuff, for sure. The calls that didn't come started there. It was the killer of my self esteem for decades. My heart wanted to be loved and connected, and when it opened to you it became vulnerable and soft. It's not broken now, by any means, just fatigued. And it understands that this is easier for you, perhaps, to not have to hide. It must be a relief.

Ah, so it is not my heart or my mind that wants to shake you and ask "what the fuck?" It is my soul. For she is the one with the sacred contract with yours. She is the one that says, Dude, what are you thinking? She is the one who heard the call from yours over lifetimes and keeps showing up for you. She smiled when shortly after your return from Tucson your soul couldn't walk away from me for three hours let alone three days. And weeks? No way. Your soul "slapped you around", I believe you said, and told you to protect this, that it mattered. And you did. And it grew, this connection, this trust. A strong belief took hold in me that we were building something ahead of us as we dismantled what was broken and no longer worked in our lives. I believed that each brick we pulled from the wreckage of our marriages we could pay forward to lay side by side as a foundation built of wisdom, knowledge and the lessons of a thousand mistakes, the mistakes that we made with those who were not right for us or with us. I believed that even if this would never become a house in which we would dwell together, it would at least be a temple of What We Have Learned, and our deep connection would always endure.

And of course it will. The support continues as I wait and wonder how you are—the hardest part of this silence, really, because I really care how you are. I will stay a little mad at you until I hear from you again. Call it ego, call it what you may, but I feel a little abandoned and I don't like it. I have things happening here that I would like your support with, too. We were the daily touchstone for each other for months and I feel cut off from a supply that sustained some of my joy. Your brilliant words of wisdom about ruby slippers and All That I Am have made the journey more magical. That is the thing that feels ripped away. Your deep knowing of me, and the love and support from my dearest of friends.

I miss you.

_____

Subject: re: mornin'
Date: Sun, 28 Feb 2010 9:50 AM
From: Mark
To: Lisa

What was the date of that journal entry?

_____

Subject: re: mornin'
Date: Sun, 28 Feb 2010 9:58 AM
From: Lisa
To: Mark

Feb 4th.

Your memory of leaving Boston really struck a chord with where I am now with Zac. He's getting the keys to his life . . . and I will really miss him.

A few more chuckles reading your letter to Randy -- the health food discussion reminds me of your occasional *fuck that health food shit* declaration over the years. Somehow that makes whatever is about to be consumed more decadent. You pondering your potential narcissism made me laugh out loud. You? Really?

Good reality check sets in while reading of your sunset drive to Mt. Diablo with "the wife". Sounds lovely. And there is not an ounce of disdain in those words, really. As I check in with myself about how I feel reading about your family life as told to your old friend, I find that I am not jarred by your words or even unsettled. This is your life. Drives at sunset with your wife, organic shopping and cooking, raising your daughter, a desire to keep your body strong and healthy . . . You *are* getting some of what you want.

I liked hearing you reminisce about your travels through the desert, of grooving with music, of being you. The way that you summed up your unwillingness to sell your soul or forgo your health for the almighty dollar rang pure and true. I hope you can go back and read it and give yourself a break, given how you felt a couple days ago. I know the work thing plagues you now, but you have good stuff going for you, too. You are a powerful guy. It's all about choices, baby, choices.

OK, so I have had my fix for now, for sure. Your turn to share your thoughts about what I've shared . . .

ciao for now

_____
Subject: re: mornin'
Date: Sun, 28 Feb 2010 12:33 PM
From: Mark
To: Lisa

OK, back . . . sent you the Randy letter with Mariah making breakfast right behind me. We had a quick tug-of-war just minutes ago about staying home while Savannah goes off to do horse chores. Haven't even had a chance to read your stuff until now, so here goes. Oh, but before I get to your stuff, I wanted to let you know something about the contents of what I wrote to Randy . . .

That day of driving up to Mt. Diablo with Mariah was not some romantic, oh-we're-so-happy event. It was my idea, and I suggested it as a safe, neutral way of passing time while Savannah was at the barn. Anything Mariah and I do together, one-on-one, always involves the risk of some sort of tense, unpleasant interaction. That drive was my way of taking the lead on doing something together, knowing it had low-risk tension possibilities.

But thanks for the feedback, just the same. It was sweet . . .

_____
Subject: re: mornin'
Date: Sun, 28 Feb 2010 1:01 PM
From: Lisa
To: Mark

I get it. I'm not surprised that this is the reality for you. I kinda knew that. You're welcome.

_____
Subject: re: mornin'
Date: Sun, 28 Feb 2010 1:24 PM

From: Lisa
To: Mark

I have another journal entry for you:

Feb 1, 2010
I wander around my house enjoying each room, all this space. I wander
around on Craigslist looking at the potential places that I could call home
in California and wonder how much space I can afford. Then I stop. Why
spend all this time looking at places that I can't go look at yet? They will
be long gone. I have to sell my house first, I have to get Zac settled first, I
have to move there first. I may as well be climbing Mt. Everest. Such a
long steep climb I have ahead of me and even my ruby hiking boots will be
challenged by this trek. I sigh. Quit your whining, Lis! In due time all will
be revealed. You are so incredibly lucky to have choices, options, many
options. Lucky Girl With Options, like a new tribal name, I claim the
moniker and smile. I like it.

I dreamt last night that Mark sent me a card. It started with My Dear
Friend Lisa . . . then talked about a project that he was working on. He
included thumbnail photos and the first one was of him inside a birdcage.
The door was open and he was sitting on the perch. I started waking up
then, drifting to the surface but wanting to read the rest of the card. I
couldn't stay down long enough to read it and started finishing the dream
in waking mind, like a screenplay. I didn't want to be left hanging. I knew I
was waking up and I had to let it go unread. But the vision of that tiny
picture is etched in my mind . . . him swinging on the perch looking at the
open door, like the horse in his story that realizes there was no gate in the
paddock.

You show up in dreams a lot. I had one the other night that I saw you and
you were pregnant. Weird, but it seemed to make sense. Birthing
something.

_____
Subject: Done any shopping lately?
Date: Sun, 28 Feb 2010 1:31 PM
From: Mark
To: Lisa

Been working on a response to your first journal thingy . . . you're gonna
love it . . I'm cracking up: You are SO busted . . . Here you go:

First of all, I didn't "rip away" nothin'. I took *nothing* away from you in the
time you didn't hear from me. All of your references to what you were
missing were things that were *given* you, and I most certainly did not take
them back, or take them away, or withhold them from you. I think you

were dead-on accurate in realizing it was daddy stuff, not Mark stuff.

The body of what you wrote is a reminder to me - and now, to you - that if we truly believe The Universe is Lord and Master of this unique relationship we have, then feelings of being left behind or neglected or forgotten or not cared about . . . they're misplaced. They are most certainly of the ego, which is fine because we're not gods, so going all human on one another is to be expected. And then forgiven.

And another thing: Regardless of how things seem *today* it doesn't mean shit. This journey isn't even close to being over, as though it were heading for some final, solid resting place. "Universe relationships" are made from the finest, select Brazilian Cherrywood: how *dare* you accuse me of having switched to Pergo while I was away!

Speaking of which: I, *ahem,* notice you did a little Pergo shopping yourself while I was gone . . . *ahem . .*

So look . . . this is so much fun to be in touch with you again. Reading all that you wrote makes me want to repeat, for myself as well, that there has to be a certain amount of detachment from outcomes here if we're really gonna buy into the Universe thing. History says it's all good, and that maybe we *get it*; not in the way you or I think we get it, but the way, um, God wants us to get it. That's the slightly trickier detachment part I'm talking about. If we agree to let The Universe run the show, we shouldn't get pulled out of our centers when there's a sudden script change. Which, come to think of it, is probably not the case anyway. *Script change?* Nah. Not enjoying the role we're playing is one thing, but it takes some balls to accuse The Universe of getting something wrong . . .

_____

Subject: re: Done any shopping lately?
Date: Sun, 28 Feb 2010 1:52 PM
From: Lisa
To: Mark

Laughing my ass off . . . Damn you're good. That's why I missed you. Shit.

Are you alone?

_____

Subject: Re: Done any shopping lately?
Date: Sun, 28 Feb 2010 2:05 PM
From: Mark
To: Lisa

OK, what? You wanna talk on the phone? Go for it . . .

_____

Subject: re: job news
Date: Mon, 1 Mar 2010 9:12 PM
From: Lisa
To: Mark

Had a great day. Good client stuff. One session was with a fellow student
of our high school English teacher (who is very young and cool guy at 65).
She is 29 years old and leaving in two weeks for her new adventurous life
in Portland. He gave her a few sessions with me as a going away gift.
Cool, huh? So we had our last session today (she is also a writer) and she
mentions that she is having dinner with him tonight and I said, "Where? I
am so needing a break." And she said, "Seriously, would you come? Let's
surprise him!"

What a blast we all had. Dinner, wine and lots of chatter about high
school, our parallel paths to the West Coast, and him looking so cute as he
watched his protégés - over a couple of generations - whoop it up and vibe
on how cool he is, chatting about their lives, writing, and life.
Imagine Sandra Bullock, Drew Barrymore and Tom Skerritt at dinner.

I love my life. I am so glad you're back in it. I know you never really left.
But welcome back anyway.

twenty-one

Subject: it's only money, right?
Date: Fri, 5 Mar 2010 3:05 PM
From: Lisa
To: Mark

Had a meeting with the realtors today and not happy with their assessment.
As a result of that meeting I realize that my house is only worth what
someone is willing to pay for it, and that amount is a mystery right now.
This is all starting to push in on me as I take big leaps and have to choose
people to trust who I don't even know. I am so aware of not wanting to
make decisions based in fear, and I'm feeling how big these choices really
are. And it is all leading towards really, *really* big choices.

Need perspective check right away . . .

Subject: your turn. . .
Date: Sat, 6 Mar 2010 7:15 AM
From: Mark
To: Lisa

Still need perspective? I can probably help. Let me support you this time. Writing you some perspective notes right now. Phone OK after 9.

Subject: re: your turn. . .
Date: Sat, 6 Mar 2010 7:56 AM
From: Lisa
To: Mark

We can talk later if OK with you, that would be great.

So I have been researching comparable houses in my area, which is tricky because we have such a big, unusual house. Having created the in-law setup for mom is an awesome feature, but we found out that, because of zoning, we have to take out the kitchen I put in. I'll have to sweet talk Dave or pay someone. *Ugh.*

Then there are the real estate agents we have interviewed so far: two older women, who I didn't really care for, who said they would list it for what we think is a reasonable price, and a great Hispanic couple, who suggested a price 20% less. Love them, but not their price. We have a third realtor coming today who actually listed this house many years ago and reminded us that it sat for nearly a year before *we* bought it.

My mom just wants it sold fast because she already bought a place and can't keep paying for two places. Of course, I am in no rush. I have to wait till Zac graduates and goes off to college before I can make my big move and . . . *hey everybody!* . . . I said when I came back from my visit in October that I would like to move back to California in a year or so, once Zac is in college. Now all this has been set in hyper-speed motion and I have to just hang on.

But, hey. . . it's all happening the way it's supposed to, right? The Universe is in charge, right?

Subject: perspective #1
Date: Sat, 6 Mar 2010 8:04 AM
From: Mark
To: Lisa

Right, the Universe is in charge.

Here's a little perspective based on your disappointment upon getting a reality check on the value of the house . . .

The real estate agents (strangers) you're somewhat reluctant to put your faith in are not your friends; their primary motivation is to make money off the sale of your house. It's in their interest to make the quickest sale possible so they can collect their commission and get on to the next sale.

And you can bet they've already sized you up the way a car salesman would, processing bits of personal info about your situation, your needs, what kind of timeline you're talking about. I think it would be wise to assume that, for all their reassurances to the contrary, you're being played a little bit. They want their money too, and it's a pretty good bet they know how much they can make off of your house, and already have a number in their head that *they* can live with, commission-wise . . .

Not sure how accurate my assessment is, but it would be cool if you could start thinking about how to play *them* to *your* advantage.

_____
Subject: re: perspective #1
Date: Sat, 6 Mar 2010 8:12 AM
From: Lisa
To: Mark

I know! Excellent point, for sure. And I believe that about the couple, especially him. I'm not shy about giving my opinion regarding what I know (*duh*) so figuring out who is best to play to our advantage is exactly what I need to do. I have not gotten my head around what the strengths (and maybe more importantly, weaknesses) of each of them might be. That is something I would like to bounce around with you.

AND there is this feeling that I need to be able to control the flow of this in some way, which is really absurd because there are so many variables. I have to make sure everyone gets settled in *their* thing, then I get to go do *my* thing, but I can't even really plan much of that right now. I'm glad I have the trip to California soon so that I can go soak up the energy of *my* *thing* and bring it back to all this. I think it will help.

So, of course you see this is not really all about how much money we can get for the house . . .

_____
Subject: re: your turn . . .
Date: Sat, 6 Mar 2010 9:11 AM
From: Mark

To: Lisa

I'm back . . . where were we? Better yet, just call.

_____
Subject: Yes!
Date: Sat, 6 Mar 2010 4:00 PM
From: Lisa
To: Mark

OK, third realtor was the charm. Great guy, knows his shit, knows the inspector here in town and suggested listing at the price we want. Signed. Done.

Gotta love that Universe.

_____
Subject: re: Yes!
Date: Sat, 6 Mar 2010 4:25 PM
From: Mark
To: Lisa

Hell yeah . . . *That's* what I'm talkin' about . . .

_____
Subject: signs
Date: Mon, 8 Mar 2010 3:14 PM
From: Lisa
To: Mark

The For Sale sign is now planted on my lawn.

I'm on my way.

_____
Subject: re: signs
Date: Tue, 9 Mar 2010 8:45 PM
From: Mark
To: Lisa

Sorry 'bout not getting back to you. *Oooff* . . . long, busy days. 100 mile round-trip commute every day; bunch of stuff in the air at the job about who's doing what, how much to get paid, yada-yada. The long-term prognosis looks good though, so I'm just doing it all one day at a time.

So, hell yeah, sell that thing! That was quick. Very cool the way everything lined up once you got some perspective. Has there been an internal change as well? I mean, it's REAL now: the house is on the market, and the next owners can find you now that you've announced you're ready for them to come and get their house.

Savannah and I home alone for the moment. She's in the next room, playing piano, creating the coolest soundtrack as I sip wine and write to you. Nice moment. Glad to have you here . . .

_____
Subject: re: signs
Date: Tue, 9 Mar 2010 9:38 PM
From: Lisa
To: Mark

Ah, nice to be there . . . sounds lovely.

Yes, they can find their new home now with the big-ass sign out front announcing its availability. The inspector comes on Thursday morning with the realtor, so we'll know what has to be done. Very real, indeed. The inner shift is real, too. Lucky Girl with Options has stopped by to gloat. Ha! She said it was getting her on the phone with you that got the ball rolling to get what I want. She's back out there by you already, measuring the new place so I know how much stuff I can bring :-)

Keep the faith about the job . . . remember how mahvelous you are, dahling.

Big, long hug.

_____
Subject: Mornin'
Date: Wed, 10 Mar 2010 5:41 AM
From: Mark
To: Lisa

My mind is whirling a bit . . . Got a call last night re: my job, which is halfway done. Starting today, there's a fixed amount of money - labor cost - available to complete the job. It's up to me to finish the job any way I want to, so the more I'm willing to do on my own, the more money there is for me. Plus, I get to make my own hours.

The office sprung this news on me late last night. The Change I've been asking for is here.

Oh, and thanks for the inspiration. Perfect timing . . . again.

_____
Subject: re: Mornin'
Date: Wed, 10 Mar 2010 5:49 AM
From: Lisa
To: Mark

Sounds like you are starting to get what you want, especially having the pressure off about your time. This is close to having your own gig and still be on a payroll. It is up to you how much and what kind of work you are willing to do. Fair enough.

_____
Subject: re: Mornin'
Date: Wed, 10 Mar 2010 6:09 AM
From: Mark
To: Lisa

Yeah. Next one should be even better.

Gotta run. Starting to come around to Facebook again. Long way back to update everyone. Haven't looked at it for months. Who ARE all these people?

Later

_____
Subject: re: Mornin'
Date: Wed, 10 Mar 2010 6:52 AM
From: Lisa
To: Mark

Here is the link to the Facebook photo album of My Tribe circa 1987. The pictures were in a "box with God". . . a shallow box I recently found in the basement containing pictures of all my California friends and Gram's crucifix. Great shots! Love the one black and white one I took of you in the rocking chair.

_____
Subject: re: Mornin'
Date: Wed, 10 Mar 2010 8:11 PM
From: Mark
To: Lisa

Wow, great pics. Got a kick out of being remembered as the Massage Guy. I wouldn't mind going back and reliving those years again . . .

_____
Subject: re: Mornin'
Date: Wed, 10 Mar 2010 8:17 PM
From: Lisa
To: Mark

They were good ones. If we knew then what we know now I wonder what might be different. Those pictures are of some of my dearest friends. No wonder God was in the box with them. It feels so right to be going back to My Tribe in California.

OK, so add that question to the next hang time with wine: *If we knew then what we know now, 25 years later, what might we have done differently?* I'm gonna really let that one simmer.

Hmmm.

———

Subject: re: Mornin'
Date: Wed, 10 Mar 2010 8:42 PM
From: Mark
To: Lisa

Simmer, no shit. Knowing what I know NOW?

One thing is that I would have asked for more money to do massage at One Pass. I would have been able to continue living in the Niles cottage. If I knew then that there was a writer in me and made enough money to stay in that Niles house I doubt I would have entered acupressure school (where I met Mariah). *Ooof . . .*

———

Subject: re: Mornin'
Date: Thu, 11 Mar 2010 5:37 AM
From: Lisa
To: Mark

Good morning.

I would have written more too, made it a real priority. I journaled last night about that question after I wrote you. In the end, each *different* choice I might have made undid another part of my life, like pulling a thread that unravels a sweater. In the end I wouldn't have wanted to change too much as the ripple effect got *huge* and it stopped looking like my life. Would it have been a *better* life? Maybe. But boy, there are things I wouldn't have wanted to miss. Lots to talk about there.

———

Subject: re: Mornin'
Date: Thu, 11 Mar 2010 5:45 AM
From: Mark
To: Lisa

Mornin' . . .

Yup. That's the thing about going back in time: One different choice creates an entirely new and different trajectory. Even now. We won't know for years how the seemingly little choices we're making on a daily basis are affecting our future . . .

twenty-two

Subject: good afternoon
Date: Thu, 11 Mar 2010 12:36 PM
From: Lisa
To: Mark

So, the inspection went well. I am excited to report that there were no big surprises. A few minor electrical things, back porch needs additional railing (I already knew that and Dave will do it). The inspector is still undecided on how much of my kitchen will need to be removed. All in all it was encouraging. :-)

_____

Subject: good evenin'
Date: Thu, 11 Mar 2010 8:19 PM
From: Mark
To: Lisa

Watched *Mostly Martha* the other night, the original movie in German that was later made into English as *No Reservations* with Catherine Zeta Jones and Aaron Eckhart. Both are great. Saw the U.S. version first, but the original was more intense. Highly recommend both.

What was the name of that movie about the guy who writes a book about his friendship with the girl he'd known a long time?

_____

Subject: good mornin'
Date: Fri, 12 Mar 2010 4:47 AM
From: Lisa
To: Mark

The movie was *Carolina*.

Subject: re: good mornin'
Date: Sat, 13 Mar 2010 5:38 AM
From: Mark
To: Lisa

I'm here for the next hour. Just went out to the truck to get something and saw a gorgeous pre-dawn fingernail moon hanging in a clear sky . . . wow . . nice start . . .

Sending you a Craigslist ad from a remodeling company, looking for a guy like me. I've answered *dozens* of ads like this with no results. Maybe this is the one?

Subject: re: good mornin'
Date: Sun, 14 Mar 2010 8:33 AM
From: Lisa
To: Mark

Good morning. That ad does sound like a perfect job for you. Hope they at least call you.

Too much fun with my sister & co. last night. Those girls are crazy during St. Patty's Day celebrations. Stayed over at their place. Feeling rough this morning. Argh.

Subject: mornin'
Date: Mon, 15 Mar 2010 5:53 AM
From: Lisa
To: Mark

Hey there. Hope your week starts well. I assume you are still on the job from last week? Maybe you'll hear from the Craigslist ad folks. I'd be curious to see if your boss ups his offer if you get a better one with another company.

Subject: re: mornin'
Date: Mon, 15 Mar 2010 7:14 PM
From: Mark
To: Lisa

. . . in the middle of cooking, so more later, BUT:

A breakthrough . . . Just in the last few hours it's come to me how to use this remodeling company in a win-win way where I make WAY more money, and the boss is cool and happy as well: *I gotta get him to let me manage my own jobs*. He sells them, and I take it from there. Then they all just leave me alone to do my thing. No headaches for him once we agree on a percentage of the job he pays me, in exchange for giving him problem-free, quality work.

How much would he pay to have that, do you think?

Gotta go . . . probably not back til the a.m.

_____
Subject: re: mornin'
Date: Mon, 15 Mar 2010 8:08 PM
From: Lisa
To: Mark

Hmmm, good thinking. I guess the question is what does he bid labor at now as a percentage? Does he do a day rate, or a per-guy, per-hour thing? Do you have an idea from doing your own jobs what it would be worth to him?

_____
Subject: evenin'
Date: Tue, 16 Mar 2010 5:52 PM
From: Lisa
To: Mark

Steamed crab . . . wine flowing. Winechat by chance?

_____
Subject: re: evenin'
Date: Tue, 16 Mar 2010 7:02 PM
From: Mark
To: Lisa

ugh, I wish . . . slamming down some food before heading downstairs for rehearsal. It's been go-go-go all day, even right now . . .

_____
Subject: house update
Date: Thu, 18 Mar 2010 5:28 AM
From: Lisa
To: Mark

Mom closed on her townhouse yesterday and we were all there last night. Wow, she is really moving! No one has looked at my house yet, though it may be me holding it back as to not have this all happen too soon. Maybe? I keep thinking *it will sell in May or June,* so to have someone buy it now would not be good. That's the story today, anyway.

Hope all is well in Busyland :-)

Subject: re: house update
Date: Thu, 18 Mar 2010 5:48 AM
From: Mark
To: Lisa

Busyland not much fun.

Girls doing a horse thing this weekend, leaving tomorrow. I have a gig on Saturday, so I'll be around. Gig tonight. Tomorrow after work I have the house and the evening to myself. We'll play catch up then . . . winechat.

Subject: a bit o'cool news
Date: Fri, 19 Mar 2010 4:31 AM
From: Lisa
To: Mark

So, I went to see a client yesterday who is moving to L.A. She was showing me her place and all the things she needs to sell or put in storage and there was the writing desk I've been wishing for! Looks like it came out of a Tuscan farmhouse. I'll tell you more tonight. I am so excited!

Subject: re: a bit o'cool news
Date: Fri, 19 Mar 2010 8:05 PM
From: Mark
To: Lisa

so call me already . . .

Subject: good mornin'
Date: Sat, 20 Mar 2010 7:35 AM
From: Lisa
To: Mark

Awakened to an inch of snow on the grass. I plan to be inside most of the day drinking tea, getting over my cold and staying cozy. For some reason I've had three coaching sessions pop up for today at the last minute, semi-emergency in nature. I will conduct most of this biz on the couch in my jammies. Gotta love it. It has hit me that your mention of the new moon energy is in line with a lot of these calls. New beginnings. Even if the people I coach are *in reaction* to them, the others involved are just having to deal. Wow. I want to talk about that.

Talking on the phone last night was awesome.

Subject: re: good mornin'
Date: Sat, 20 Mar 2010 7:37 AM
From: Mark
To: Lisa

tea chat?

_____
Subject: way mornin'
Date: Sun, 21 Mar 2010 1:49 AM
From: Mark
To: Lisa

mornin' . . . it's 1:45am here, just home from the gig: freakin' *awesome*!

I'll get to bed around 2:30 probably; having a bite to eat before bed . . .
check in later.

_____
Subject: re: way mornin'
Date: Sun, 21 Mar 2010 5:58 AM
From: Lisa
To: Mark

That's *great!* Can't wait to hear all about it . . .

_____
Subject: teachat?
Date: Sun, 21 Mar 2010 7:54 AM
From: Mark
To: Lisa

wow . . . big sleep . . . for *me*. Must have needed it (duh).

_____
Subject: I need some good vibes
Date: Mon, 22 Mar 2010 5:19 PM
From: Lisa
To: Mark

Hey. Long, long kinda tough day. Lots of coaching and a call from my doc
to come in tomorrow for some tests. Really mustering every good, positive
vibe I've got, but could you send some, too, please? I need all the good
juice I can get.

I know I will be alright. Right? Right. Right? I know I shouldn't be scared.

but I'm scared.

_____
Subject: re: I need some good vibes

Date: Mon, 22 Mar 2010 7:00 PM
From: Mark
To: Lisa

just got in . . . five minute call . . . Girls home soon, and won't get computer time for the rest of the evening.

Or write to me about what's up . . .

_____
Subject: re: I need some good vibes
Date: Mon, 22 Mar 2010 7:27 PM
From: Lisa
To: Mark

Sorry I missed the phone window . . .

OK, so I had a routine pap last week and it came back with abnormal cells. I have a colposcopy test tomorrow. This could prove to be *nothing*. I am certainly putting all thoughts on that being the case. A couple things drag me into a scarier place, though. I have one first cousin who died of cancer at 49 and another who is battling it now at 50. I dodged a bullet already, with a benign breast biopsy 10 years ago.

I know this is crazy thinking and that I'm *fine*. I have way too much to do with my life!

I will know more later tomorrow but probably nothing definitive and it is all the waiting that makes me crazy. I feel really by myself with it all even though I have lots of friends and family support if something is bad. But it's *not*. I know that. I'll be fine.

I'm just a little scared.

_____
Subject:
Date: Tue, 23 Mar 2010 6:02 AM
From: Mark
To: Lisa

Scared seems appropriate . . . but . . .

Whatever's really going on with the body is already there. If it's something, or nothing, that condition is already there. The fear and the worry comes from anticipating the worst.

Of course there were "abnormal cells " . . . There's no one else like you.

Let go.

What time do you go in?

_____
Subject: re:
Date: Tue, 23 Mar 2010 6:38 PM
From: Lisa
To: Mark

Aww. Thanks, that's sweet. I know it's all OK. I just hate not knowing, ya
know? 1:30 pm my time. Send me hugs, please

_____
Subject: well?
Date: Tue, 23 Mar 2010 2:49 PM
From: Mark
To: Lisa

How'd it go?

_____
Subject:
Date: Tue, 23 Mar 2010 3:24 PM
From: Mark
To: Lisa

heading out in 15 minutes (5:40 your time) Call?

_____
Subject:
Date: Tue, 23 Mar 2010 7:49 PM
From: Mark
To: Lisa

Uh-oh . . .

_____
Subject: re: well?
Date: Tue, 23 Mar 2010 9:13 PM
From: Lisa
To: Mark

Hey. Just got home.

Had my appointment and all is OK for now. Biopsy with a 7-10 day wait
for results but the doc feels that this is not likely a big deal and, if it is, it's
early enough to fix. (Sigh of guarded relief . . .)

Then I went grocery shopping and nearly broke down in the dairy aisle.
Huge emotion that comes up now even as I write this. Huge. Lots of stuff.

I called my friend Janet from the store and said, "I had a biopsy today and I am coming over for a hug." We had wine and dinner and a great evening together. I love her.

I'm still emotional and near sobbing as I write this for so many reasons. God, I wish I could talk to you. Thanks for showing up with the time you had, you have no idea what that means.

Subject: re: well?
Date: Tue, 23 Mar 2010 9:18 PM
From: Mark
To: Lisa

We'll have to chat later. Can't do much tonight. Write to me about it, if that helps . . . I'll respond in the morning.

hug.

Subject: re: well?
Date: Tue, 23 Mar 2010 9:26 PM
From: Lisa
To: Mark

Thanks. I don't even know what to say except I really wish I could talk to you and I *can't* and that I can't is harder than some of the rest of this. I hate *that* most of all. There is so much that happened today and the big thing that has flashing lights around it is that the person I feel like I need, who is there for me in some real way, is the one I can't call. *Fuck*. But it is the way it is. If I was a guy friend, or a Horse Club mom or a colleague I could call you. But because I have been your friend for decades, and I'm a girl and you care about me, we aren't allowed to have a phone call when a life-changing moment occurs and you could be supportive when I need *you*. I'm sorry but this feels so crazy to me.

Subject:
Date: Tue, 23 Mar 2010 9:50 PM
From: Lisa
To: Mark

OK, pulling my shit together . . .

Sorry for the rant about not being able to talk to you. My feelings are valid but I signed up for this, as seemingly silly as the rules are. As for Dave, I hate that I even called him tonight, but hey, I was feeling way vulnerable and he's there in that way that Pergo is designed for – a substitute for the real thing. Not so much this time, it turns out. Bad time to find out that he

233

is really isn't there when it counts. Really good to know, of course, that I was right. I know that not counting on him is a good idea.

So I count on me. And I pray that all will be well enough to get my ass to the West Coast where I will still count on me but the view is better. I am not whining, really. But boy, did I get to see who I am today and what I need to remember about the life I have created. I really might want to think about why I have men in my life who aren't able to take care of me. For whatever reason . . .

_____
Subject: re:
Date: Wed, 24 Mar 2010 5:28 AM
From: Mark
To: Lisa

I'm here. Never left. Nice rant. How you doin' this morning?

_____
Subject: re:
Date: Wed, 24 Mar 2010 5:30 AM
From: Lisa
To: Mark

I must say that this experience has really been about me looking at other things in my life beyond this health thing. Good stuff for me to see. Most of all that life is short and can be even shorter than we think. I see the people who really care about me, like you, checking in, looking for news. And who doesn't really care? Dave, who didn't call me back. Of course in the end, that was what I focused on and after a long, emotional day I fell apart. There are plenty of reasons I looked more to you for support in all this, even more so after so much time talking recently. I got a little spoiled. I knew you would listen. Thanks for that.

_____
Subject: re:
Date: Wed, 24 Mar 2010 5:34 AM
From: Mark
To: Lisa

An appropriate response, if you ask me. Life-changing events create a "re-set", and everything gets sorted out in a big way. Emotional earthquake? Anything with a well-built foundation is left standing.

_____
Subject: re:
Date: Wed, 24 Mar 2010 5:36 AM
From: Lisa
To: Mark

God, I love you.

How are you, by the way?

Hey, if there is a chat opportunity please let me know. I have missed the last couple chances, but please keep trying. I really would love to hear your voice.

Subject: re:
Date: Wed, 24 Mar 2010 5:43 AM
From: Mark
To: Lisa

I'm okay. Job work/pay thing still squirrely. Had some space to walk around the groovy downtown area near this job yesterday, sat at a window eating carnitas tacos for lunch while drawing up sketches of an entertainment unit I'll be doing as a side job. You were there. We were in Borders at 11:30 PT.

Subject: re:
Date: Wed, 24 Mar 2010 5:46 AM
From: Lisa
To: Mark

:-) I love that alternate reality so much more than where I was instead, here, at that same time in the doc office, having an awkward, uncomfortable procedure.

Subject: re:
Date: Wed, 24 Mar 2010 5:49 AM
From: Mark
To: Lisa

. . . or, actually, you were HERE, and the doc appointment was the alternate reality. Just ask LGwO . . .

Subject: re:
Date: Wed, 24 Mar 2010 9:53 PM
From: Mark
To: Lisa

If the Universe has our back anyway, then why do we fret the day-to-day shit? I'm down with Eckhart Tolle: the present moment is where it's at.

And keeping in mind my own spin: *It's all temporary; even the good stuff.*

So 'let go' is a temporary watchword to get me through my days, and come Friday I'll move into letting go of the entire week, and move into how I want to spend the weekend. It's high Spring out here, so something outdoors seems appropriate.

_____
Subject: re:
Date: Thu, 25 Mar 2010 5:09 AM
From: Lisa
To: Mark

You told me to *let go* when I was going for this test and I really did. I let go of fear, of outcomes, of stress . . . and in the end, what it did was open the space where I could *let in* the lesson and the growth that the experience was *really* about. I've been simmering in that for a couple of days. Most of what happens *is* temporary, exactly. It also can be transforming in unexpected ways if we allow it, if we let it in. And the doors fly open, right? Cosmic door bells are ringing everywhere right now . . .

Ding-dong. *Honey, can you get that? Your future's here.*

_____
Subject: winechat?
Date: Thu, 25 Mar 2010 5:25 PM
From: Lisa
To: Mark

I'm overdue . . .

_____
Subject: re: winechat?
Date: Thu, 25 Mar 2010 7:45 PM
From: Mark
To: Lisa

OK, go.

_____
Subject: Great news
Date: Fri, 26 Mar 2010 4:19 PM
From: Lisa
To: Mark

I got a call from the doc today and the test was negative for anything bad! I am so relieved. She said come back in three months for another pap just to keep an eye. Whew.

I was out shopping when I got the call. Life is short. Lucky Girl with Options was egging me on and we found a fantastic Lucky Brand purse (yeah, it's really named that) that we *had* to have even though it was $60 and doesn't hold a lot, but it is so *us*. And hot shoes, of course. What is a shopping spree without shoes? *And* a lime cashmere and silk scarf that I would have never bought for $35 but *what the hell*. I deserve it. Feels great against my neck.

All in all I spent about $200 that could have been a night on the town to celebrate my long, healthy continued life (if I was still with Dave) and instead I celebrated with *me*, and my fab alter ego LGwO. I feel so good.

Thanks for being our BFF. :-)

hugs.

_____
Subject: re: Great news
Date: Fri, 26 Mar 2010 7:50 PM
From: Mark
To: Lisa

Love that . . .

And yeah, about your test results: *WHEW*!

_____
Subject: re: Great news
Date: Fri, 26 Mar 2010 8:20 PM
From: Lisa
To: Mark

Thanks, yeah it's a relief.

Tomorrow I go to a write-in at the library. Looking forward to meeting new writers and hanging out in Oak Park. I love that library.

So lots of talk about me this week . . . how are you doing?

_____
Subject: re: Great news
Date: Fri, 26 Mar 2010 8:29 PM
From: Mark
To: Lisa

I'm OK. Long work days with frustrations. But a good mindset to deal with it. I mostly don't give a shit about the money or the company, and I just make a point of doing good work, getting along well with the customer, and will deal with the money later. 'Letting go' is working.

Gorgeous spring days out here. Gonna spend the weekend near the ocean. Food, nature, maybe some music . . . ready for a break.

Don't have time here to hang and write at length. Shit. Sounds like fun. I'll get back to you on Monday probably . . .

Be well.

———
Subject: re: Great news
Date: Fri, 26 Mar 2010 8:31 PM
From: Lisa
To: Mark

You, too. Enjoy.

———
Subject: re: Great news
Date: Fri, 26 Mar 2010 9:49 PM
From: Mark
To: Lisa

I really want to do the winechat thing when you're here next week. I may have to play hookie for a day.

———
Subject: re: Great news
Date: Sat, 27 Mar 2010 5:43 AM
From: Lisa
To: Mark

Sounds good to me. Couldn't think of a better reason to play hookie :-)

twenty-three

Subject: Greetings
Date: Mon, 29 Mar 2010 5:20 AM
From: Lisa
To: Mark

Good mornin'. . . How was your trip?

Subject: re: Greetings
Date: Mon, 29 Mar 2010 5:33 AM
From: Mark
To: Lisa

Very nice. Sunny and warm at the coast; we found a nice bed and breakfast almost by accident; garden art and antique store; roller coaster at the Boardwalk; great dinner; drove home, then picked up Savannah at the barn and over to my sister's house for a party (my niece is getting married in October).

So, yeah . . . nice relaxing weekend. And fun, too. But . . . well . . . not romantic.

Subject: re: Greetings
Date: Mon, 29 Mar 2010 5:55 AM
From: Lisa
To: Mark

Good to hear it was nice. As for romance . . . oh, well . . .

I feel all better and healed and back to myself. Better, even. I spent an industrious day yesterday cleaning the basement. Argh! Good to have it in better shape, but I was furious by all the crap Dave had left behind and the pockets of mess to clean up. Whatever. The writing group was not too exciting, but I did read aloud my story so far (lots to winechat about). I read parts to my mom this weekend and she loved it! That was cool.

Lots of sessions in these next few days till I leave. I'm getting excited about my visit.

Subject: apts
Date: Mon, 29 Mar 2010 6:05 AM
From: Lisa
To: Mark

Looking on Craigslist for Bay Area places I might want to live. I want to talk over a map when I see you so I can look in the right areas and stay out of the 'hoods. Are you still working in San Jose this week?

Subject: re: apts
Date: Mon, 29 Mar 2010 6:46 PM
From: Mark
To: Lisa

Yeah, working in San Jose area probably til Wednesday for sure.

Nice place you found on Craigslist, by the way . . .

___

Subject: read first. . .
Date: Mon, 29 Mar 2010 7:02 PM
From: Mark
To: Lisa

I need a big favor right now . . .

This company sucks to work for, and I want out. Sure, I got side jobs to hold me over for a week or three, but I'm done making a living at carpentry. I just want to do it when I feel like it, and not because I *have* to. The favor?

Run this whole work issue of mine by your psychic friend. I mean, *what the fuck?*

I need this bullshit to be over. I want to be happy making better money at something I'm great at.

___

Subject: re: read first. . .
Date: Mon, 29 Mar 2010 7:05 PM
From: Lisa
To: Mark

OK. I'll see if she can do a channeling about it before I get there.

Do you hate it as much when you work on a job for yourself, meaning no company breathing down your neck? I'd be curious to know if she sees you working on your own.

___

Subject: re: read first. . .
Date: Mon, 29 Mar 2010 7:13 PM
From: Mark
To: Lisa

Working alone on side jobs is fine; I create my *own* headaches, which is pretty rare . . .

___

Subject: re: read first. . .
Date: Mon, 29 Mar 2010 7:13 PM
From: Mark
To: Lisa

Another thing: To get me through the next 24 hours, I need to be reminded of what's REALLY going on here. I've been under the spell of being pissed off enough to pull the plug on this guy's business - turns out he doesn't have a contractor's license - but not sure of the karma backlash . . .

_____
Subject: re: read first. . .
Date: Mon, 29 Mar 2010 7:33 PM
From: Lisa
To: Mark

OK, so you hit it on the head with the karmic backlash. Not worth it. I totally got that hit and you want to stay away from bringing someone down for being a greedy idiot. Still not worth it. Better to let the anger fuel you to go find the thing you really want to do and then do it. Channel it for your good, not his bad, right? How does him going down serve *you?* Convince me. If you can't, then I stand by my gut.

Everything is moving towards being who you are, doing what you want in a world that *gets you* and appreciates your gifts. You are a rock star. Be one. Period. The end.

_____
Subject: morning. . .
Date: Tue, 30 Mar 2010 5:36 AM
From: Lisa
To: Mark

Outta your funk yet? Hope so.

_____
Subject: re: morning. . .
Date: Tue, 30 Mar 2010 6:05 AM
From: Mark
To: Lisa

Yeah, somewhat. Not looking forward to pulling up a newly-laid fake laminate piece of shit crappy cheap floor, to replace a piece in the *middle* of
the room that got mysteriously chipped over the weekend. *Ugh* . . .

_____
Subject: re: morning. . .
Date: Tue, 30 Mar 2010 6:07 AM
From: Lisa
To: Mark

That sucks.

I sent Kathy an email last night and I will talk to her early tomorrow morning about your request for her insight.

_____
Subject: Kathy
Date: Wed, 31 Mar 2010 5:28 AM
From: Lisa
To: Mark

Mornin'.

I just talked with Kathy for half an hour and some interesting things came up. Lots of notes to share but the gist of it is that you are here to create. You are capable of being a master carpenter and you have a love of working with your hands that you need to remember. This job right now is for you to find your love of creating again. I remember a piece you wrote about that and will try to find it. It was a beautiful description of building something *lasting*. Kathy said, "He is a beautiful soul. How blessed these families are that they have Mark's energy in their homes. It's amazing." You need to connect with that. It's a big gift that you are *not* running things with your boss right now. Don't do it. More side work is coming this summer so hang in with this company till then, and even part-time, through the end of the year. There are viscous layers that have built up over the past 6-7 years that need to be peeled back to reveal who you really are. You can't just say "fuck this!" and walk out on the boss anymore than you can on your marriage. Peeling it all away steadily is the ticket.

She saw a see-saw and you are down at the bottom and Savannah is up in the air. She said you need to balance yourself out to find your center but it's hard to do that while holding her up there. This is part of the deal right now in the choices you make: all the ways you are supporting her keep you down on the ground. This is not bad, it is just what *is*. But you can lift up off the ground a little at a time and balance out and she'll be OK.

The big news? You are here to help people. To inspire people (I could have told her *that*). Your writing is part of that . . . but not while you live there. You may do coaching, not one-on-one, but with groups doing workshops. Speaking, too. She saw me as a catalyst for this, and when I move there it will feel like you have two lives, and it will draw out the inspirational guy even more, peeling back more layers.

There's more. I'll share it when we talk. For now, get in deeper awareness when you are creating and seek to attract cool, beautiful projects. They're on their way.

_____
Subject: re: Kathy

Date: Wed, 31 Mar 2010 5:32 AM
From: Mark
To: Lisa

thank you thank you thank you thank you thank you thank you

_____

Subject: re: Kathy
Date: Wed, 31 Mar 2010 5:35 AM
From: Lisa
To: Mark

Oh, and music is another way you create and that looked to be a great outlet for you right now. Seems timely with the new band coming together. She said you are not ever going to be a guy who does just one thing.

Of course not. With all your talents, why would you? :-)

_____

Subject: visiting hours
Date: Wed, 31 Mar 2010 5:48 AM
From: Mark
To: Lisa

Remind me of the details of your arrival tomorrow . . .

_____

Subject: re: visiting hours
Date: Wed, 31 Mar 2010 6:09 AM
From: Lisa
To: Mark

I arrive at 1pm in San Francisco. I will be heading to the East Bay and staying at Mary's. Meet for a drink at the Bistro at 3?

_____

Subject: tomorrow
Date: Wed, 31 Mar 2010 6:42 PM
From: Mark
To: Lisa

Hey, that would be great.

See you *TOMORROW*!

_____

Subject: mornin'
Date: Fri, 2 Apr 2010 5:33 AM
From: Mark
To: Lisa

Talked to the boss last night about getting a check from him later today. The office is not far from where you are. Lunch together?

———

Subject: re: mornin'
Date: Fri, 2 Apr 2010 5:48 AM
From: Lisa
To: Mark

OK, I'm free after 1.

———

Subject: bang!
Date: Fri, 2 Apr 2010 7:32 PM
From: Mark
To: Lisa

Got my check after lunch with you. *bang!*
Got "permission" to do a side job next week, then start a new job the following Monday. *bang!*
Deposited the check 5 minutes before the bank closed. *bang!*
Called my electrician to say I'll have money for him tomorrow. *bang!*
The girls not home til after 8, so went to the gym. *bang!*

"What did you always want to BE?", she asked, cocking the trigger.

"Me!", he answered, looking her in the eye, fearless.

She lowered the gun slowly, nodding, "Good answer."

———

Subject: mornin'
Date: Sun, 4 Apr 2010 1:32 PM
From: Mark
To: Lisa

Just now getting some alone time . . .

Been spending the morning drawing up the last details for the job next week. I think I'll start Tuesday: rains are coming, yard work needed badly here, and time to gather materials.

That was some gig, some evening . . . I mean, really, it was kind of otherworldly. All new environments - playing music by the ocean, at night, with you in the audience - all so unfamiliar and stimulating; almost no point of reference because it's so new. Big fun, big feelings . . . big, deep . . . *everything*. It's a bit sad though, to have to leave those moments so soon, rather than get to linger, hang out, and let those moments *breathe* . . .

There were still dust motes floating in the airspace . . . microscopic bits of stuff stirred up from thrashing and driving the band from behind the drums, particles of *bang!* that wouldn't settle to the tabletops and carpet for hours. Oh man . . . the ocean; the music; the passion; the energy . . . all coming together, funneling down from the cosmos to a pinprick point on the Earth. *Love* that you were there.

Raining here now. Nice. Heading for a hot bath before finishing up my drawings and estimate.

Let me know about Thursday for breakfast.

Hug . . .

_____
Subject: good evenin'
Date: Sun, 4 Apr 2010 10:16 PM
From: Lisa
To: Mark

OK, so we need to talk soon. Talk about things being thrashed and shaken up. The producer friend I'm staying with wants to pitch me for a TV show. Big. Huge. News. She mentioned this a few years ago and I wasn't ready then. I think I'm ready now. Or *soon* . . .

Let me know if there is any time tomorrow for a phonechat. I'd love to get your thoughts.

_____
Subject: mornin'
Date: Mon, 5 Apr 2010 6:38 AM
From: Mark
To: Lisa

Holy shit! Awesome! Check emails for call time. I'm 'off' today. Let's meet for tea chat.

_____
Subject: Thurs breakfast?
Date: Tue, 6 Apr 2010 6:42 PM
From: Mark
To: Lisa

Rushing tonight . . . quick dinner, then rehearsal, up early tomorrow to hit Home Depot before going to the job. The new client with the kitchen remodel is set up for a 5pm meeting. Good luck at your speaking engagement.

Thursday breakfast before you fly out would be cool. I'm working on that side of the bay.

gotta run . . . *(pant, pant, pant . . .!!!)*

_____
Subject: Thurs breakfast?
Date: Wed, 7 Apr 2010 6:32 AM
From: Mark
To: Lisa

Thurs AM: Bay Diner, San Mateo, if you can make it. They open at 7am

_____
Subject: re: Thurs breakfast?
Date: Wed, 7 Apr 2010 4:01 PM
From: Lisa
To: Mark

I'll be there . . .

Hope your day was as good as mine. Off to my gig soon. Ready to rock.

See you at 7am.

twenty-four

Subject: Mornin'
Date: Mon, 12 Apr 2010 5:43 AM
From: Lisa
To: Mark

Back home, yet it doesn't quite feel like home anymore. I met up with Zac and we spent the rest of the weekend at Karen's in Nashville. It was gorgeous and lots of fun. We also got to check out his college and his place at his Dad's. All good.

How are you?

_____
Subject: re: Mornin'
Date: Mon,12 Apr 2010 10:44 AM

From: Mark
To: Lisa

Mornin' . . .

Home for the day to do taxes. Rain all day yesterday and today. Nice.
Prolongs the spring for me. I have just GOT to go out and play in it
somewhere, sometime soon. Too much *doing* for my tastes, but happy to
have re-established my work-when-I-want-to pace. More work offers
coming in, and cash keeps showing up, like, hundred dollar bills . . . and
then to come home to Mariah repeating: *I'm broke*. Ugh.

Gigged last night in SF with the new band. A few magic moments,
musically, along with the rain coming down outside the entire time. Nice.

Weird that I've had so little interest in writing lately, but I notice that my
thoughts often drift back to Kevin and Cody, sitting there in that Flagstaff
cafe, waiting for me to move their lives along. Got really nostalgic for
them the other day when I flashed on how great it would be to bolt for the
desert *right now*, searching out wildflower displays, taking pictures,
camping, and writing. That life is so *me*. Speaking of which . . .

This whole idea of this other Self, down inside of me, wanting out? That
really passionate guy with so much talent and potential? I got another big
hit of the drummer version of him last night when there are these
spontaneous moments of my playing that come from a whole other place
inside of me, and I do these great things with the groove and feel of the
song that seem like I've wrapped the whole band inside of what I'm
playing. It's solid and strong, and I'm *leading* the band with what I'm
playing. And in those moments I can feel how it's exactly the same guy
who's lurking down inside of me, in part holding back, and in part just
ready to *bring it* when participating in something creative with others who
are either doing the same, or who are doing something that inspires *that
guy* to show up.

. . . like owning a Porsche, and discovering one day that, hey!, there are
three more gears in this thing! What the-?

Seems like a long time ago that you were here. The memory lingers, but
that aura of fun, bliss and creative stimulation wears off, like the week
after coming home from a tropical vacation. And right now, outside the
window, the rain just keeps on coming . . . and after-breakfast walks on the
sunny side of the street are just fond memories now. Kind of sad . . .

Back to taxes. This was my one break, taking some time to say more than
'hi', before having to stay with it without interruption. Sounds like your

travels all went well. Glad to hear how Zac is settled and that it's all good for him out there. Then you get home, and whoa . . . not feeling like home so much now, is it?

You're brave to move about in the world and in your life the way you do, bolstered by inspired confidence. Perhaps you don't experience your actions as brave; maybe a better word is: *intentional*. Yeah, intentional . . .

But I gotta tell you: There's something way hot about going into the Land of New with just a magic wand, some ideas, and some cash . . .

_____
Subject: re: Mornin'
Date: Mon, 12 Apr 2010 10:52 AM
From: Lisa
To: Mark

Hey . . .

I really needed this reminder. Great to hear about *that guy* and the drumming and desert and the brave girl with her wand :-)

Just got a call from the realtor and there's another showing of the house set for tomorrow, so that's a bright spot.

Other than that, I'm having a tough day.

Talked with my coach friend Michele who wanted to hear about my trip and offered some perspective about my coming-home-funk. I know this is the crash from the high . . . like you said, a little sad.

It's *all* temporary, right? Even the good stuff. Some sage soul told me that once.

_____
Subject: you there?
Date: Tue, 13 Apr 2010 5:46 AM
From: Lisa
To: Mark

mornin'. . . feeling better. It is lovely here . . . magnolias next door are in bloom . . . the pussy willow is blooming . . . tulips are up. It was great being in the country at Karen's in Tennessee, hiking around and hanging with peacocks.

Today is the house showing at 1:30 my time. Please send out some good vibes and pass it on if you see Lucky Girl with Options. I know she's back there by you. Look for her sitting in the window of a coffee shop, laughing and having breakfast with Creates with His Hands . . .

_____

Subject: re: you there?
Date: Tue, 13 Apr 2010 11:09 AM
From: Mark
To: Lisa

Neck deep in taxes. Sending juju at 1:30.

You packed yet?

_____

Subject: re: you there?
Date: Tue, 13 Apr 2010 12:58 PM
From: Lisa
To: Mark

They are here looking at the house now. Turn on the juju. Dave is here working and may be putting out the vibe for me to *not* sell the house. Argh.

_____

Subject: re: you there?
Date: Tue, 13 Apr 2010 6:12 PM
From: Mark
To: Lisa

Kind of a cool music thing happening out here: The country band (Calico) plays near Santa Cruz on the 24th. *Hell* yeah! Music, friends, wine . . . awesome!

Sell the house yet?

_____

Subject: re: you there?
Date: Tue, 13 Apr 2010 6:31 PM
From: Lisa
To: Mark

No, they didn't want it. I'm a mess. Too much drama. Dave is coming on strong and I am being tested in ways I can't even understand.

"You have never looked so good to me. You're such a catch. What happened to us? And now you're moving to California," he said.

Uh, yeah.

I'm an emotional mess. You are looking like premium, high grade superior Brazilian Cherrywood right now. And yes, I *know* you are not available.

But *really?* A mere idea is better than what I am dealing with here in reality. These last several hours are some kind of trial by fire. God wants me to really walk my talk. This last week is coming back to me *big time.* I know who I am and what I want.

Stick around, please.

I need to stay real right now.

Subject: where did I leave off?
Date: Wed, 14 Apr 2010 5:54 AM
From: Lisa
To: Mark

Oh, geez. That was some night.

So my last email left off with me being really emotional after that *long* talk in which Dave finally steps up and says all the things I thought I wanted to hear a year ago. They might have mattered then, but not now. I am still done. It all still comes across as *fake.* The thing that really got me was him saying that I never looked better than right now, " . . . so beautiful and vulnerable, and that makes me feel strong. I could never feel strong around you, Lis."

That broke my heart a little. It was never my intention to evoke weakness in him, or anyone, and I like to believe that I have the ability to bring out the *strengths* in someone. I know I do that with my clients, and with friends like you. I hope with Zac. It just felt really bad to think that's how he feels. Yet he was suggesting, on the other hand, that I stay, which makes no sense, and I have no intention of doing, of course. It sounds like manipulation, right? I know he is feeling the true loss of me now. I said that I need to go and make my own fresh start . . . *back to where I was before husbands and kids.* I actually have that phrase on my dream collage. California is where I am the happiest and feel like I belong. I think he gets it; I hope so. He said he didn't feel worthy to try to make me stay. Sad.

The whole night became very surreal, talking until it had turned dark and then we went inside and he was downstairs in the basement for awhile. That's when I sent that email to you. He came up and said he didn't want to make the long drive home after drinking too much wine so I let him sleep in the spare room. All very weird.

Very cool to hear about the Calico gig. Fun :-)

I really would like to chat when you can. There is a clearing opportunity to process here and I would really appreciate talking with you.

Subject: re: where did I leave off?
Date: Wed, 14 Apr 2010 6:57 AM
From: Mark
To: Lisa

That was some night alright . . .

Doubt that we'll get a chance to chat today. Mariah is dragging her tax feet
- *I'm* done - and she and Savannah leave tomorrow morning for a three-day
horse gig . . . far away. The completion of taxes, the switching of vehicles,
and the packing of camping gear need to be accomplished, all with the
familiar push-pull of the Bulldozer and the Porsche.

Take notes gather topics, distill your needs . . . I will be so there for you
tomorrow.

Subject: re: where did I leave off?
Date: Wed, 14 Apr 2010 7:24 AM
From: Lisa
To: Mark

thankyouthankyouthankyou I am off the next two days and it will be 80
degrees here. Lots of time enjoying my yard, where I will write and we can
talk and all will realign. New moon, too. Hope you have a good day today
in spite of the push-pull . . .

May the Porsche be with you

hug.

Subject: re: where did I leave off?
Date: Wed, 14 Apr 2010 7:54 AM
From: Mark
To: Lisa

LOL! *May the Porsche be with you* . . . great . . .

Subject: mornin'
Date: Thu, 15 Apr 2010 6:21 AM
From: Mark
To: Lisa

Leaving soon to spend the day rebuilding my mom's back fence. I'll check
in again when I get home, around the PST dinner hour.

Winechat.

Subject: re: mornin'
Date: Thu, 15 Apr 2010 3:41 PM
From: Lisa
To: Mark

Just came back from the chiropractor for an adjustment. Lower back is really tight . . . base emotions and all that, makes sense. But my neck is loose and adjusted beautifully.

Well, Lisa, your lower stuff is holding on and taking its time releasing. But at least you have your head on straight.

Yes indeed, Doc, I do.

Talk to you tonight.

Subject: Hey
Date: Fri, 16 Apr 2010 6:41 AM
From: Lisa
To: Mark

Good mornin'. . . Fun night. Great chat and loved swapping all those pictures.

talk later . . .

Subject: re: mornin'
Date: Fri, 16 Apr 2010 6:36 PM
From: Mark
To: Lisa

Just got in. Heading for the tub. Call sometime after 7, k?

Subject:
Date: Sun, 18 Apr 2010 8:34 AM
From: Mark
To: Lisa

oooff . . . just got up . . . late gig last night . . . teachat?

Subject: inspired morning
Date: Mon, 19 Apr 2010 7:36 AM
From: Lisa
To: Mark

Hey you . . .

Great convo with Kathy this morning. Awesome start to the day. She said I really need to be writing, as that is a huge part of my future.

_____
Subject: re: inspired morning
Date: Mon, 19 Apr 2010 7:57 AM
From: Mark
To: Lisa

Sounds all good. Gone all day w/ new job, working for the Remodelers From Hell . . .

later . . .

_____
Subject: re: inspired morning
Date: Mon, 19 Apr 2010 7:59 AM
From: Lisa
To: Mark

Remember how great it is for your customers to have your energy in their house and enjoy what you can of the work.

_____
Subject: inspired afternoon
Date: Mon, 19 Apr 2010 6:13 PM
From: Lisa
To: Mark

We dropped the price on the house today! Let's just get this done, I say. . . Ma wants it sold yesterday.

Did you fill the owner's house today with your juju?

_____
Subject: re: inspired afternoon
Date: Tue, 20 Apr 2010 6:12 AM
From: Mark
To: Lisa

ugh . . .

Exhausted. Good Calico rehearsal Sunday, but very tired from the whole weekend by the time I got home. New job yesterday morning: complicated, many hoops to jump through, but nice folks. The house overlooks the Bay from the hills above Berkeley.

Very tired through the day. Didn't get to the end-point I thought I would. Left at 4:30, got home with enough time to eat, then back out again to a rehearsal.

No mood for juju. Sleep. Quiet. Must . . . recharge . . . batteries . . .

Heavy rain this morning.

———

Subject: re: inspired afternoon
Date: Tue, 20 Apr 2010 6:22 AM
From: Lisa
To: Mark

Oh, hey did Savannah end up taking first place with her horse show?

———

Subject: re: inspired afternoon
Date: Tue, 20 Apr 2010 6:30 AM
From: Mark
To: Lisa

yup

———

Subject: re: inspired afternoon
Date: Tue, 20 Apr 2010 6:42 AM
From: Lisa
To: Mark

Of course she did! Great!

I came across a 'hand reading' a Bay Area client of mine did for me last year. My 'gift markings' all indicate speaking, writing, counseling, leadership. Very cool stuff. She was at my talk in San Jose.

Hey . . . a hand reading . . . what a perfect gift for my dear friend Creates with His Hands . . . hmmm, maybe for your birthday :-)

———

Subject: re: inspired afternoon
Date: Tue, 20 Apr 2010 6:33 PM
From: Mark
To: Lisa

Having my hands read: bring it.

———

Subject: bits of bang!
Date: Wed, 21 Apr 2010 6:27 PM

From: Lisa
To: Mark

Only client today rescheduled to next week, giving me all day free. *bang!*
Mom is free to go down into the city with me to the discount fabric
warehouse to scope out fabric to reupholster my furniture. *bang!*
Find 25 yards of the perfect sand-colored heavy cotton fabric I want to use
for an unbelievable $3.95/yd. *bang!*
Decision made and a fun day with Mom on an adventure. *bang!*
Steak swimming in awesome marinade. *bang!*
Wine flowing, music going. *bang!*

No one home. Blast the tunes. *Serious* dance jam. Feel amazing. Life is
good.

Off to grill my steaks.

___

Subject:
Date: Thu, 22 Apr 2010 6:06 AM
From: Lisa
To: Mark

Mornin' . . .

I woke up very early with a strong sense that you needed support, positive
energy . . . you still feeling depleted? I pulled a Rune asking: *what is Mark
experiencing*? Pulled Joy reversed - long, slow birth . . . *everything is a
test.* Then asked: *how can I help him*? Pulled Harvest (yet again) - patient
perseverance, cultivate with care, encouragement of success, One Year.

Sending water and sunshine. Whatever shit shows up is just fertilizer.

hug.

P.S. The train is coming . . .

___

Subject: thanks
Date: Thu, 22 Apr 2010 6:08 AM
From: Mark
To: Lisa

Shit as fertilizer . . . That's good. Great *bang!* story, by the way . . .

Sorry to miss out on the evening. Never went on the computer after
coming home. Went to the gym after work, which turned out to be a really
good thing; this remodeling company . . . *ugh.* Lot of effort going into

255

keeping my cool and letting things go, so the gym was good for my head. I came out feeling relaxed and hungry, with enough time to make a nice dinner before the girls came home. Savannah ended up not having her usual Wednesday piano lesson, so there was no rushing to eat and get out the door as per usual. Made a fire, watched *The Blind Side*. Then came the moment when Savannah brought her homework out so she could do it in front of the fire, and there we all were: everyone relaxed and comfortable, and no tension in the house . . . due, in large part, to having used some of my own healing juju to calm the mother/daughter sniping that had come in the door earlier. The moment of witnessing Savannah being in the same room with us, doing her homework by the fire, was the moment I lost interest in the half-baked movie and just grooved on the harmony in the room, a harmony that I could take some responsibility for. I went to bed, leaving the two of them to their comfort zones.

It's been cold and rainy every day this week, the kind of weather that really can affect my mood, especially while having to deal with this knuckle-headed company. The best part of the work day is when I'm done, and drive off. Another full week of this to go . . .

_____
Subject: re: thanks
Date: Thu, 22 Apr 2010 6:22 AM
From: Lisa
To: Mark

Glad to hear you sounding better . . . nice that you had a harmonious evening. I haven't seen *Blind Side* but it's on my Netflix.

I had a nice evening to myself, then with Zac when he came home at 9. The steaks were awesome :-) Zac loved his and he sautéed baby portabello mushrooms and a sweet onion. Mmmmm

twenty-five

Subject: hi. gotta run
Date: Fri, 23 Apr 2010 3:16 PM
From: Mark
To: Lisa

I've been missing out on my usual routine of teachat in the morning, then being home at a reasonable hour to do some winechatting before dinner, and now I have one minute left before I have to pick up Savannah from school and take her to the barn . . . and then to my mom's birthday dinner . . . and then the Calico gig tomorrow afternoon in Santa Cruz.

More rushing than I planned on, and no time to respond to your letters and support. I'll be back when there's a pause in the action.

_____
Subject: making it happen. . .
Date: Sat, 24 Apr 2010 7:18 AM
From: Lisa
To: Mark

Up early, ready *to move.* Did a sage cleansing to completely release the house (and remove all the Dave energy that was here the last couple days with his *I-don't-want-you-to-go* vibes) and now I am sorting stuff to get rid of while listening to a song on the Calico CD . . .

"The way it was just can't compare to the way it can be. . ."

Oh, yeah.

Since I can't be at your gig today I thought I would still have a listen to you guys here. A friend in Santa Cruz may come to your gig. She's in my "tribe". LGwO will be there, of course. Look for her and give her a wink, will ya? She'll like that.

_____
Subject: re: making it happen . . .
Date: Sat, 24 Apr 2010 8:59 AM
From: Mark
To: Lisa

Mornin' . . . ah, space . . .

Totally exhausted by the time we got home at 11 last night. Parked the car, got out, walked into the house, dropped my clothes on the floor, and got in bed before Mariah and Savannah were even in the house . . . and . . . woke this morning from a dream that ended with me on the ground, on my knees, sobbing, next to a homemade-looking white box/casket that had Mariah inside. Wow.

_____
Subject: re: making it happen. . .
Date: Sat, 24 Apr 2010 7:54 AM
From: Lisa
To: Mark

Wow. Crazy dream.

Subject: The Calico gig
Date: Sat, 24 Apr 2010 9:14 AM
From: Mark
To: Lisa

Turns out Mariah will be coming with me today. Looking forward to
meeting your friend, but wish it were under, uh, better circumstances . . .
especially since she's a tribal member. I'll bet there's some great winechat
potential there, which probably won't get to happen. I'm realizing that I
had a hand in creating it all. The stage is set, the players have been lined
up, and the show begins when I pull out of the driveway at noon . . .

Subject: re: The Calico gig
Date: Sat, 24 Apr 2010 9:46 AM
From: Lisa
To: Mark

I had a feeling that Mariah could be going. Just felt it. Maybe it's not
meant to be that you get to be 'just Mark' in a room with my peeps there.
Maybe Mariah's soul is telling her to go 'supervise'. . .

Subject: re: The Calico Gig
Date: Sat, 24 Apr 2010 10:13 AM
From: Mark
To: Lisa

ooh yeah, good reminder. It should be interesting having some tribe juju in
the room for the evening. I've asked them to be there for a reason; they're
agreeing to come for a reason; we all need to know one another for a
reason.

Looking forward to writing you tomorrow to tell you the reason . . .

Subject: re: The Calico gig
Date: Sat, 24 Apr 2010 10:23 AM
From: Lisa
To: Mark

I can't wait . . .

On this side of the world . . . I packed up a bunch of stuff for the garage
sale on this chilly, rainy day. Just had a hot shower and am having lunch. I

have a channeling session with Kathy later this afternoon. Dinner plans with writer group tonight.

A cool synchronicity: Zac's Welcome packet for college came today alongside my Coastal Living magazine. Nice.

_____
Subject: re: The Calico gig
Date: Sat, 24 Apr 2010 11:08 AM
From: Mark
To: Lisa

Yeah, tribe support. I was thinking the same thing.

So I made myself some breakfast and went out to the sunny back deck to eat it, thinking about manifestation, creating my reality and being powerful, yada-yada . . . and how I would really rather Mariah stay home for this gig.

I sit back, visualize driving there alone, being there without her, and being free to hang out with new and old friends as *me* . . .

I come into the house to Mapquest directions to the gig and discover that I have to leave by noon. Mariah is doing horse stuff with Savannah, and is already a bit bent that I pushed on her to make sure she'd be ready to leave at 12:30. I just left her a message to be ready to leave at noon - very doubtful - or drive herself there in a separate car. She will be very upset.

She's not supposed to be there.

_____
Subject: re:
Date: Sat, 24 Apr 2010 12:04 PM
From: Mark
To: Lisa

leaving now . . . alone.

_____
Subject: hey. . .
Date: Sat, 24 Apr 2010 7:11 PM
From: Lisa
To: Mark

Hope you are coming off a great night.

So, my night took an interesting turn as my dinner plans fell through just as I was leaving the house. I was initially bummed - all dressed up with nowhere to go - but then realized that having the night with myself was just fine. I'd had an incredible session with Kathy and it gave me time to process it. I changed into comfy clothes and curled up on the couch to do some reading and chill. Zac just called to say he and his friend Tyler are coming home with a pizza and a movie. Life is good. I am imagining you and the band grooving on playing together, the crowd dancing and laughing and everyone there having a great time. Wish I was there, too, and I am in spirit. Looking forward to hearing all about it.

Lots to share about the Kathy call. My "Faith Flame" was the focus of much of the reading and it had been flickering up and down all week, more than I realized. My soul kicked my ass a little bit about letting *anything* sway my decisions. I need to let go of some beliefs, behaviors and feelings and my new life will pull me forward easily. It came across strongly that I would be there by August. Trusting the Universe came across as something I am *great* at telling others to do and have to remember to do myself (OK, you're laughing, I know you are).

Your soul showed up strong and in good spirits. "He's stronger than he's ever been," she said. She said that you loved how I expected you to bring your greatness, and I brought it out in you, yet I didn't devour you like other women may have in your life. I told her about the dream you had and she said it was all symbolic: Death of The Marriage. We can talk more about that if you want.

I'm not supposed to worry about my work at all and keep focused on the move. I had an epiphany about how I am dismantling my Midwest life, which has served my family well, and am now rebuilding my brand new life on a foundation that's nearly 30 years strong. What was it that you said once? Oh, in my emotional earthquake *that which is built on a strong foundation will still be standing*. It's all about foundations, isn't it?

Subject: tribal feedback
Date: Sun, 25 Apr 2010 2:19 PM
From: Lisa
To: Mark

So I heard that my friends had a great time. Can't wait to hear more from your end.

Subject: everything ok?
Date: Sun, 25 Apr 2010 6:24 PM
From: Lisa
To: Mark

Please say a quick hey. Weird not to hear something yesterday. Check in, 'k?

─────

Subject: re: everything ok?
Date: Mon, 26 Apr 2010 5:11 AM
From: Mark
To: Lisa

No, no . . . all is well. Never got a minute alone yesterday. Not one.

The short story is I had drinks with your Tribe after the gig. That was
great, but I never got more than a couple of minutes of one-on-one
conversation with your friend Melissa. I was eager to hang with her more.
I followed her clan to a noisy techno bar, went to buy her a drink, and
while waiting for it, she came up alongside me. There was this moment
when we were sipping wine and starting to connect . . . or so I thought. We
chatted a bit, going into spirit talk, and then she moved onto the dance
floor with a girlfriend, so I wandered around a bit, taking the place in:
twenty-somethings everywhere, industrial concrete decor, loud, shitty
techno music . . . not my scene, but was willing to hang to get to know her
better. But she was there with *her* friends too, and after a few minutes of
taking all this in I realized this was not going to be the time or place to
really connect with her, not to mention that I wasn't so sure she and I were
even on the same page with the tribal connection thing. My vote would
have been to take her away from her friends and have her to myself for an
hour, but it didn't feel like a reciprocal thing . . . so I abruptly called it a
night . . .

. . . but not before going down the street to an all-night taqueria to eat fish
tacos. And even while sitting there, I kept glancing up and looking out the
window, hoping maybe the Tribe would pass by. . . but nope.

Shit.

Oh well . . . I had a good time meeting and hanging with them. I was up
for much more than what took place, but the vibe and energy in that
industrial techno bar . . . *ugh*.

─────

Subject: re: everything ok?
Date: Mon, 26 Apr 2010 6:26 AM
From: Lisa
To: Mark

She definitely caught enough of your vibe to understand why I know and
love you. It sounds like the circumstances were not ideal.

So in the end did you come across the reason they were there? Why you
created *that* night?

_____
Subject: re: everything ok?
Date: Mon, 26 Apr 2010 6:44 AM
From: Mark
To: Lisa

I'll have to get back to you on that: House waking up.

Later.

_____
Subject: winechat
Date: Mon, 26 Apr 2010 6:10 PM
From: Mark
To: Lisa

Home now. You there?

_____
Subject: pergo-tory
Date: Mon, 26 Apr 2010 8:59 PM
From: Mark
To: Lisa

Glad we got to chat . . . "juju girls" . . . that was so funny, it bent me in
half, laughing . . .

(I'm riffing now . . . no idea what's coming . . . winechat mode still in
effect. Girls gone for an hour, so I'm with *you* now . . .) As to the reason I
created that evening . . .

Contact. Stimulation. Memories. Attraction. Possibilities. Alcohol. Time,
space . . . new faces, old faces, familiar faces, desire, hope,
disappointment, joy, music, connection, food, alone, waiting, support,
pain, letting go . . . ah, yes . . . letting go . . . letting go . . .

"Letting go of outcomes" . . . So in one respect I cast a fistful of Rune
stones that evening . . . didn't pull any one in particular . . . which now
makes me think that the evening could be considered *The Night of the
Blank Rune*: any number of events or outcomes were possible, and
regardless of the number of options available that evening, I forced
nothing, tried to make *nothing* go my way. I brought all these people
before me just to see what might come of it. No pre-determined outcome,
no forcing of my will, just being with what was happening in front of me,
and making all my decisions in the present moment, available and ready
for anything, then making choices based on what was happening. I could
go with the flow, or insert my influence to effort a desired outcome. I
chose the former, all night long.

Result? By not exerting my influence to create a specific outcome, I ended up being with my Self. The two of us went out for some fish tacos, and ate them while yearning for some contact.

So why not *create* contact? I could have, right?

Well, I made myself available for contact, and there *was* some, but it didn't satisfy. Unconsciously the need was deeper. Hanging out in a noisy techno bar - The Pergo Club - didn't feed any part of me. The people who seemed to be OK with Pergo Bar ended up not being people I could hang with for very long, and THAT makes sense. I wouldn't consider them the Pergo Clan, but they lost me - no, *I dropped out* - because of the Pergo *scene* they had gravitated to.

So I pulled myself out of pergo-tory and went off to find some fish tacos at The Brazilian Cherrywood Room. And nobody followed me there.

I created the evening in hopes of making deep connections, while being conscious of not forcing an outcome. Options for deep connections were few, and the one significant possibility for connection - Melissa - had aligned herself with a Pergo-tolerant tribe. No reflection on her, mind you, but I just can't do Pergo for more than a few minutes.

_____
Subject: re: pergo-tory
Date: Mon, 26 Apr 2010 9:27 PM
From: Lisa
To: Mark

Nice word . . . pergo-tory.

Contact. Stimulation. Memories. Attraction. Possibilities. Alcohol. Time, space, . . . new faces, old faces, familiar faces, desire, hope, disappointment, joy, music, connection, food, alone, waiting, support, pain, letting go . . .

Hmmm . . . that sounds just like a recent week *I* spent with you . . .

_____
Subject: re: pergo-tory
Date: Mon, 26 Apr 2010 9:27 PM
From: Mark
To: Lisa

yup. the original juju girl . . .

_____
Subject: re: pergo-tory

Date: Tue, 27 Apr 2010 5:30 AM
From: Lisa
To: Mark

I need to finish our phone conversation today if we can. Things left unsaid.
My upset over your casual remarks about what might have happened if
you were alone with my friend, on the heels of all the lovely time we just
spent together, well, there's more for me to say about how that made me
feel. See what you can do, OK?

_____

Subject: re: pergo-tory
Date: Tue, 27 Apr 2010 5:51 AM
From: Mark
To: Lisa

Sure. I'll make a point of knocking off work by 3:30 or 4 today.

_____

Subject: home now
Date: Tue, 27 Apr 2010 4:43 PM
From: Mark
To: Lisa

OK . . . Let's do this.

_____

Subject: Hey
Date: Wed, 28 Apr 2010 4:22 PM
From: Lisa
To: Mark

A lot has been said and while I sort out my feelings I want you to know
that yours matter to me, too.

Are things gonna be weird with us now for you?

_____

Subject: re: Hey
Date: Wed, 28 Apr 2010 8:15 PM
From: Mark
To: Lisa

yup.

_____

Subject: re: Hey
Date: Wed, 28 Apr 2010 8:26 PM
From: Lisa
To: Mark

Seems we have an opportunity to lose something or to gain something. Is that all you want to say?

_____
Subject: re: Hey
Date: Wed, 28 Apr 2010 8:49 PM
From: Lisa
To: Mark

Yeah, for now. Gonna bury myself in work for a few days . . .

twenty-six

Subject: wanna chat?
Date: Fri, 7 May 2010 7:22 PM
From: Mark
To: Lisa

give a call if you get this before 9:30 your time . . .

_____
Subject: I'll send this in the meantime
Date: Fri, 7 May 2010 7:23 PM
From: Mark
To: Lisa

(written 6:00am this morning)

I don't even know where to start . . . or what to say. Swear to God, I don't. Even now I'm just typing without a clue as to what's coming next, but there's this version of me - the one you had breakfast with in San Mateo in April – who's fully aware there's something really wrong here. One day LGwO and CwHH are making plans for world domination and the next day Mark and Lisa are at an impasse over . . . *what?* Nearly two weeks go by and I still can't tell you what it is exactly that had me dropping out, to step back and wait, fully expecting that within a few days it would come to me why things should be so different after trying to sort out feelings of hurt, anger, trust, expectations and . . . and *what?* Savannah walked in on the middle of our sorting process and suddenly I had to hang up. Not being able to stay with the conversation and find some sort of resolution turned out to be a huge mistake. My belief that answers and understanding would float to the surface in a day or two was wrong. It never happened. I swear to God, Lisa, absolutely nothing came up to inform me, guide me, or help me make sense of what happened during that phone call. Three, then four days passed, and I still didn't know what I wanted to say to you. It was very, very weird.

(7:20 pm)

Just sent you an email, asking you to call . . .

_____
Subject: re: wanna chat?
Date: Fri, 7 May 2010 7:41 PM
From: Lisa
To: Mark

just got your message . . . offer still on?

_____
Subject: re: wanna chat?
Date: Fri, 7 May 2010 7:43 PM
From: Mark
To: Lisa

oh yeah. Christ, but I miss you . . .

_____
Subject:
Date: Sat, 8 May 2010 5:58 AM
From: Mark
To: Lisa

Trailering a horse for someone early this morning . . . a quick fifty bucks, and a break from my daily routine. Also: horses, and some alone time to write while waiting to return to our barn. Done by 10am or so.

Not enough time here to tell the story of Thursday's mental earthquake. Foundation still intact, but geez, what a fuckin' mess.

Felt much better after our chat last night, only to have the evening ruined by yet another . . . *ugh* . . . never mind.

Off to pre-dawn horse thingy. :)

_____
Subject: re:
Date: Sat, 8 May 2010 6:09 AM
From: Lisa
To: Mark

Tell me more about the quake or save it for a chat. Cold day here . . . good for clearing stuff to get ready for the garage sale, do Zac's grad party invites, cook.

The picture is from last weekend with Mom & my sister at a family event. Nice one.

_____
Subject: re:
Date: Sat, 8 May 2010 10:28 AM
From: Mark
To: Lisa

Love the pic. Nice vibe. Everybody happy.

The quake: too strong a metaphor for my headspace that day. More like . . . uh . . . being too hard on myself, and guilt-tripping myself for not being more productive with my time that day. Wrote about it this morning at the horse thingy, and realized I mentally talked myself into a depression, instead of cutting myself some slack for the stressful and problematic two weeks I'd been under the spell of. Keeping my chin up, looking for the perks and the silver lining in a very difficult and challenging remodel was like being in some kind of spiritual gym: *No pain, no gain.* Best part of the day was driving away.

_____
Subject: re: I'll send this in the meantime
Date: Sat, 8 May 2010 10:49 AM
From: Lisa
To: Mark

A couple things come up as I read what you sent last night about not having answers come to the surface *easily* . . .

First, there are no easy answers to a complicated situation. Whatever guide you follow that leads you to drop out is not a nice guide. Sorting it out by yourself may not be what needs to happen. We need to sort it out *between* us.

Yes, all those things you mention have come into question . . . hurt, anger, trust, expectations. I have pondered them all by myself these couple weeks. I wished after we hung up last night that I had had more time to share that. Much more to say. The changes in me as a result are good for me, maybe you, too.

Let's continue talking . . .

_____

Subject: re: I'll send this in the meantime
Date: Sat, 8 May 2010 12:35 PM
From: Mark
To: Lisa

Yeah, well, great. Here comes the adjustment period of getting used to the new tone of this relationship. Looking forward to when these *changes* have had their full effect . . . whatever that turns out to be.

Fuck.

_____
Subject: re:
Date: Sat, 8 May 2010 2:11 PM
From: Lisa
To: Mark

Huh? C'mon, change can be good. Let's talk.

_____
Subject: re:
Date: Sat, 8 May 2010 4:21 PM
From: Lisa
To: Mark

I gotta be honest . . . your email is really bothering me. It feels like there was a context that you read into my note that I didn't mean to convey. It's like you're angry at me again. So, whatever tone you hear, would you please tell me what it is because I really didn't intend to send a bad vibe. In fact, after our conversation last night I was feeling good about reconnecting with you. You were the one who went away, remember? I know this may not be an easy weekend to get time to yourself, so when you can please reply and if a call can happen, that would be great. You said it best: we didn't really get to finish the conversation that ended so abruptly a couple weeks ago . . .

I hate this, too.

L

_____
Subject: re:
Date: Sat, 8 May 2010 9:21 PM
From: Mark
To: Lisa

Just now getting some alone time . . .

I'm not angry at you. Sorry you had to wait so long to hear it.

268

It's the tone, the adjustment, the newness of the re-set . . . It's a setback for me. I just need to deal with it, that's all. *It's here. deal with it.* So . . . I'm dealing with it. Therefore: *fuck.*

The cautiousness, the stepping lightly, the monitoring of thoughts, the choice of words and their repercussions . . . and yes, yes, yes, no easy answers to complicated situations, yada-yada . . .

I'm just venting for two - no, wait, *three* - reasons: three weeks of a sucky remodel company; a big reset with you; and the woman I share a house with. *grrrr* . . .

I blame the moon. Another week and a half til the new moon, a cosmic reset. In the meantime: a period of adjustment, realignment, and the hashing out of things. *After enlightenment, the laundry.*

Plus, there's a whole thing about the I Ching that came up a couple of days ago, about the need to step into the role of being a leader, guide, and inspiration for others.

I'm smack in the middle of losing confidence that all this stuff taking place right now is headed for some higher, better place. That's my depression talking, mind you, and these last several days of going in and out of feeling confident - and then pessimistic - have me yearning for a gifted therapist, a sign from God, and/or an evening of hedonistic sex.

The inside of my head is a terrifying place these days . . .

_____
Subject: re:
Date: Sat, 8 May 2010 10:19 PM
From: Lisa
To: Mark

Lots to say, yes. The re-set? I really need to talk it out more with you. I can't do eggshells either. We need to finish that conversation.

I know a good therapist in the East Bay. I'll check in with her if you're interested. What if the sign from God is the change you resist that will lead you to the higher, better place as an inspirational leader? You can end up isolated, or put yourself out there. Your choice. And the evening of hedonistic sex? Well, I could use one of those myself.

All this to say that there are options and answers buried in the drama , the misery, the waiting, the sorting. All is being revealed, Mark. All that is good is worth waiting for, fighting for, fixing, choosing boldly. Stepping into the role means . . . taking steps. Baby ones, all the time. And yes, how you are living is a big part of your problem. *Big.* The sucky job doesn't help either but it's easier to leave.

_____

Subject: mornin'
Date: Sun, 9 May 2010 5:59 AM
From: Lisa
To: Mark

A new day. . . :)

_____

Subject: re: mornin'
Date: Sun, 9 May 2010 6:00 AM
From: Mark
To: Lisa

amen, sista . . .

_____

Subject: mornin'
Date: Sun, 9 May 2010 6:07 AM
From: Lisa
To: Mark

Can we talk like us for a minute . . . no *cautiousness, stepping lightly, monitoring of thoughts . . .?*

_____

Subject: Re: I'll send this in the meantime . . .
Date: Sun, 9 May 2010 6:47 AM
From: Mark
To: Lisa

yeah, writing you right now . . .

Am I resisting change? I thought I was just pissed about the timing of it.

The gist of the message from the I Ching was *Innocence*: Let go, let things be, the Universe has the first move, etc. It was a blissful moment when I threw the I Ching that day, which, by the way, was in the middle of my absence, and partly a reaching out to comprehend what was going on with me. I was home alone, spent a few hours cleaning my room and desk space, then I sat at my neatly-ordered desk for an hour, with my journal and the I Ching. It came out in my writing that, for an hour, I had exactly the life I wanted: A quiet home in the 'country' with lots of open space, and the freedom - for an hour or so - to use this quiet time any way I wanted. And there I was, completely absorbed in my 'studies', literally studying my relationship to the world and the people in my life. That's when I threw the

I Ching. It was awesome. It was the last time I felt happy and contented . .
.

So I took the message to heart. And since that day I've been doing a lot of letting go, trying not to manipulate events to my will, but paying attention to open doors and opportunities . . . and impulses that won't quiet down. Like asking you to call, so we can begin to rebuild.

Subject: mornin'
Date: Sun, 9 May 2010 6:50 AM
From: Lisa
To: Mark

Look, I missed you, too. And what I missed is precisely what I am hearing you say has *changed*: talking easily about everything, having each other's back, being in sync and connected like we are. The changes that have happened for me didn't diminish that. It honors it. We haven't even gotten to that part in our conversation and I need to ask if you know when you might be able to talk. There is a reason that we are coming to this place *now* . . .

Here's the thing: not talking to you at all was better than thinking we are now in an abbreviated, eggshells place. I want to hear 99% of what you are thinking in your terrifying head. Uncensored. Our relationship has become what it is now because it *changed* over the years. I think of all we would have missed if we had just stayed the buddies we used to be in the 80's. Would you trade all that for the comfort of telling me any thought that comes into your head about my friends without any consequence? For that 1% of what I prefer you keep to yourself?

We will keep growing and that changes us, individually and with each other. *We* define who we are. The lines had gotten pretty blurry between us and I found out where my line in the sand is, what I can live with and what I can't. I may not have had a right to get so upset but I felt the way I did and was glad I could speak up about it to be true to myself.

It's all for a reason. That's all I know. We can't go backwards, and I wouldn't want to. But the step back was good. And hearing your voice the other night was good, too. We have reached a precipice that oversees all that we have journeyed through on our way here. As I make my way back home to California, what our relationship looks like needs to be defined. It doesn't need to be a *certain way*, it just needs to be clear for both of us where we stand so that we are both honored, supported, and true.

Subject: re: mornin'
Date: Sun, 9 May 2010 6:54 AM

From: Mark
To: Lisa

Excellent. well said.

_____
Subject: Re: I'll send this in the meantime . . .
Date: Sun, 9 May 2010 6:59 AM
From: Lisa
To: Mark

I agree with the letting go and yet there needs to be some sort of action to get you out of the stuck place like you were last night . . . *the job* . . . *the wife* . . . the same place you talked of five years ago exactly. It breaks my heart for you. The non-efforting only goes so far before you must take a step towards the change, the new life. The leader needs to step onto the path and walk forward.

_____
Subject: re: mornin'
Date: Sun, 9 May 2010 7:00 AM
From: Mark
To: Lisa

YES!

_____
Subject: Re: mornin'
Date: Sun, 9 May 2010 7:07 AM
From: Lisa
To: Mark

I think of all we would have missed if we had just stayed the buddies we used to be in the '80's. Would you trade all that?

You know, I have this sense that you might wish we could go back to just being the friends we used to be . . .

_____
Subject: re: mornin'
Date: Sun, 9 May 2010 7:10 AM
From: Mark
To: Lisa

Uh-oh . . . We are so not on the same page. Never had that thought. Not once.

twenty-seven

Subject: Lucky Mom with Great Son
Date: Sun, 9 May 2010 8:58 AM
From: Lisa
To: Mark

Aww . . . Zac brought me a bear and roses of every color for Mother's Day.

_____

Subject: pages. . .
Date: Sun, 9 May 2010 3:11 PM
From: Lisa
To: Mark

So, I have been thinking about being on the same page, and what page that might be. I have come to believe it might be found in *Bridge Across Forever*, like maybe in chapter 32 when Leslie gives Richard the 'out' to be just friends. Not because she wants to, but to be fair, given how she can't be really okay about his other women and still be true to herself. Or page 356, that's a great page. You'll like it, too. I am reading it with new, older and wiser eyes, and I love it even more. I love them.

If you pull out the book to read that chapter and page, as I suspect you will, read the foreword that Richard wrote at the very beginning. The last paragraph made me smile, as if written for us. We've walked through these pages together for decades . . . maybe not always on the same page but at least in the *same book*.

_____

Subject: re: pages. . .
Date: Mon, 10 May 2010 5:33 AM
From: Mark
To: Lisa

What's up with Austin, Texas? Any bells go off when I ask you that? Big, out-of-the-blue hit of Austin yesterday. Took my mom to see *Wicked* in S.F. for Mother's Day. What a blast. I sat next to a guy who lit me up about Austin.

_____

Subject: re: pages. . .
Date: Mon, 10 May 2010 5:43 AM
From: Lisa

To: Mark

Austin . . .Wizard Academy. Funny, since you were off to see the Wizard.

Subject: got phone?
Date: Mon, 10 May 2010 6:25 PM
From: Mark
To: Lisa

call me

Subject: article
Date: Tue, 11 May 2010 4:51 AM
From: Lisa
To: Mark

Check out this article about Living Out Loud. I loved it.

Subject: re: article
Date: Tue, 11 May 2010 5:38 AM
From: Mark
To: Lisa

There's been a black and white picture on my dresser for years of my dad holding one-year-old me on his lap; there's a big smile on my face as he's looking down on me. Stuck to the glass at the bottom of the frame is a cut-out of some words I put there years ago, which reads: *If you ask me why I came here, I will tell you: I came to live out loud.*

Chat tonight very possible. I should be home b'twn 5-6 CA time.

Subject: got wisdom?
Date: Wed, 12 May 2010 11:48 AM
From: Lisa
To: Mark

More frustration with my realtor . . . agonizing while purging my stuff. . . need more comfort than a handful of dark chocolate espresso beans could provide.

Subject: re: got wisdom?
Date: Wed, 12 May 2010 6:26 PM
From: Mark
To: Lisa

Ah, grasshopper . . . the wheel turns, but the spokes move not . . .

. . . when one is at one with All That Is, one becomes the oneness that permeates all the oneness that there is . . .

. . . as the grass grows to meet the enthusiasm of the cow's teeth, the wine in my glass rushes toward the oblivion that holds within it the juju which only those of the JuJu Tribe can know.

Subject: hey there
Date: Thu, 13 May 2010 5:41 AM
From: Lisa
To: Mark

LOL ahh . . . what a trip it all is. Stormy here, and cold. Good burrow-under-the-covers morning.

OK, so I fired our realtors and hired the older ladies Mom liked. They will list on Craigslist and anywhere I want, do a bilingual flyer to hand out and do an open house. LGwO has arrived and taken over :-) All systems are *go* . . .

Subject: Have a nice day. . .
Date: Sat, 15 May 2010 2:01 PM
From: Mark
To: Lisa

Well now, things can change dramatically in an instant, can't they?

Got 3 hours sleep after the Thursday nite gig w/ the blues band. Had an 8am meeting w/ one of my new customers on Friday morning. A bit nervous about whether or not she'd go for my estimate. She said yes to everything right away, and gave me a deposit to get things started. *Bang!*

Went to my 2nd new customer nearby and dialed in the details and estimate for all I'll do there. Big job, plenty of cool, tricky, artsy carpentry for six weeks. Good gig. *Bang!*

Then . . . *ugh* . . . time to get paid from Mike, which is always a *negotiation* because of his, um, unique style of bookkeeping: I tell him what he owes me, and he tries to pay me less.

The first half-hour was him behind his desk, me sitting across from him, haggling over money he owed me. Soon we're off into the problems and inefficiencies of his company. I'm so clear about where the problems are I hold back nothing, reminding him of the three times I've offered to help fix things, but he blew me off. At this point in our talk he's beside himself with stress, rubbing his face in his hands, going out of his mind reminding himself of all the shit that's wrong and how nearly a million bucks a year (!) is being wasted on various things.

Now he's asking me to step up and help him. *Now* he's realizing that I just might be the guy he's needed all this time. *Now* he's pushing on me a bit to say yes but I have to tell him it's too little, too late: I'm booked with my own good-paying jobs for the next month or three, thank you very much, sorry buddy. And by the way, the salary you're offering me to help slay your dragons ain't gonna cut it.

45 minutes have passed. The bank closes in an hour, and I need my money.

I finally get from him *most* of the money he owes me, and then . . .

I tell him about people and integrity and having heart and *you and I aren't done yet*, and don't worry about anything because the people you need to turn this around are on their way to you, and I'm probably going to be one of them but not for a couple of months, and here's the number of the one guy I know and trust who MIGHT be willing to work with you to turn your company around. He calls the number right away, leaves a message about how I'm sitting there with him, and to call back because he thinks we can all work something out . . .

I get up to leave, but before I go I stick my neck out a bit, and tell him to lean on his faith a little more, and to ask God to send him the people and the resources he needs to bail him out . . . and then to let it go.

So, just before I left, he said he felt relaxed for the first time in months. He seemed bewildered. I told him that from this moment on his company was pointed in a new direction, and that everything was going to be fine, saying:

"When you come to work tomorrow, don't give this stuff a second thought, and don't burden yourself with what to do about any of it. Ask God for help, let the rest go, and handle whatever is in front of you at the moment to the best of your ability. The rest will take care of itself. The people and the answers you need are already on their way."

He came out from behind his desk and hugged me . . .

Cashed the check. Paid my electrician. Collected Mariah and Savannah and went out for dinner. Got home, went to bed, and slept for eight hours, the first time in months . . .

Then this morning I get a call from the one guy I trust and care about in this business, whose number I'd given to Mike. He's interested, he says, but only if he'd get to work with me (neither one of us wants the gig by ourselves). He said he wanted to talk with me more about it on Monday, and we both agreed to think about it some more.

Awesome.

So I ended my day with a decent-size check made out to me, two months worth of good-paying side jobs ahead, an offer to help turn a company around with a team of guys who, together, could *absolutely* pull it off, and the witnessing of my boss' transformation from stressed and burdened CEO to grateful everyman.

All in all, not a bad day.

_____
Subject: re: Have a nice day. . .
Date: Sat, 15 May 2010 2:38 PM
From: Lisa
To: Mark

Just getting to your email now . . .

I signed with the new agents. They are psyched to sell my house so I am in the Bay Area by 8/15. In fact, we had the contract only go for 90 days as that is all I will need them for to make that happen.

You *rock.*

When I got to the part where you completely transformed your boss's world *with your words* . . . I let out a big, deep throaty YES! (big grinning over here as I write this!) I can feel a really cool buzz going on inside, *feeling* your joy and the power rising up in your soul, and oh man, it feels really good to be reading this.

The brokering of these guys to turn this company around, and the knowledge that you can be as much a part of it *as you want,* and do all the other great, kick-ass work you will do for good money, fuels your ability to have choices. How does it feel to get what you want?

Yes, things sure can change dramatically in an instant. *Shit happens yes, but cool shit happens, too.*

_____
Subject: re: Have a nice day. . .
Date: Sat, 15 May 2010 5:55 PM
From: Mark

To: Lisa

It was hard trying to convey in an email what took place in the talk with my boss. I was in there for well over an hour, and the shift from where we started to where we ended up was just this beautiful, beautiful thing. I wish you could have been a fly on the wall to witness the transition.

The weird, sad part about that whole event in the office: I started relating the story to Mariah later during dinner, but never got to the magic part of the story because she interrupted me with her low opinion of him, and after a couple of tries I let it go. She just couldn't hook into what was special about my meeting with him. I never got far enough into the story for her to *get it,* and celebrate the great things that are yet to come.

It was hard having to wait so long to relate the story to you . . .

_____
Subject: re: Have a nice day. . .
Date: Sat, 15 May 2010 6:03 PM
From: Lisa
To: Mark

You're invoking your magic. I love that you couldn't wait to share it with me. Can't wait to hear you tell me more . . . *magic-chat.* We can celebrate the great things to come . . .

_____
Subject: re: Have a nice day. . .
Date: Sat, 15 May 2010 7:34 PM
From: Mark
To: Lisa

Be sure to seek out and drink: Grassi Cabernet, 2005, Napa valley . . . best wine I've had in quite some time. A gift from the remodel customers.

Savannah's being dropped off at a movie, meeting up with girlfriends after a long frustrating day for her of clipping (shaving and grooming) a high-spirited horse. Grilled gorgonzola/mushroom hamburgers, and made french fries from the red potatoes I pulled out of the garden 10 minutes earlier. *Hell yeah . . .*

Magic-chat . . . that's one for the juju book . . .

gotta go

_____
Subject: re: Have a nice day. . .
Date: Sat, 15 May 2010 8:05 PM
From: Lisa

To: Mark

ughhhhh . . . I want to hang here longer, enjoy it.

Savor the wine . . . *magic-chat* soon . . . logging in the juju book for later .
. .

What you did with your boss was the ultimate stepping up, Mark . . . into
who you are, why you are here and where you are headed. You are *That
Guy.*

You know, we came to this brink, right? Where something shifted and it
felt really jolting, and then *awful,* for a time? As much as we both hated it -
differently - returning from it has brought us another level deeper in
knowing each other, I think. Closer maybe. You feel that, too? Like God
knew we needed something to remind us about the *magic* . . .

_____
Subject: Dot connecting
Date: Sun, 16 May 2010 7:30 AM
From: Mark
To: Lisa

In my little rant a week or so ago I remember being pissed off that, even
though the changes were *probably* a good thing, I had yet to be in the zone
where I trusted it, welcomed it, and could embrace it. *I fucked it up!* etc . . .

But now, with time, talk, and transmutation, I can look backwards and see
how the dots connect.

So, yeah: closer.

_____
Subject: re: Dot connecting
Date: Sun, 16 May 2010 7:38 AM
From: Lisa
To: Mark

Yeah, right? It feels good, really does.

Gorgeous day. I'll get a good walk in today. Cooking dinner with Zac as he
asked to me to get skirt steak and limes to make something he wants to
cook. God, I love him. Magic chat *soon* . . . I got used to the phone time
and liked it.

_____
Subject: re: Dot connecting
Date: Sun, 16 May 2010 7:45 AM
From: Mark

To: Lisa

Yeah, phonechat tomorrow. Today I'll be at a horse show all day then a gig in SF with the horn band at 8.

Skirt steak and limes . . . Oh, yeah. Tribe food. Good boy.

twenty-eight

Subject: More dot connecting
Date: Sun, 16 May 2010 8:54 PM
From: Lisa
To: Mark

I am reading John Welwood's *Journey of the Heart: Intimate Relationship and the Path of Love,* the book you gave me 20 years ago in your Survival Kit gift when I left California. Whoa. I read it so long ago, and I was so different then. It's like reading it for the first time. As I skim through it I see that it has surfaced often in two decades: yellow highlights appear on pages where the wound of abandonment is addressed and validated, a salve for me in times while healing from my own. Pencil markings written by Jimmy, when I was leaving him, with starred paragraphs in the chapter Warrior of the Heart. At the end of the chapter he wrote: *I want to be a warrior of the heart.* I was already living back in Chicago when I discovered that comment. It was too late of course, and it was already too late when he wrote it.

He was never going to be the man I would live out my life with, yet it was comforting to know he picked it up that day to try and understand the realities of love. I wonder if he would have read the book had he remembered it was from you. He tore up an 8x10 photo of you and me taken years ago. I found it in a box recently in four jagged pieces, and actually taped it together. He never understood our friendship.

So while lying in bed last night I was reading about the nature of path, creating space and welcoming awareness . . . yeah, yeah, yeah . . . Relationship 101 stuff, yet beautiful in its reminder that love is not easy and when we resist that truth we suffer more. When we give up the notion that it *should* be easy and we allow love's rough edges and rawness, we experience the wonder that loving someone deeply opens up.

My heart, wide open from your story about your boss and how it affected him *and* you, wanted more - the graduate-level love stuff - I wanted to be on *that page*. I took a breath, closed my eyes, and randomly opened the book to a beautiful passage about male power and a man's ability to act on convictions based in truth. When a man brings *that* power into relationship he brings, " . . . a strong, steadying influence that allows a woman to relax and blossom."

Ahhh.

OK, now we're talkin' . . .

When I opened that lovely gift from you 20 years ago - "one of the best gifts ever" I have said many, many times - we were sitting in the same room beside our future spouses, not knowing what journey of the heart *really* lie ahead for us.

_____
Subject: Notes from the Cool Mom files?
Date: Sun, 16 May 2010 11:10 PM
From: Lisa
To: Mark

A box of a dozen cool condoms: $7

A teen baby mama: Thousands of $$ and control of your life

Being able to show your Mom the box of cool condoms and laugh about it: priceless

OK, so Zac comes home with his friend Jessica and says, "Mom, you have to see this box of condoms. It's hilarious!"

OK, Zac . . . Sure, show me.

He proceeds to open this cool looking tin that says ONE on top. In it are a dozen round condoms with graphics on each and clever names like: ONE time at Band Camp (with a picture of a saxophone) ONE with Nature (florescent green) . . .

It was hilarious. I wrote all the names in the juju book. How cool that he felt comfortable enough to share that with me (it may be really inappropriate of me, but I don't know or care). Then he made us dinner, rocking the Tribal skirt steak. We hung out watching Glee on her laptop. It was really great. I will miss him a lot. Yet, it's all OK. I am reveling in the moments we are having now. I'm ready to let go; he's ready to go out in the world. A man with the keys to his life . . . and a box of very cool condoms. Geez.

_____
Subject: re: More dot connecting
Date: Mon, 17 May 2010 6:54 AM
From: Mark
To: Lisa

house awake. check in later. don't respond to this.

great emails, by the way! phonechat coming . . .

_____
Subject: Mornin'
Date: Tue, 18 May 2010 5:39 AM
From: Mark
To: Lisa

About the book I gave you and how it's hitting you now: I like the bits from the book about the masculine and feminine dynamic. Bittersweet story of Jimmy's efforts to embrace the warrior-of-the-heart ethic.

And it's great to hear how different things are with the new agents re: your house. I'll try again tonight for phonechat.

_____
Subject: re: mornin'
Date: Tue, 18 May 2010 5:50 AM
From: Lisa
To: Mark

That was such an interesting "random" page to turn to. Nice stuff. Yeah, I would love a phonechat. Feels like a while since the last one. All good over here. Lots of clients yesterday, more today. Off Wed/Thurs to work on the house. Dave coming today to finish ceiling fix and then I will paint it tomorrow. Weird energy there; he has barely called since you resurfaced and I think he gets it that *I'm gone*.

_____
Subject: got phone?
Date: Tue, 18 May 2010 5:29 PM
From: Mark
To: Lisa

Hey . . . wanna winechat?

_____
Subject: re: got phone?

Date: Tue, 18 May 2010 8:15 PM
From: Lisa
To: Mark

OK, a loose end that we didn't get to on our call . . .

What you said to me is true: my connection to you is deeper than just showing you who you are, over and over. I don't fully understand it, but I am willing to honor it. I'm here by myself a lot and think about that, especially after our calls that end too soon when there is so much more to say.

_____
Subject: hey
Date: Wed, 19 May 2010 5:51 PM
From: Mark
To: Lisa

Nice chat last night, and yeah, just got started. Too short . . . but big fun.

Gotta run. More tonight, maybe. Long day tomorrow: after work, a gig in SF, so I'll go straight to the gig from the job, then up early Friday again.

Off to shine some light . . .

_____
Subject: contemplate this one
Date: Wed, 19 May 2010 5:51 AM
From: Lisa
To: Mark

Look up your birthday from the site for the book *The Secret Language of Birthdays* . . . wow

_____
Subject: re: contemplate this one
Date: Thu, 20 May 2010 5:35 AM
From: Mark
To: Lisa

Wow is right . . . Holy shit . . . That birthday thing is awesome. Send me yours, too.

_____
Subject: re: contemplate this one
Date: Thu, 20 May 2010 2:55 PM
From: Lisa
To: Mark

The guys who wrote the birthday book, Gary Goldschneider and Joost

Elffers, have *Secret Language of Relationships*, too. I ordered it today. Should be interesting.

Weird day. Painting ceilings (I hate painting), cleaning floors (I hate cleaning), laundry (hate too strong a word for laundry, but . . . not fun exactly) Emotions all over the place; Zac pushing limits of how cool he wants me to be *(Can I have a beer pong tournament at our house, Mom, please? There will be designated drivers.* Uh, I don't think so. *We'll stay in the garage, no one in the house.* Uh . . . no, I don't think so. *But, Mom!) Argh.*

Feeling out of sorts, restless yet lethargic. I want to get on with it all already. And the next minute, I just want to take a nap. I am taking care of everything and everyone. That's OK but it would be nice to be taken care *of*, too.

Are we having some whine with that winechat?

Uh, yeah.

―――――

Subject: hey, psssst . . . . . wanna?
Date: Fri, 21 May 2010 7:17 PM
From: Mark
To: Lisa

. . . chat?

―――――
Subject: re: hey, psssst . . . . . wanna?
Date: Fri, 21 May 2010 10:54 PM
From: Lisa
To: Mark

Per your suggestion, I listened to Antoine Dufour while I let our conversation sink in. Writing in my journal, trying to remember what I said just before you said, *You have a lot to write about.*

Let go.

I know, I know.

I listen for a while to the Swell Season, then, wanting to hear *Falling Slowly*, I put that title in Pandora as a station . . . and . . . that's it. With each song the tears come . . . the answers come and *I let go* . . .

―――――
Subject: re: hey, psssst . . . . . wanna?

Date: Sat, 22 May 2010 7:18 AM
From: Mark
To: Lisa

So . . . got answers?

_____

Subject: re: hey, psssst . . . . . wanna?
Date: Sat, 22 May 2010 7:30 AM
From: Lisa
To: Mark

kinda, I guess . . . I'm even more emotional today.

_____

Subject: hey, psssst . . . . . wanna?
Date: Sat, 22 May 2010 7:37 AM
From: Mark
To: Lisa

Teachat?

_____

Subject: re: So...got answers?
Date: Sun, 23 May 2010 3:08 AM
From: Mark
To: Lisa

3 am . . . just home from the Napa gig. Should be up around 8.

_____

Subject: found a bit of my birthday meaning
Date: Sun, 23 May 2010 8:43 AM
From: Lisa
To: Mark

Day of The Hellraiser: Deeply meaningful . . . gritty determination . .
crushing defeats . . . indomitable spirit. . .

_____

Subject: re: found a bit of my birthday meaning
Date: Sun, 23 May 2010 9:55 AM
From: Mark
To: Lisa

Sounds like someone I know . . .

House awake now. Won't be able to hang til later.

Picture of my girl from her prom . . .

_____

Subject: re: prom pic
Date: Sun, 23 May 2010 10:18 AM
From: Lisa
To: Mark

Wow . . . gorgeous. Zac's is next week . . . same colors, only he picked a
white shirt with his tux.

_____
Subject: re: prom pic
Date: Sun, 23 May 2010 10:28 AM
From: Mark
To: Lisa

Yeah, Savannah looked amazing. I don't see her boyfriend very much, but
not until I uploaded the pics did I notice something about him that bugs
me: his eyes. In most of the pics where he's looking into the camera, his
eyes look . . . dead . . . or something. They had a good time though, and
got home on time. All seems well. She's headed for the barn soon, but is
being picked up by a friend.

How was your chat w/ Kathy?

_____
Subject: mornin'
Date: Mon, 24 May 2010 5:43 AM
From: Lisa
To: Mark

You see a phonechat today? I would love to finish the thread from
yesterday. I have some good juju for you from Kathy :-)

_____
Subject: re: mornin'
Date: Mon, 24 May 2010 5:52 AM
From: Mark
To: Lisa

Mornin' . . .

Yeah, phonechat should happen. I go back to Job From Hell today to do
some loose end stuff, so I doubt it will be a long or full day. Can't wait to
hear all about juju. I've been on another page registering for the
Mendocino men's retreat in August.

Gray and misty here this morning. Rains keep comin' and goin', keeping
things green longer than usual. Had a 'moment' yesterday: shaking out rugs
over the back fence, looking out onto the open, green pasture, breeze
blowing the tall grasses with a lovely hissing sound . . . I paused, leaned on

the fence, and stood there with this idiotic grin on my face . . .

Good shit.

Spent all day yesterday doing house and yard work. Lovely, idyllic spring day. Good vibes with music and cooperation, only to have it fall apart on the way to see *Robin Hood* at the end of the day when . . . *ugh* . . . tell you later.

_____
Subject: re: mornin'
Date: Mon, 24 May 2010 5:56 AM
From: Lisa
To: Mark

I did yard work too, and spent much of the day out in 80-degree sunshine. Nice. Cool about the retreat. It fits the juju story well . . .

Light day for me, more sunshine. I will take another walk/jog on my creek trail (about 2.5 miles). I will miss that spot, a short walk from my door but the SF Bay, redwood trails and rolling hills seem way better.

_____
Subject: sheesh. . . finally
Date: Mon, 24 May 2010 5:52 PM
From: Mark
To: Lisa

Just got in. Ringy-dingy?

_____
Subject: probably will be mornin'. . .
Date: Mon, 24 May 2010 8:42 PM
From: Lisa
To: Mark

Hey, so before I go up to bed I wanted to download the rest of the juice from our phone call . . . all those cool, good, true vibes. Nice stuff. Really *good.* Feels like another layer of breakthrough happened today, feeling right and real and on track. You are so a part of it, Mark. It makes me happy that you are in this with me. It was impossible to know when we met those many years ago what was ahead . . . and yet, we knew . . . *something.* I feel blessed, and as you have said, *called,* to use my voice for the good of many, to wake them up. Thank you for waking *me* up that first week I arrived in the Land of Oz. Without the Wizard, Dorothy was lost. She needed a force to bring her along the Yellow Brick Road. I wouldn't be who I am without you in my life.

you are loved.

twenty-nine

Subject: here I am
Date: Tue, 25 May 2010 6:48 AM
From: Mark
To: Lisa

Went for a walk w/ Mariah last night and talked to her from *that place*: clear, truthful, grounded, unemotional, suggesting she practice more loving kindness. I threw the I Ching before getting in bed . . .

I was about to include the journal entry I wrote this morning about the conversation we had, but . . . *nah*. I will say, though, that the last few things I said to her really had an effect. She hasn't spoken to me since. The I Ching, by the way, was in answer to a general question about the day and evening: *Given the current state of affairs in my life, what is the correct action for me now?*

#20, *Contemplation*, and # 64, *Before the End* . . .

Subject: re: here I am
Date: Tue, 25 May 2010 11:35 AM
From: Lisa

To: Mark

Wow. Yeah, that was right on, that reading. You are ready, my friend, for the changes you have been asking for. Nothing short of divinity is at work. That's how it goes. It's always at work and we can walk around unconscious or answer that call . . .

Hello?
(recorded message) This is the Universe calling and I have some very important information for you, please hold the line. Someone special will be with you shortly . . . Hey, Dude! God, here. I've been calling you and I keep getting voicemail. Nice to finally hear your voice last night. You so rocked. Keep up the good work and seriously, when you see my number, please pick up.

_____
Subject: re: here I am
Date: Tue, 25 May 2010 8:54 PM
From: Mark
To: Lisa

Finally got in 45 minutes ago. Just starting dinner here, flour on my fingertips . . . Savannah in the tub, me cooking, Mariah out. Wow, what a day. It's late there, I know . . .

Many treasures today. The homeowner at the job *gave* me: 3 laptops, a home theater speaker system, big-ass TV . . . cool shit. Getting the electronics dialed in for my new space!

_____
Subject: re: wow
Date: Tue, 25 May 2010 9:09 PM
From: Lisa
To: Mark

NICE! Ask and ye shall receive. I love it. The Universal Relocation Program LOL. Go enjoy your dinner with Savannah. Let's try to talk tomorrow.

_____
Subject: The Soul of Change. . .
Date: Wed, 26 May 2010 6:06 AM
From: Mark
To: Lisa

There should be a guy's version of *Eat, Pray, Love* . . .

When I sent in my deposit for the men's retreat I also ordered a 4-cd set of Michael Meade's "The Soul of Change", which came in the mail yesterday.

I was listening to some of it while cooking and eating . . . go to mosaicvoices.org and order it. Now. Just do it. Trust me.

Going to Arcata on Sunday for a big-money gig with the blues band. Driving up with the keyboard player, leaving at dawn for breakfast at The Bluebird Cafe in Hopland at 7, then the gorgeous drive north. After breakfast we'll head into the redwoods: two musician friends, two awesome playlists on two iPods, and three hours of drive time. Weather forecast: sunny and warm.

Heading out now, looking forward to listening to Meade during the drive across the bay . . . at sunrise . . . towards San Mateo, where tribal elders have been known to gather for food and magic-planning. . .

_____
Subject: re: The Soul of Change. . .
Date: Wed, 26 May 2010 6:06 AM
From: Lisa
To: Mark

I'll order the CD. Have a good one. Catch up with you later . . . let's try for winechat.

Oh, and the guy version of *Eat, Pray, Love*? Write it.

_____
Subject: re: The Soul of Change. . .
Date: Thu, 27 May 2010 8:34 PM
From: Mark
To: Lisa

Dusty, labor-intensive day. Cuts and scrapes on my hands; cutting stucco with a diamond blade; satisfying work, lovely couple to work for, and the Japanese grandparents are in town to help with the new baby. All very sweet. Talked about music with the husband. Nice connection, he and I.

Listened to a LOT of Michael Meade today. Journaled a chunk about his stuff . . . hooo-wee, you are SO going to love this. Very inspiring.

_____
Subject: re: The Soul of Change. . .
Date: Thu, 27 May 2010 9:08 PM
From: Lisa
To: Mark

<grinning> nice . . .

I ordered it and sat for a moment, a bit surprised that I just did it because you told me to. *Trust me*, you said, and I plunked down my money without question. *Then* I listened to the clip. You're right. I will love it.

_____
Subject: re: The Soul of Change. . .
Date: Thu, 27 May 2010 9:41 PM
From: Mark
To: Lisa

Just finished dinner. Savannah cleaning tack, and Mariah home soon.

All this rush-rush doesn't sit well with me. No time to digest the Meade stuff I listened to today. It helps to write about it in an email and get your feedback and reaction. There was a great moment when he discussed the soul's *need* to change, but . . . *ugh* . . . not enough time to hang out with it now. Need a bath in a bad way, and Savannah will take over the computer soon to complete a homework assignment. Try again tomorrow.

Interesting how small the chat window has been the last two days.

Holy shit: It's almost midnight there . . . ugh.

_____
Subject: re: The Soul of Change. . .
Date: Thu, 27 May 2010 9:51 PM
From: Lisa
To: Mark

Still here . . . catching up on some stuff; waiting up for Zac who should be home at midnight.

I know what you mean. Window only cracked open . . . lots to talk about. That's why through the day I send snippets of thought to talk about later, like the Meade stuff. I can't wait to get the CDs.

Yeah, we'll try again tomorrow.

_____
Subject: cool a.m.
Date: Fri, 28 May 2010 6:09 AM
From: Lisa
To: Mark

Nice start to the day with Zac whooping it up in the hall and heading out at 7:30 to have breakfast with his friends to celebrate. "High School is OVER!!" he said, pulling me into a bear hug and lifting me off the ground in a spin. He is so psyched. Big Day. Prom tonight :-)

Clients and cleaning on my agenda today. Tomorrow the realtor is having an Open House!

How 'bout you? Another long day ahead?

_____
Subject: re: cool a.m.
Date: Fri, 28 May 2010 6:33 AM
From: Mark
To: Lisa

yeah. everybody up.

later . . . : (

_____
Subject: re: cool a.m.
Date: Fri, 28 May 2010 7:06 AM
From: Lisa
To: Mark

Hey, I hear you . . . remember: *temporary* :-)

Enjoy what you can of the day and keep that Soul stuff buzzing with Meade's voice in your ear. Looking forward to hanging out talking about it soon, especially after I get mine and listen to them.

Sending good juju. Full moon this week, too, that usually makes you a bit . . . *ugh.*

It, too, will pass

_____
Subject: OMG!
Date: Fri, 28 May 2010 12:22 PM
From: Lisa
To: Mark

So I got my *Secret Language of Relationships* book today. I heft it out of the box, this huge book of over 800 pages and putting it on my lap I randomly open it to somewhere in the middle to . . .

July 11-18 and December 19-25 - "Bringing Out The Best"

Noooooo!!! You've got to be kidding me! I shouted, out loud, HA! There it is in front of me - our birthdays - out of thousands of combinations in this book, on the page I opened to. Unbelievably cool.

Strengths: *encouraging, appreciated, admired.* The whole profile is completely right on.

On the facing page is you and Savannah: Strengths: *varied, dramatic, colorful*

Subject: re: OMG!
Date: Fri, 28 May 2010 6:25 PM
From: Mark
To: Lisa

this is really interesting stuff . . . can't believe you cracked the book open to our birthdays . . . holy shit.

got wine? got time?

Subject: teachat time. . .
Date: Sat, 29 May 2010 9:09 AM
From: Mark
To: Lisa

Morning errands done. Makin' breakfast . . .

I'll be leaving for the Arcata gig tomorrow at 6am your time. Won't be back til Monday evening.

Saw the pics of Zac. Looks much older than just a few months ago. And boy, does he look like you: the eyes, nose, and mouth . . . there you are.

Subject: mornin'
Date: Tue, 1 June 2010 5:55 AM
From: Lisa
To: Mark

Hope you had fun at your gig! Busy weekend of gatherings here. It was really nice. One of the best parts were the drives listening to Meade . . . holy shit. Need soulchat ASAP! Lovin' it.

Subject: Blame it on the moon
Date: Tue, 1 June 2010 6:09 AM
From: Mark
To: Lisa

Heading out early to get a jump on the coming week, in which I am already behind schedule, and I didn't realize it til just last night. Son of a bitch.

Nice road trip to and from Arcata. Got underway as planned on Sunday, great breakfast at the Bluebird, perfect weather, gorgeous drive heading north. Passed the time going back and forth with our iPods, playing two songs each, all the way up to the gig.

Nice gig, lovely setting in the backyard of a private winery. Gig over by 8 pm. Back to the hotel room and in bed by 11. On the road by 10 the next morning under gray skies, DJ games resumed. Dropped Matt off in SF, and home by 6pm, wiped out from the road. Everybody tired and behind schedule from a long weekend of early risings and setbacks: Savannah, in first place after her first day at the horse show, was eliminated on the second day when her horse refused a jump on the cross-country course. She did NOT take that well, of course - from 1st place to eliminated . . . *ouch!* It took all the fun out of the rest of the event. She came home to homework and sleep deprivation.

Gray and cold today. Waning moon cycle. Sure feeling it . . .

Check in later. Knew you'd love the Meade stuff.

_____
Subject: hey!
Date: Tue, 1 June 2010 6:09 AM
From: Lisa
To: Mark

Ouch about the job pile-up and sorry to hear about Savannah's event. Try not to go too far down the moon slide. You'll finish that job and get started on a new one before you know it.

One of my clients has been approached about doing a reality TV show set in her office. She is shooting footage this week and she sent me the screen treatment from the producer. Pretty cool! She's trying not to buy into the raunchy MTV factor and instead show her staff as successful young adults. She hired me to coach all five of them this week to prep them for the shoot.

_____
Subject: oooff
Date: Tue, 1 June 2010 6:54 PM
From: Mark
To: Lisa

Just got in. *oooff* . . . tired . . . Rehearsal in an hour . . . *oooff* . . .

Everybody cool with everything in the work world so far.

Love hearing about your coaching gig with the office staff. I notice you keep drawing closer and closer to Big Media . . . as it should be. You gonna get some screen time out of that gig?

Leaving early every morning this week. This is gonna be one of those weeks where we don't get to play together much. Tomorrow night is my last free evening, then comes a gig every night thru Saturday, with a recording session on Sunday, and long work days each day.

It's been rough not having the space to really drop into the Meade material with you, or myself even. The drives home while listening to Meade bring up all kinds of things and I long to sit quietly to write or reflect a bit. I'm always listening to his stuff when I'm in motion.

_____
Subject: re: oooff
Date: Tue, 1 June 2010 7:07 PM
From: Lisa
To: Mark

Yes, she's talking about possibly bringing me down for the pilot. I've been listening to Meade, oh man. I want to talk about it with you so bad.

Zac's high school graduation is *tomorrow*. Wow.

Thanks for the heads up about the week. We'll talk soon. Pick a chat, any chat. Write as you can.

_____
Subject: rejuvenation. . .
Date: Wed, 2 June 2010 5:44 AM
From: Lisa
To: Mark

Today is Zac's graduation. Such an important day. It's really *his* day, though he's not nearly as excited as I am. It is more *meaningful* for me. A rite of passage, a chapter complete, a new beginning for both of us. It may be more so for me because I never had a high school graduation day of my own. Ah. There's something to that. Getting him to this point in his life on my own. . . feels *big*.

At any rate, a big day at our house. Feeling *good*.

_____
Subject: re: rejuvenation. . .
Date: Wed, 2 June 2010 8:55 PM
From: Mark
To: Lisa

You there? Just got in the door . . . have 5 min to chat.

_____
Subject: Magic

Date: Thu, 3 June 2010 5:57 AM
From: Mark
To: Lisa

Drama: Savannah comes in the door crying last night, followed by a stern-looking Mariah, who has (rightfully) pulled the plug on Savannah's quest to hang out with her boyfriend at his house Saturday night. So Mariah's bent because Savannah's upset with her.

I take a bath. Mariah comes in to gather my support of her decision, but even that conversation is charged with her irritability. Oh great, thanks for dumping on my bath time. *Oooff* . . . Later, I sat on the back deck where it's cool and quiet, considering the day, and the hectic week ahead. Ah! To the I Ching . . .

41, Nourishing, and #27, Decline. Essentially all is well, lay low, chill, and ride it out: things are as they should be. You'll be fine. Go to bed.

Alarm goes off at 5am, waking me from an awesome dream in which I'm levitating and manipulating small objects through the air with my hands, a la telekinesis . . .

Damn right I'm gonna be fine.

_____
Subject: re: Magic
Date: Thu, 3 June 2010 6:34 AM
From: Lisa
To: Mark

Teen drama . . . it's a bitch. It's part of the initiation towards adulthood to separate from your mother. They'll be fine, ultimately.

My night? Well, the last two guys left Zac's graduation soiree here when the parents of one came to get them at 4am. Though I agreed to it, I did not like he and his friends partying here. It was so uncomfortable and won't happen again. Being the cool mom is not cool for the mom. Zac knows this will not be the way that we spend our summer. Argh. I am exhausted after only a couple hours of sleep. Need coffee.

Oh, but the pride and joy of watching him graduate last night was worth all the rest! Really. Wow, so great. And now life goes on. Funny, the moments get built up, they happen, then on to creating new moments.

What a cool dream, Magic Man, and the I Ching reading seems right on. *The pendulum continues to swing.* You will be way better than *fine.*

Off to grocery shop with Zac for the family graduation party here on Saturday.

_____
Subject: Proud moment
Date: Thu, 3 June 2010 9:51 PM
From: Lisa
To: Mark

Here's a pic taken at graduation last night. Great talks with Zac today. We had a blast shopping and cooking together, then watched a movie. It all works out in the end, it really does. Even when things look less than good they have a purpose. I feel better about having had the uncomfortable night last night when his friends were here and they were drinking in the basement. Even though I took their keys and thought it would be OK - nothing *bad* happened - it turned out not to be so OK *with me,* after all. Good lesson.

Off to bed. I have a session at 8:30 my time. Hope your day and gig were good and these long days aren't kicking your ass too bad.

'nite

_____
Subject: mornin'
Date: Fri, 4 June 2010 5:20 AM
From: Lisa
To: Mark

More Meade magic: *We all get older but we don't all get elder. . .* Talk about tribal. God, I love this guy.

How're you today?

_____
Subject: re: mornin'
Date: Fri, 4 June 2010 6:01 AM
From: Mark
To: Lisa

Graduation pic is good. He's his mother's son, alright . . .

Heading out the door after 3 hours sleep . . . *oooff.* No idea when I'll get back tonight. I've been pretty good with just riding out this phase: do what I gotta do, so I can do what I *wanna* do . . .

_____
Subject: all we've got right now. . . solo winechat
Date: Fri, 4 June 2010 10:11 PM
From: Lisa

To: Mark

Random thoughts . . .

Sitting on the couch while I listened to the CD of my last session with
Kathy. Oh, man it's all so good. I kinda dozed off towards the end of it and
was awakened by the next CD in the changer - Journey's *Infinity*. Ha! That
was the most played album I owned at 17, Zac's age. Yeah, I want to get
home to my city by the Bay.

Throwing I Ching while I listen . . . *What do I need to know?*

#54 Subordinate ~ #40 Liberation

The gist is that I am not in control of a single thing. I need to remain
passive for now and cling to long term ideals. This will carry me across
this difficult time with a clear purpose.

_____
Subject: re: all we've got right now. . . solo winechat
Date: Sat, 5 June 2010 6:25 AM
From: Mark
To: Lisa

Dontcha just love the I Ching . . .

Consulting it the other night sure helped me get through the last two days.
With the sleep deprivation, long days of nose-to-the-grindstone carpentry
projects, and household dramas all coming together to form a perfect storm
of potential stress, I was able to keep my cool and calm my mind while
taking care of the business at hand. Kind of remarkable, actually: Inspired
by the I Ching I made a point of letting all of the extraneous shit go, and
just focused on doing what I could and had to do. Got into a Zen-like state,
a combination of being too tired to *care* about any of the bullshit stuff, and
calmly go from point A to point B, then to C and D, and accomplish quite
a bit . . . doing nice work as I went, by the way.

More later. House awake, and I'm off soon.

_____
Subject: re: all we've got right now. . . solo winechat
Date: Sat, 5 June 2010 7:09 AM
From: Lisa
To: Mark

Zen is good. Day off tomorrow to recharge, yes?

Zac's graduation party this afternoon with lots of great food we have been making - should be fun . . . especially hoping it doesn't rain. About 35 people should be here.

Catch up later.

_____
Subject: re: all we've got right now. . . solo winechat
Date: Sat, 5 June 2010 8:26 AM
From: Mark
To: Lisa

Tomorrow's recording session was canceled, so yeah, a day off . . . sort of.

Now I'm available to take Savannah to a horse thingy tomorrow morning, back home by 2.

Missing winechat . . .

_____
Subject: re: all we've got right now. . . solo winechat
Date: Sat, 5 June 2010 8:32 PM
From: Lisa
To: Mark

Whew! Party over. It was a really nice time. He was thrilled and made out well. Now that this is over it feels like one step closer towards the move. The house can sell any day now. I keep feeling that the family who saw it last week will be back.

Hope the gig went well. Horn band tonight, right? Bet sleeping till you wake up sounds like heaven about now. I have had a very busy coaching week and actually have a couple sessions tomorrow morning. Good week, though really crazy from adding the graduation and party prep. But all that pomp & circumstance made it worth it :-)

_____
Subject: Here I am
Date: Sun, 6 June 2010 8:41 PM
From: Mark
To: Lisa

I know, I know . . . *where IS he?*

He is sleeping three, four, or five hours a night and having to work long days to keep up with scheduled projects that he's already behind on - but has kept all involved parties cool - and then, on his one day off, had to get up early for a half-day horse gig, *then* spend the next six hours running errands, finally coming in the door at 7:30 pm. All together now: *UGH!*

Quick . . . where's the wine, and where the HELL is that Lucky Girl with Options chick?

Subject: re: Here I am
Date: Sun, 6 June 2010 8:50 PM
From: Lisa
To: Mark

Lucky Girl is standing by with wine in hand . . . say when :-)

Subject: good morning!
Date: Mon, 7 June 2010 5:37 AM
From: Lisa
To: Mark

Winechat Probability Quiz:

A. Tonight for SURE

B. Looks good, plan on it

C. Let's try, we'll see

D. No way (but wish I could!)

Subject: re: good morning!
Date: Mon, 7 June 2010 5:41 AM
From: Mark
To: Lisa

Ha, funny girl . . . I choose C, "Let's try, but we'll see". Day of the mantle: must build and install before coming home. Start new ($$$$) job tomorrow.

I didn't mind being up early yesterday to join the troops for the horse thingy. In fact, I was thinking some time with horses and being outdoors would be a nice change, even therapeutic. But it's a lot of tagging along behind the lessons as they move from place to place on the course, then stand around and watch, then move to another location as they practice getting over certain obstacles, etc . . . an hour and a half of this, then hike back to the truck, sit around for another hour while the horse is cooled, cleaned up, the legs iced, then wrapped before making the drive back to the barn. During this cool-down time I just wander or sit around, grooving on the scene and the scenery: horses with their riders scattered around the 200-acre facility, the views of the surrounding hills to the west, all of this in 80-plus degree heat this particularly fine day.

So because of the over-stimulation of the prior week I sit in a folding chair, close to where Savannah is tending to the horse at the end of her lesson.

Sitting is good. Sitting is needed. Lots of sitting. Especially on this day, when the sun is hot, my hat has been thoroughly soaked in a water bucket, and the water is dripping off the rim onto the back of my long-sleeve white shirt. Drip, drip, drip . . . sit, sit, sit . . . doze, drip, sit . . . doze, drip, sit . . . high point of my day.

Eventually we head out, and after the horse is back in its stall at the barn it's another few hours of running around before coming home. I go straight for the wine, and shoot off a quick hello to you.

Bath. Bed. Dreamless sleep.

Subject: re: reminders
Date: Tue, 8 June 2010 6:13 AM
From: Mark
To: Lisa

Came in the door at 9:30 pm last night. So close to being done with the job. Now comes the tweaking, dialing in, finalizing last minute details. Everybody anxious to finish and move on, but not before all the bases are covered. More discipline about staying present, and resist the temptation to hurry.

Subject: re: reminders
Date: Tue, 8 June 2010 6:25 AM
From: Lisa
To: Mark

You are an inspiration with your Zen get-it-done-right attitude, my dear. I love it. I will apply it where I can in my world. And I'll remind you of it in a couple weeks should you spin into a less groovy place ;-)

Oh and by the way, I have to tell you that your past few emails feel they are from *That Guy*.

Just had to share.

Subject: Zen letters
Date: Tue, 8 June 2010 7:31 PM
From: Mark
To: Lisa

Gee, thanks. In fact I made a mental note at one point that I've been running a nice creative energy these days and have the kind of work life I insisted on several years ago. I have no problem working long and hard hours to earn a living as long as the work is connected to who I am in some way, and serves as an outlet for creative self-expression. Your feedback to me about my Zen mode feels really good and validates where I've been with myself lately.

thirty

Subject: Hey
Date: Wed, 9 June 2010 5:56 AM
From: Lisa
To: Mark

AH . . . what a gorgeous morning . . . and Meade, oh, man. Listened to Power, Money & Sex . . . gettin' some of *that*, oh yeah . . . came back and did a little dance jam in the yard before coming in . . . Outkast *Hey Ya* . . . Duffy *Mercy* . . .

Soaring on the 220 energy grid today. How 'bout you?

_____
Subject: re: Hey
Date: Wed, 9 June 2010 5:56 AM
From: Mark
To: Lisa

Writing, but we are not on the same grid this morning. I'll just bring you down, and now I see that I really shouldn't send it. You're not gonna wanna hear about bullshit stuff w/ Mariah, so how 'bout we try again later?

_____

Subject: re: Hey
Date: Wed, 9 June 2010 5:59 AM
From: Lisa
To: Mark

You're wrong about that. I was looking for a conversation with you after my walk and this is where you are. So please don't "protect" me from your dark stuff, 'k? Thanks.

_____
Subject: ok, you asked for it
Date: Wed, 9 June 2010 6:10 AM
From: Mark
To: Lisa

Mornin' . . .

Don't feel very witty or chatty this morning. I really need to go to bed earlier. It didn't help to end the night with a "conversation" with Mariah about Savannah's boyfriend stuff. Mariah makes no bones about her disapproval, and wants my support in dealing with it. Well, okay, but the conversation we end up having is all over the map and rife with defensiveness and raised voices as we ultimately end up talking about our own communication issues. I don't even try to invoke Meade's info, that there's a whole other dynamic going on that involves a certain *necessity* for the two kids to come together and learn and work some things out, plus the connection between our marriage and Savannah's choice of men. I don't even go there.

Look, I'm pretty sure this is not the morning email content you were looking forward to after your walk.

_____
Subject: re: ok, you asked for it
Date: Wed, 9 June 2010 6:14 AM
From: Lisa
To: Mark

So, the boyfriend thing: I have found with Zac that having frank chats makes for a more honest reality. You have either instilled in Savannah values that steer her to make good choices or you haven't. I believe you have but there comes a time when she needs to test drive them away from you both. It's scary out there, yes, but she is a good girl and needs to be trusted to show trustworthiness.

_____

Subject: winechat. . .
Date: Wed, 9 June 2010 8:06 PM
From: Mark
To: Lisa

Just came in the door. Up for it?

_____
Subject: re: winechat

Date: Wed, 9 June 2010 9:42 PM
From: Lisa
To: Mark

Argh. Conversation interuptus . . .

So, first I want to say that I hate that our call left off on a heated note. The intensity with which I was sharing my thoughts was not unlike when I coach and want to make a point. Sorry. I can come across a bit *passionate*. I can't state enough that the road ahead is not an easy one. It's hard. I have been through it and it is not a pretty thing.

_____
Subject: Welcome to my secret world
Date: Thu, 10 June 2010 5:53 AM
From: Mark
To: Lisa

I Ching last night:

#15, Moderation, changing to #63 After The End . . .
Everything speaks to the coming changes and reminds me to lay low, keep from doing or reacting with extremes, and to maintain a modest and disciplined attitude.

oooff . . . a bit early for me to go deep and mine for gold. And thank you for the feedback about our too-short winechat. That "meltdown", that place you find yourself in that overwhelms and feels like a mix of joy and grief? I've been popping in and out of that state since before the Apollo Years. Being a witness to it while it was happening to you made me feel like you just stepped into my secret world.

_____
Subject: I Ching
Date: Thu, 10 June 2010 9:44 AM
From: Lisa
To: Mark

I asked *What is the significance of my connection with Mark last night?*

#26 POTENTIAL ENERGY changing to #43 RESOLUTION

Wow. Now the "meltdown" make perfect sense. All this stored potential energy needs resolution that must spring from the heart and be voiced. And, like you, the timing is of vast importance.

So, Kathy JuJu called this morning to say that she got a big hit yesterday that I need to do more in the house to prepare for the Open House on

Sunday, that it is imperative that I see it SOLD and shift the energy in some bigger way. I told her how funny that yesterday my Feng Shui client was here and she told me to move around all this furniture, take out rugs, etc. So I did that. It was exactly what Kathy was feeling I needed to do. Perfect. I need to see the house packed and ready to move. I need to pack boxes *TODAY* and call the movers to schedule for mid-August estimates.

Kathy told me about a client of hers who was waiting to hear about an adoption she wanted so badly to come through. She told her to get up early each morning, even at 3am, and go to the nursery to take care of her baby as if it was already there. Within weeks she was a mom.

So, acting *as if* is key. Keep doing things in your world that are in line with your new life.

_____
Subject: packing music
Date: Thu, 10 June 2010 2:48 PM
From: Lisa
To: Mark

CD's from you were in the changer, September Songs and March '06 (you do make the best mix tapes), when I started packing. Tears keep on coming. *Big* change coming. Man, oh man. Followed Kathy's advice and packed boxes of books and shoes and boots. *Holy shit, I'm moving.*

Yep. Here's to the coming changes. I know the next several days are long ones . . . stay close as you can.

Send juju, please.

_____
Subject: Hey
Date: Sat, 12 June 2010 3:26 PM
From: Mark
To: Lisa

Gig last night after work. Thursday night the horn band was AWESOME! Band sounded fat and smokin' hot. All the players knew it . . . and ran with it. Packed the house by the end of the second set . . . holy shit, what a night.

Just had another "talk" with Mariah, but kept totally solid, clear, and grounded. She can't get to me anymore. I'm on the other side now, listening to her rap from there, so no need for me to get jacked up.

Pulled the I Ching out when she went to the store a bit ago and came up with # 51 (*Shocking*) and #16 *(Harmony)*.

gotta go

Subject: re: Hey
Date: Sat, 12 June 2010 3:50 PM
From: Lisa
To: Mark

Oh, that's wonderful . . . *shocking harmony* . . . I love it.

Incredible moments here in the last 20 minutes. My emotions are running
so high today. I got your note, read the I Ching book, dove into another
pool of emotional waters, and then the phone rang. It was a dear friend I
have not seen in a few years. She's an energy healer who I did a lot of
work with several years ago (she's known you quite well over the years as
that guy with the Big Energy). She called out of the blue with an urgency
to connect with me right then, just as I was feeling the need to connect
with someone *tribal*. There she was saying, "Get in your car and meet
me!" So I am off to have wine and deep conversation to share *it all*.

See ya later with the goodies that come from it.

Subject: good mornin'
Date: Sun, 13 June 2010 6:40 AM
From: Lisa
To: Mark

What a wonderful evening. So much to share about the synchronicity of
things. My friend has been recovering from a fire at her condo where she
lost *all her stuff* . . . wow. Talk about perspective. We talked about my
current events, my connection with you and this divine calling.
Unbelievable. Best over a chat, I think. Any free time today? You subbed
for that new band last night, right? Would like to hear about that, too.

Subject: Ching Chat
Date: Sun, 13 June 2010 8:16 AM
From: Mark
To: Lisa

Mornin' . . . Got home a little after 2. Yeah, subbed for a new band last
night. Bass, guitar, drums, and a *killer* female vocalist . . . wow. Great gig.

I didn't have time yesterday to mention another interesting I Ching thing:
Found a scrap of paper in my I Ching book from May of '04 - #2 *(Natural
Response)* and #49 *(Changing)*. Essentially, it supports me landing where I
am *now*.

_____
Subject: re: Ching Chat
Date: Sun, 13 June 2010 8:27 AM
From: Lisa
To: Mark

Wow, that's incredible. It's finally "later", huh? Only took six years LOL

OPEN HOUSE TODAY! Send sell-the-house juju!

_____
Subject: Ching Chat
Date: Sun, 13 June 2010 8:28 AM
From: Mark
To: Lisa

got chat time? Call.

_____
Subject: re: Ching Chat
Date: Mon, 14 June 2010 5:55 AM
From: Lisa
To: Mark

Mornin'. . .

Been giving some thought to your comment on the phone yesterday . . . *is it doubt or impatience?* It is definitely impatience, which is one of my lifelong challenges. I am not naturally a patient girl. In Liz Gilberts' book *Committed*, I read last night how Liz and Felipe revealed their worst traits to each other, out loud, and the acceptance that came from still loving someone with the ugly truth hanging out there. It was the best thing she has written in this book, so far. It made me think about my own faults, and impatience came to mind easily (along with a bunch more, of course). I'm not impatient about everything, though. I think it shows up most when I am excited about something and I *can't wait* to get started. Yet once under way, I like to savor. I don't tend to rush *through*, just *to*. Hmmm.

You, on the other hand, can be amazingly patient. The I Ching mirrors that for you. You believe that five or six years ain't shit when you have a lifetime - or several - to have, be, or do something you want, right? I am seeing the gift in that today and not scratching my head as much as I used to, wondering *what are you waiting for?* I see you closing in on the end zone of your dream and the momentum that is building under the surface is now visible to me; you are *there*. I have watched for a very long time, sometimes from the sidelines, sometimes playing alongside you, and I have *patiently* looked forward to celebrating your victory.

Now I just have to learn how to do that for me.

___

Subject:
Date: Mon, 14 June 2010 6:11 AM
From: Mark
To: Lisa

Mentally a rough second half of the day yesterday . . .

Mariah in an upbeat mood after being home for a while from the barn chores in the morning. Ran errands together, one of which was to the place we get organic soil for the garden boxes I built. Great place, with tons of landscaping supplies and all kinds of stone for walls, gardens, floors, etc. Of course Mariah is pointing out all the cool stuff and what we could do with it, ideas and projects that "we" should do, and boy, is she in a good mood to be looking at all this stuff - with me - but I'm reserved, pulled in, and not exactly meeting her in the same place since I'm intending to leave soon.

Man, it's just weird having a completely different world going on inside of me from the one going on inside of her. We may be looking at the same thing at the same time, but we're both seeing something different. And I'm the only one aware of it.

. . . and it's unusual to witness her being upbeat and happy.

I nap for an hour, then write for a bit when the girls go out for an hour. Once home, Mariah gardens til sundown, very much into it.

Dinner, *Avatar*, and bed . . .

oooff . . .

___

Subject: re:
Date: Mon, 14 June 2010 6:48 AM
From: Lisa
To: Mark

It could be that the more she plans things with you the more she feels you will be there later. I know this well. I've been in relationships where I felt the guy wasn't really gonna stay. I just *knew* and still planned weekend getaways three or six months out. Sometimes they happened, most times they didn't. I went on one trip with girlfriends and another one alone when the guy had bailed before the trip.

Enjoy her good moods while they show up. It's great that she is finding joy in the garden. Wouldn't it be nice if she is finding some inner joy of her own? Holding a place for *that* would be a good thing.

_____
Subject: re:
Date: Tue, 15 June 2010 6:09 AM
From: Lisa
To: Mark

Woke up this morning thinking about the price of the house. I made coffee, Zac's lunch, and sent him off to work, then sat down and did some house math. Just how much do I need to sell it for to get some decent $$ in my pocket? Not as much as I thought. In fact, *way* less.

So the price of the house will be dropping today.

Oh! Cleaning my office yesterday I found a file folder called Go Deep. In it were inspirational articles, notes, the poem *The Invitation*, a 12-page letter from you that accompanied the CD I happen to have in the changer *right now*. And the freakin' craziest thing? A check for $150 dated the *same date* as your letter to me - March 22, 2006

What great stuff.

_____
Subject: re: Hidden treasure
Date: Wed, 16 June 2010 4:33 AM
From: Mark
To: Lisa

Aww . . . thanks for the desk tour . . .

Speaking of treasure, I'm looking forward to pulling down my box of journals and checking the timeline of my New Mexico campfire journal entry and the date when you first came to California. Was it October '82?

_____
Subject: re: Hidden treasure
Date: Wed, 16 June 2010 4:33 AM
From: Lisa
To: Mark

I did that yesterday and found the journal from March 22, 2006 . . . oh, man. The day before was all about *you*.

Yeah, I arrived 10/3/82 and that Apollo gig where we first met was within the first week or so.

_____
Subject: re: Hidden treasure

Date: Wed, 16 June 2010 4:52 AM
From: Mark
To: Lisa

I think my New Mexico trip was August or September, but not sure of the year. Haven't been home alone long enough to pull down the journal box. Kind of exciting to find out how that all fits.

_____
Subject: re: Hidden treasure
Date: Wed, 16 June 2010 5:12 AM
From: Lisa
To: Mark

You know, it takes real courage to dream the way we do and believe that we can actually create it. Not for the faint of heart, this path.

Yet, others like Marianne and Meade all prove it can be done . . . *really well*. They beckon us, even *dare us* to do our own version. Our resonance with them is not to follow them but to be guided by them to where they are. "Come here," they say, coaxing us with their brilliance and courage, "You can do this, too."

_____
Subject: check it out
Date: Wed, 16 June 2010 5:16 AM
From: Mark
To: Lisa

Read Jon Carroll's column at SF Gate about Abby Sunderland, the 16 year-old girl who tried sailing around the world by herself . . . wow.

_____
Subject: re: check it out
Date: Wed, 16 June 2010 5:25 AM
From: Lisa
To: Mark

I have been following Abby. What a story. I agree with him that we as parents can ultimately do nothing to protect the safety and lives of our children. All we can do is teach them right, but they are going to make dangerous choices if they want to. As a mother whose son was hit head-on by a drunk driver only a month after he got his license, I have to say that you trust God a whole lot more when He allows your kid to walk away from something dangerous and into his long life. Some parents are tragically not as lucky. But it's not luck. It's fate and destiny. That day convinced me that we are not in control, we really aren't, and we are *all* here by the grace of God.

Though not sure I would have let Zac sail around the world at 16 :-)

Subject: 6/24/82
Date: Wed, 16 June 2010 12:03 PM
From: Mark
To: Lisa

That trip to New Mexico was on June 24, 1982.

The journal ends on October 15, and the next journal begins the following December . . .

Re-reading some of the journal entries from that trip was . . . well, it made me yearn to be out in nature for days at a time, wandering, walking, writing, hiking. Boy, I was really fortunate to have even had that experience. I'll send some entries later.

We can chat while I have lunch if you want. 20 minutes worth . . .

Subject: re: 6/24/82
Date: Wed, 16 June 2010 12:05 PM
From: Lisa
To: Mark

Sorry, got a client call.

Subject: re: 6/24/82
Date: Wed, 16 June 2010 2:16 PM
From: Lisa
To: Mark

Late June '82 . . . that was when the overwhelming pull to California occurred for me. My girlfriend Kathleen (who was with me when I met you at the Apollo gig) had moved to California in the spring and I wanted to visit so bad but I didn't have the $$. For months I saved every penny to 'get to California' and by the end of that summer I decided I needed to just *move there*. Sight unseen. I just *knew*. I was living in a little basement apartment alone, I had just broken up with my boyfriend and bought a new car. In fact, I remember I had a little less than $500 to my name. I brought the car to the dealer and just gave it back before I left.

Subject: Hey Yoda
Date: Fri, 18 June 2010 6:17 AM
From: Lisa
To: Mark

Woke up blue today . . . can't tell why. A bit concerned about my light client schedule (light $), can't get Jimmy to call me back about important stuff (like health insurance for Zac). Worried about the house sale, or lack thereof. It's all money stuff, I see now.

It's not like me to wake up feeling this way. And with my mantra of *I have plenty of money* I have not worried about money in a long time.

Argh. I hate feeling like this!

I need cheering up. Please enlighten me if you can, Yoda.

Oh, and I colored my hair last night and for the first few days I look like Morticia Adams till I wash it a few times. I hate that, too.

Waaaaaaaaa

Subject: re: Hey Yoda
Date: Wed, 16 June 2010 6:17 AM
From: Mark
To: Lisa

Impatient for *change*, are we?

I know: I'll change my hair color and the price of the house. Then I'll change my mind about my money mantra by not really believing it for a while. While I'm at it I may as well act as though all of this is a permanent situation. Come to think of it, I haven't worried about the small stuff for quite a while. Hmmm . . . think I'll try that and see if it helps . . .

Whoops! Hey! What the f- . . . ? It's not helping! Shit . . . Let's see . . . I know! I'll doubt myself! No, wait . . . did that already. I vaguely remember that it didn't help things either . . .

Christ, where the hell is that Girl With Options? Ugh, the way she comes and goes around here like she owns the place and doesn't have a care in the world. Probably off somewhere with that Creates with His Hands dude, or dancing by the creek, or writing in her JuJu Book, or coaching some pro athlete, or (ugh) walking on a California beach and acting all, like, awesome, or happy, or some woo-woo shit . . .

Fuck it. I'll send Mark an email and see what he *thinks . . .*

Subject: re: oh, and. . .
Date: Wed, 16 June 2010 6:30 AM
From: Lisa

To: Mark

I freaking love you.

Laughing my ass off.!!! You're the best.

_____
Subject: re: oh, and. . .
Date: Fri, 18 June 2010 7:51 AM
From: Mark
To: Lisa

Savannah officially done with school. Yay. Nice evening here last night, with everyone hungry (Tuscan chicken - the 500-degree iron skillet thing), Savannah on my lap at the computer, the two of us looking up how to say "good morning" in Russian . . . then ate dinner while watching *Twilight*. Ugh, what a boring, downer movie. Fell asleep 1/2 hour in, went to bed.

Okay, now it's time to go set up my shop on the lawn and get back to the cabinets.

Be of good cheer . . .

_____
Subject: re: oh, and. . .
Date: Fri, 18 June 2010 7:59 AM
From: Lisa
To: Mark

Nice to have the kids off school; no homework stuff, etc. Zac is loving his day camp counselor job. He has the 10-13 year olds. Pool all day yesterday. Cool gig. Off to do two sessions . . . both guys . . . then *whatever I want*.

_____
Subject: chat
Date: Sat, 19 June 2010 1:08 PM
From: Mark
To: Lisa

Need some chat. Can ya?

_____
Subject: re: chat
Date: Sat, 19 June 2010 1:20 PM
From: Lisa
To: Mark

Sure, call ya in a few.

Argh. No power here since yesterday afternoon. Getting email on my phone. I'll sit in my car and get cool while we chat!

thirty-one

Subject:
Date: Mon, 21 June 2010 6:14 AM
From: Mark
To: Lisa

Nice weekend here, punctuated with good music and a bit of work . . . and a lot of yawning. After talking with you Saturday I decided *not* to take on the wall unit project for the picky customer.

_____
Subject: the beauty of power
Date: Mon, 21 June 2010 8:51 PM
From: Lisa
To: Mark

. . . as in electricity, on a very humid day. . . *finally* have our power restored after 3 days. It's lightening and storming again. Praying that the power stays on . . . but loving the vibe.

Nice chat tonight. But too short.

_____
Subject: Ugh
Date: Tue, 22 June 2010 9:55 AM
From: Lisa
To: Mark

Frustrating day so far.

College snags with Zac's financial aid. Then the push-pull with him these days that can be so upsetting, yet I understand all too well. The key is not taking his withdrawal so personally. It's his way of growing up, I know that.

I know you leave for Oregon early tomorrow for the rest of the week.

Subject: Zac
Date: Tue, 22 June 2010 11:02 AM
From: Mark
To: Lisa

Tricky place for you to be in now, with Zac. When you were telling me the story last night I thought right away of the Keys To His Life thing. From over here it looks like you want to *give* them to him, but he wants to *steal* them. Even when he knows you give him a lot of freedom and leeway he still manages to fuck with you over going after what he wants. Seems like a power struggle of some sort, which, by the way, makes perfect sense: What better way to sharpen your "negotiating" skills than to mix it up with other powerful people . . . a formidable adversary.

I think in *his* mind he's already gone . . .

Subject: re: Zac
Date: Tue, 22 June 2010 11:09 AM
From: Lisa
To: Mark

Yes, yes and *yes*. Exactly. Zac needs to feel like *he* is in control of his life. So even when I give him space, he pushes the envelope for *more*. You are right about his being already gone. He's a college guy now, don't you know, and he doesn't need things like curfews, limits, or *Mom* . . . till he *does*. Like taking care of all the college paperwork, buying things like food and having a place to come home to.

It's interesting about the college stuff because that's where he is looking to me Big Time to guide him, asking, "What do I say when I call the adviser? How do I do the orientation thing online?" He has always looked to me to take care of that stuff and now is the time where I am trying to get him to do some stuff on his own. I don't want him to be one of those guys who looks to his smart woman to take care of things (like his Dad was).

Subject: re: Zac
Date: Tue, 22 June 2010 11:15 AM
From: Mark
To: Lisa

ooh, yeah, good one. But he IS a bit of a player, and probably knows he can turn on the charm to bend unsuspecting women to his will. OR . . . he'll be the smart guy, and won't have a need to use The Force for evil.

Hopefully this dynamic with you two will find a middle ground over the summer. Soul stuff going on, you know, so yeah, don't take any of it personally.

_____

Thanks for the reminder. Yeah, I have to just chill. The soul stuff is very true. His and mine. In the end we will grow through it.

TRUE about the player thing. Though I think he will use the Force (mostly) for Good.

_____

Welcome back. You should be on your way home about now, I think? Hope all went well and that Savannah was happy with her results.

So, news to report from here . . .

Work continues to be slow and I am not freaking out about it. I am spending time reading, going to the gym a lot, time with friends, watching movies, a bit of writing and overall house stuff. It feels good to have space in my days during the summer. Zac is barely around, working full time days and hanging with friends at night. We are getting all his college classes signed up this week.

Good news: We had an open house yesterday and there is a young couple wanting to make an offer! They are meeting with a loan officer tonight, so we will see if they qualify. I feel the sale of the house coming soon.

The big lunar eclipse on Saturday sent my emotions flying for a couple of days. Did you feel it, too? Boy, lots of *feelings*. Interestingly, I went to my cousin's wedding reception that night, a cool event at a funky art gallery in the city. The toasts were all about how these "two great friends *for fifteen years* finally found their way to a life together . . ." Seriously? Fifteen years ain't shit. LOL

That about sums up my week. How 'bout yours?

_____
Subject: mornin'
Date: Tue, 29 Jun 2010 6:52 AM
From: Mark
To: Lisa

12-hour drive back from Oregon yesterday, and after unloading horse, trailer, and truck it was 11pm here when I got to take a bath and crash. Didn't get to check (45) emails til this morning. *Oooff*, busy week ahead.

Oregon trip had a lot going on. We were on the outskirts of Philomath, near Corvallis, and tent camped the whole time. Many pics, mostly of Savannah, who, by the way, had a rough time of things. She was in first place at the end of her first day, then was thrown off her horse on the second day. Not hurt, but come off your horse and you're eliminated. Second time in a row of going from first to eliminated. Heart wrenching to watch her suck it up as she walked across the course with her horse, fighting tears, and having spectators tell her *good job, honey* as she walked past them, stone-faced.

Funky moods through the week as Mariah micro-managed things on a daily basis. Four days spent barely enjoying myself. Lots of naps, laying low, taking pics, walking at pre-dawn before anyone awake. Love Oregon. Green, lush, and clean. Love the drive, too. 108 degrees near Shasta on the drive home, then 67 degrees back in the Bay Area.

Busy week ahead, starting today. Lots of catching up to do with rehearsing with 2 bands, gigging every day but Wednesday, truck repairs, job requirements . . . *wham,* welcome home!

Glad to hear about the house offer. This may be the one, eh?

Lunar eclipse felt here as well. Rough. No magic for miles around.

Ciao. Don't forget to breathe.

_____
Subject: re: mornin'
Date: Tue, 29 Jun 2010 7:02 AM
From: Lisa
To: Mark

Hey there, nice to see you :-) Lots to chat about. Magic is coming *back* . . . Sorry to hear about the problems for Savannah. Glad she didn't get hurt.

The funky mood stuff and the moon sounds like it made for long days, but in a beautiful place, at least. I'm hoping to get out of Dodge myself and up to Door County in late July to see Kim. I was there a year ago this week and my, oh my, has my life changed. I had just left Dave and I was sad, miserable, heavy and craving change.

Today I am free, happy, healthy and moving forward in every way. What a difference a year makes! I couldn't have anticipated *all* the changes coming, as my move to California wasn't even on the radar yet. All that has transpired since then couldn't have been seen, even in the clearest crystal ball. *Whew*. It's interesting how the ripple effect of my changes have reached the lives of others. And the beat goes on.

There is no word yet about the potential buyers. Not looking too promising. But I have to believe the right buyers are on their way. The time will be right, too. I have faith. *Breathe*. (thanks for the reminder)

Off for a walk on this gorgeous day. Really looking forward to our next chat. *Bring it.*

___

Subject: re: mornin'
Date: Tue, 29 Jun 2010 6:44 PM
From: Mark
To: Lisa

A quick hello while upstairs from a Calico vocal rehearsal. Horn band showing up in a couple of hours. *Oooff. . .*

You sound great. Feels like I've been away a long time.

___

Subject: Hi there. . .
Date: Wed, 30 Jun 2010 5:41 AM
From: Lisa
To: Mark

Busy music night, huh? You sound less than thrilled, understandably after such a long day traveling on Monday. My day wasn't quite as groovy as it started out. I caught up on emails, puttered around and didn't accomplish much. Lost my *oomph* somewhere mid-day. Drank wine with a friend on the patio last night and grilled out, that was cool.

Yeah, it does feel like you have been away a long time and that you were *far* away. A chat would be good today. I am free for most of the day (again, *argh*).

___

Subject: re:
Date: Wed, 30 June 2010 8:36 AM
From: Mark

To: Lisa

chat? give a call . . .

_____
Subject: my mojo is back
Date: Fri, 2 Jul 2010 5:44 AM
From: Lisa
To: Mark

The world seems to have righted itself. Nice combination of things yesterday to gain insight, perspective and a nice dose of sunshine. Glad you were in on it. Hoping your world is spinning nicely on its axis today. I have some sessions and a lunch date today (yeah! work!). Funny story to tell about last night.

_____
Subject: re: my mojo is back
Date: Fri, 2 Jul 2010 8:24 AM
From: Mark
To: Lisa

teachat?

_____
Subject: mornin'
Date: Sun, 4 Jul 2010 6:56 AM
From: Lisa
To: Mark

Happy Independence Day :-)

Hope your festivities were fun! I had a great day poolside yesterday with my friend Rene'. It was a spectacular summer day with several of us girls whooping it up. Delicious skirt steak dinner with Zac; saw the fireworks from my roof. How 'bout you?

_____
Subject: re: mornin'
Date: Sun, 4 Jul 2010 7:48 AM
From: Mark
To: Lisa

Great rehearsal on Friday nite after finishing and delivering my cabinet. Long day yesterday, mostly from setting up early for the Calico gig. Problems with the power, which set us way back, but the band sounded awesome. Mariah, Savannah and three of her friends came out for the show. Good times, mostly about hangin' with my band mates.

Not much alone time this morning . . .

Subject: Fireworks
Date: Sun, 4 Jul 2010 8:03 PM
From: Lisa
To: Mark

Even though it was hot, steamy and drizzling outside, I sat on my couch and watched fireworks in every direction around my house out the bay windows in my living room. Very cool.

I love fireworks. Tonight is mostly neighbors, but the big display was last night and I have a prime spot on the lower part of my roof. When I was about five I had a scary fireworks moment when we went to watch them at the local park near my aunt and uncle's house. It was near the end of the show and they weren't shooting high enough so there was ash floating down on top of us. I got really scared and ran crying down the street back towards my aunt's house. It's one of those childhood moments that you really remember.

Settling into change being present without much happening. I call it *invisible progress* . . .

_____
Subject: re: Fireworks
Date: Mon, 5 Jul 2010 7:51 PM
From: Mark
To: Lisa

Didn't seek out fireworks yesterday. We got our fill on the 3rd at the gig, but Savannah joined some of her horsey friends last night to hang with their scene.

Had a horn band gig in the afternoon at a nearby swim and tennis club, which was just okay music-wise. Popular event, but not many people paying attention to the band. Mariah and Savannah were there for a couple of hours, during which I sat with Savannah and we had a nice casual chat about just stuff. It was cool, watching her be comfortable with her dad, no pressure, no issues, no orders given, no questions about her plans or her friends. Mariah had gone over to talk with some band mates, eventually making her way back to Savannah and I, wanting to know: *What are you guys talking about?* apparently having noticed from afar how relaxed and chatty Savannah and I had been. They left soon after for barn chores, and to deliver Savannah to her friend's party.

Plan on winechat tonight . . .

_____
Subject: wow. . .

Date: Wed, 7 Jul 2010 11:11 PM
From: Mark
To: Lisa

Just finished downloading a bunch of stories and writings onto a disk from my old laptop. Mariah requested use of it so Savannah could do summer homework on it while they're on the road this weekend. Uh . . . okay . . .

Download to disk. Delete all. *Whew!*

And, oh boy, was there ever a lot of words written on that sucker.

Plan on winechat tomorrow nite.

_____
Subject: for winechat. . .
Date: Thu, 8 Jul 2010 1:25 PM
From: Lisa
To: Mark

I got a nice surprise from an in-person client today: she brought me a bottle of Syrah from a winery she visited on her trip to Sedona. Might bring some extra woo-woo to the winechat tonight. :-)

_____
Subject: just got in. . .
Date: Thu, 8 Jul 2010 7:39 PM
From: Mark
To: Lisa

pouring my first glass . . . chat time

_____
Subject: flow
Date: Tue, 13 Jul 2010 6:00 AM
From: Mark
To: Lisa

Yard work and a nap after our chat Sunday, then to Trader Joe's for dinner stuff before the girls arrived home. Savannah took first place at the show. Paperwork yesterday morning, followed by not finding cell phone. Still haven't found it. Work. Gym. Got home at the same time as the girls. Mahi-mahi dinner while watching *The Game*, with Savannah snuggled up against me the whole time.

Listening to Meade on the drive home yesterday, connecting with how money is *currency*, current, as in the *flow* of water or electricity . . . flow . . . and, hmm, money doesn't seem to flow much around here.

This came up for me in a peculiar way while making dinner last night. Mariah was talking about the horse show in Montana next week, and how big a deal the show is - huge, in the horse world, apparently - and wishing we could afford a hotel room instead of camping for ten days, which she then somehow associated with "white trash". . . *oooff.*

———

Subject: re: flow
Date: Tue, 13 Jul 2010 6:22 AM
From: Lisa
To: Mark

The way you tell it, there seems to be plenty of money flowing through your house. Where I come from only people with money could have a horse and travel so much in the summer, taking off all that time from work, so . . . it's all perspective, eh?

———

Subject: winechat . . .but not yet
Date: Tue, 13 Jul 2010 6:00 PM
From: Mark
To: Lisa

Had another Meade insight on the way home:

The "curse", or wound, delivered from the family earlier in life, sits right on our *gift*. For me I'm sure it would have something to do with my own dad leaving when I was in my mid-teens, so . . . what "gift" might a wound like that be sitting on?

OKAY, chat time. Phone clear . . .

thirty-two

———

Subject: Greetings
Date: Mon, 19 Jul 2010 3:02 PM
From: Mark
To: Lisa

Sitting in the Kalispel, Montana library . . .

Gorgeous drive to get here. Northeast Oregon was beautiful, especially the fifteen or so miles before crossing into southern Washington where there was the biggest spread of golden wheat I've ever seen. But western Montana was mind-blowing. Now I know what they mean by Big Sky. I also reconnected with my passion for taking long road trips into areas I've never seen before. God, I love the road . . .

Taking many pictures. Missed quite a few, though, from doing most of the driving from home to Idaho, crossing into Montana. Truck running great, and some sweet moments when we let the horse out to graze and walk. A family with two young kids pulled in, and seeing the kids mesmerized at the sight of a *real* horse - at a rest stop - was awesome.

Got here safely, but not without the usual tension. Made me crave being alone on some of these roads . . .

May or may not get another moment to write. Back to the horse park soon. Keep your eyes peeled.

Mark

Subject: Latest here. . .
Date: Wed, 28 Jul 2010 5:50 AM
From: Lisa
To: Mark

There are some potential buyers who are having a hard time coming up with a co-signer for the mortgage. Credit issues. I'm contemplating a lease purchase deal but that has risks, yet it lets me *be* the miracle they are looking for and that would be so great.

Big decisions.

Subject: long one. . .
Date: Wed, 28 Jul 2010 6:41 AM
From: Mark
To: Lisa

I'm back . . .

Montana is beautiful, yeah, but *different* beautiful . . .

The air is cleaner, the grass is a richer green color, and you can't drive more than five miles before coming across water in some form. The rivers get first place, with the lakes a close second, but only because the rivers

323

are *moving*, creating water dramas you can't find anywhere else. Montana rivers run like liquid sapphire, parallel to highways and train tracks, bordered on all sides by the healthiest groves of cedar and pine I've ever seen. We saw these images from a whitewater raft trip on our second day there - a trip set up by Savannah's trainer that included a barbecue next to the river when we came back ashore.

Never got back to the library after that one day. Spent most of my time camped out in front of our horse's stall, helping with horse chores or taking pictures. Got into a routine of waking up between 5 and 6, feeding our group's horses - eight of ' em - then walking around with my camera as the sun came up, or just walking around the grounds, taking in the views: the Rockies to the east, half an hour away; the valley we were in running north and south, thick with lush green wheat and oats, waist high and vast; and cedar-covered hills to the west. The horse facility - Rebecca Farms - is internationally famous for its horse events, and this particular one was special in that the owner flew in a fistful of Olympic riders to ride some of her horses. The upper-level competitions brought hundreds of spectators each day, many of them moneyed and local.

Savannah did well, going from second place after her first two days of competing, to fifth, after knocking down a rail on the last jump of her last event, on the last day. The only expressions of disappointment about the shift from second to fifth place came from the adults. She was beaming when the judges hung a massive fifth-place ribbon on her horse. A team she and her fellow riders created came in third overall, and Savannah was beside herself with pride to come away from such a prestigious event with *two* ribbons. Bonus moment: She won a raffle for a poster-size photo taken by one of the photo pros during the entire event. She and I hung out with the photographer to design the layout for the poster, which will be a montage of three pictures, one from each of the events she competed in. Awesome. Very happy girl.

Found my new favorite restaurant in Kalispell, "The Knead Cafe", breakfast and lunch. Saved about $1,500.00 by camping instead of hoteling, so justified eating out with that in mind.

Slept great every single night. Got rained on a couple of times, but no issues or problems with that. Those rainy moments made for dramatic skies later on, not to mention what it did to the air.

Went back to the river we'd rafted on Sunday, under clear, hot skies. Savannah joined in with some other river rats who were jumping twenty-plus feet from a bridge into the deep, cold water. Pics to follow . . .

There were unpleasant tensions in our camp from time to time when . . .

ugh, never mind. I'll just say that when the group was packing up to hit the road for home I noticed how they seemed to resist connecting and coordinating with us about which route to take and where to stop and check on the horses. We ended up taking a different, more scenic route than the others. There was no small amount of bickering between Mariah and I on the long drive. Savannah's only escape from our exchanges was to put in her ear buds and crank up her iPod. So much for the low points of the trip. *Ugh.*

More stories of course - happier ones - and cool pics, but that will come later. Time to get it together for work, plus house awake now. Look towards chat this evening. Got your email this morning. House issue very interesting. Waning moon cycle, too. Don't forget to breathe . . .

Later.

———

Subject: re: long one. . .
Date: Wed, 28 Jul 2010 6:59 AM
From: Lisa
To: Mark

Awesome to hear about Savannah's success and about the poster. You sound good, too. Can't wait to see pix. I have some, too. Yes, all this came at the full moon about the house, on the heels of a last-minute trip to Florida to meet up with Karen, which was great, by the way. We had such a good time together. The waning moon feels like it's about release and letting go, though choices still need to be pondered.

Lots of breathing today, yes. I will start with some heavy breathing . . . at the gym this morning.

Yeah, chat tonight.

———

Subject: whew!
Date: Wed, 28 Jul 2010 4:42 PM
From: Mark
To: Lisa

Okay, well, THAT was interesting . . .

I just finished a bunch of fast-paced, back-and-forth emails to a dear drummer friend, Danny, from high school days, who I haven't heard from in years, and is currently writing me from . . . Paris. He's been in Europe for the last 15 years, playing in France, England, Spain, and . . . Italy.

Chat time, yes?

Subject: Here I am
Date: Thu, 29 Jul 2010 5:29 AM
From: Lisa
To: Mark

Mornin'. . . Here is my house on Google maps. If you zoom in and look towards the left to East Drive, that is the curvy road I can be found bopping down to Taylor Swift and Fergie . . .

Thought for the day (from a postcard I saw in Captiva, FL):

"Before you can *exceed* your wildest expectations you have to HAVE some wild expectations."

——

Subject: random bits of morning
Date: Thu, 29 Jul 2010 5:58 AM
From: Mark
To: Lisa

Lovely chat last night. Boy, that was fun.

Checked out the Google map satellite to see the creek and trail better. Nice haul. Gigging tonite w/ blues band at 9, Saturday afternoon w/ Calico at an Art and Wine Fest, then that evening in SF w/ horn band.

I've been invited to play at a double-drumming gig/party in Berkeley w/ Danny and some music buddies in October. He saw my Facebook pic and said I looked "professoresque". Not a gray hair on HIS head, the fucker . . .

——

Subject: re: random bits of morning
Date: Thu, 29 Jul 2010 6:06 AM
From: Lisa
To: Mark

LOL, Professor. I love that. My friend Rene' has told me for years that she sees me with "some hot professor guy" :-) Funny.

Yeah, great chat. Time flies. Hope we can fit one in this weekend in your free time.

So the walk trail, yes, is good. I have to have a green space near my new place. Along the water, ideally. That is what I love about Alameda . . . shoreline walks from my door. Berkeley maybe. San Leandro. Oakland hills. Those are my hot spots. Can't wait to go looking at places to live!

Subject: random bits of afternoon
Date: Thu, 29 Jul 2010 12:43 PM
From: Lisa
To: Mark

Hey. . .

Great walk on the creek trail . . . gorgeous sky, sunny. Feeling lots of
gratitude. Mom came by after and she is not keen on the lease purchase
deal but persuadable, I think. The buyers are enthusiastic, yet I need more
info to feel comfortable. ARGH! I wish we just had a buyer with the
money. But where is the story in *that*? LOL

Talked with Kath this morning. Mentioned our great chat and how good
you sound. She said she got a very strong hit and to share this with you:

The Montana trip was powerful for you and Savannah. August still feels
like the right time for everyone. You will feel a deep calm and know 'this
is the moment'. Stay aware when in conversations with Mariah and look
for the feeling you had with your boss. It will be just like that. Divinely
inspired. You may feel knocked from your center when she fires back, but
you can, and will, keep your calm. Hold on to the truth that this is what
will allow all of you to move forward in your lives, and all will be well.

As we talked about last night: everybody wins.

_____
Subject: mornin'
Date: Fri, 30 Jul 2010 6:03 AM
From: Lisa
To: Mark

Hope you had a good gig. Girls Night Out w/ Rene' last night. Nice.
Struggling with the house deal. Mom is resistant and wants to lower the
price and wait for a "real" buyer. *Argh.* What to do?

Feels like I need to meet the people who want to do the lease purchase and
get a vibe, then pray I can change Mom's mind.

_____
Subject: here I am. . .
Date: Fri, 30 Jul 2010 10:12 PM
From: Mark
To: Lisa

After midnight, your time. Just came in the door. Big ol' day . . .

Finished the cabinet/arches/floor job. Good vibes, everybody happy. Collected another couple of grand. Encountered the crabby old lady neighbor down the hall as I was leaving, and stopped to thank her for her patience and understanding for putting up with my noise and mess. Totally disarmed her, and ended up having a lovely little visit with her. Heard all about her eye surgery. Sweet. It sort of tied up the whole job in one big bow, leaving a trail of good vibes behind me. Drove away feeling just great . . .

Picked up Savannah at the barn. She needed to shop for a girlfriend's birthday. There's a Target, a Whole Foods, and a Baja Fresh in the same shopping center, so she went to Whole Foods, made an awesome salad and brought it over to Baja where I'd ordered us some grilled Mahi fish tacos. Ate well, chatted, hung out . . . cool and groovy. Went over to Target. She shopped for her friend, and herself, totally digging on spending some of her summer job money. Fun. Good mood. Then took her to see *Salt*. Popcorn. Previews of some cool movies coming up.

What a blast. Nice day.

Feel that nice breeze? Chat window opening . . .

_____
Subject: big news. . .
Date: Fri, 30 Jul 2010 10:42 PM
From: Lisa
To: Mark

How fun, what a lovely time with your daughter. Nice vibe coming off that email :-)

Just wait . . . your day is about to get even better.

Wanna know now or wanna wait till chat?

_____
Subject: re: big news. . .
Date: Fri, 30 Jul 2010 10:43 PM
From: Mark
To: Lisa

NOW!! HA! Thought you were in bed for sure . . .

_____

Subject: re: big news. . .
Date: Fri, 30 Jul 2010 11:33 PM
From: Lisa
To: Mark

OK, so what if I told you that my Mom put the kibosh on the lease purchase deal and I had a bit of a meltdown because it was a tough day, what with Zac having an earache and it being $200 for his medicine and then the A/C went out AGAIN, and it's the compressor this time and could be $1000-2000 to fix, and I am so done with this house thing and *waaaaaaaa* . . .

I cried to her on the phone tonight, "Ma, you were able to just move to your new place and I am a little jealous of that and feel trapped here and this deal is the only buyers we've had so far and this felt like our people and now I can't go to California soon because you are scared they won't pay . . . and *ugh,* I gotta call you back, it's the doctor calling on the other line . . ."

And in the time it took to convince the doctor to give us the cheap, generic $15 ear drops, Mom called Dad. When I called her back she was crying, and said, "Lisa, just go. Your Dad and I don't want you getting sick over all this. After Zac goes to off college just go to California and Dad will pay your part of the mortgage till the house sells and you can pay him back then. You need to go."

What the . . .? Huh? Huge sobs . . . oh man, like relief and deep gratitude and every fiber saying *yeah.* Oh. My. God.

We hang up. *Then,* within 20 minutes, I get a call from the woman in Berkeley I had emailed on Craigslist this morning about subletting her house while she goes to Australia. I inquired about her listing in case this lease deal happened so I'd have a place to stay till I found my perfect home. She and I have a great vibe, a total fit. *This is meant to be,* she said . . .

So I have rented her house in the Berkeley Hills for the month of September and I will be *home* in California a month from today.

———
Subject: re: big news. . .
Date: Fri, 30 Jul 2010 11:38 PM
From: Mark
To: Lisa

holy fucking shit . . .

———

Subject: re: big news. . .
Date: Fri, 30 Jul 2010 11:33 PM
From: Lisa

To: Mark

. . . It's like that picture of Savannah jumping into the river off the bridge. *Wheeeeeeeeeeeeeeeeeeeeeeeeeeee!*

Subject: re: big news. . .
Date: Sat, 31 Jul 2010 12:15 AM
From: Mark
To: Lisa

Well, let's see . . .

I love the synchronicity of the day's events. Your parents' support is incredible, coming through for you like that, and so unexpected by you. Doesn't it strike you as being a bit Divine Intervention-ish?

Then the Berkeley place coming through. LOVE *that* . . .

See, this is why it's a complete waste of energy to panic or freak or worry when things *appear* to be falling apart. It's all just the setup for the upcoming payoff. The Zen move is to do the eye-of-the-hurricane thing: Notice, pay attention, acknowledge, and remember that *everything has meaning*. Stuff isn't just randomly happening TO you; you're creating the whole thing. All of it. I can see LGwO just shaking her head and rubbing her forehead when you were doing your Victim Of Circumstance Dance.

gettin' to be bed time. . . . still good, though. I'm here . . . feet cold . . . gettin' hungry . . . what's to eat?

Subject: re: big news. . .
Date: Sat, 31 Jul 2010 12:32 AM
From: Lisa
To: Mark

I'm about ready to fall asleep here, too. I will burrow under the covers and dream about my new life.

Subject: re: big news. . .
Date: Sat, 31 Jul 2010 12:39 AM
From: Mark
To: Lisa

'k. tomorrow then.

Sweet dreams.

thirty-three

Subject: re: power-less
Date: Sat, 31 Jul 2010 7:42 AM
From: Mark
To: Lisa

Weird . . . got in bed about a half hour after signing off with you, started to read for a bit, and *poof!* Power outage. Everything pitch black. Shit. I was just settling in . . . was it just our house? That would be *very* weird, and a little spooky.

Walked carefully to the front door - couldn't see shit - opened the front door: entire neighborhood out.

Huh? What's going on here? Shit, I was trying to read! I was just getting comfortable! I had a good day! I just-

Poof! Power back on . . .

Like: *Oops, sorry, sorry! Here's your power back. Won't happen again! Sorry!*

Okay, well then . . . that's more like it. Harrumph. Back to bed.

Heading out soon to take Savannah to the barn.

_____
Subject: re:
Date: Sat, 31 Jul 2010 10:48 AM
From: Lisa
To: Mark

They should know better than to mess with *your* power. LOL

I was at the gym when you emailed. Then I stopped by my Dad's to hug him and thank him. We had the sweetest visit. This is all so great.

Chat anytime.

_____

Subject: re:
Date: Sat, 31 Jul 2010 10:57 AM
From: Mark
To: Lisa

Okay, home now, but give me an hour to do a house-cleaning/ drum-loading mash up . . . then I can hang for a bit. Gotta leave for the Calico gig by 1pm, my time.

_____
Subject: spread the good vibes
Date: Sat, 31 Jul 2010 5:39 PM
From: Mark
To: Lisa

Home for an hour or so before needing to head out for SF gig . . .

Calico gig was freaking awesome. Pro stage set-up, drums sounded amazing, everyone played with heart, balance, and emotion. Good dynamics in the music . . . just a first-class performance. Very satisfying. Everyone hugging one another when arriving, so those vibes went up on stage with us. Nice.

My mom was there. Came up at the end to let me know she'd seen the whole show. Aww . . .

Several high school friends appeared again, with a few new ones. Again, much love and good heartedness. Very, very sweet to see all these familiar faces and to have all of us really enjoy being brought back together again. Yeah, something's up . . . something special is going on . . .

So more good vibes here (duh). Good friends, mom, music, hugs, memories. *DAMN*, that was good.

_____
Subject: re: spread the good vibes
Date: Sun, 1 Aug 2010 5:48 AM
From: Lisa
To: Mark

Hoping your vibe is still buzzing high this morning. Feeling good here and pulling things out for the yard sale next weekend. Getting rid of everything I don't *really* want or need. Letting go . . .

Ready for LetGoChat whenever the window opens on your end.

_____
Subject: mornin'
Date: Sun, 1 Aug 2010 8:51 AM

From: Mark
To: Lisa

oooff. . .wow, big ol' day yesterday . . . just got up . . .

Burned a lot of calories with the horn band last night. The first set with
was with the 5-piece version of the band - one sax - then the trumpet and
trombone players showed up later, and brought the house down with the
full-on horn section for the rest of the night. What a great day . . .

Look for chat around 4 or 5 your time today.

_____
Subject: hey there
Date: Sun, 1 Aug 2010 3:34 PM
From: Lisa
To: Mark

You around?

_____
Subject: re: hey there
Date: Sun, 1 Aug 2010 6:31 PM
From: Mark
To: Lisa

Yeah, hi . . . knew you'd be looking for me . . .

After the morning barn chores and bringing Savannah home to get ready
for her party, I dropped her off and was heading home, looking forward to
chat time . . .

Phone rings: Mariah is where she dropped her car for the weekend (caught
a ride with another yoga mama, which I knew nothing about), and the
battery in her car is dead. So battery drama resolved now and I have this
small window to say what's up . . .

_____

Subject: re: hey there
Date: Mon, 2 Aug 2010 11:00 AM
From: Lisa
To: Mark

Mornin' . . . actually afternoon here . . .

I made a sublet plan with the owner of the Berkeley house. I will pay a
deposit now and the balance mid-month in exchange for the key. I really
appreciate that you're willing to get the key for me and see that the place

actually exists. Let me know your dates for Meade. I think it is Aug 17 - 22? She would like the $$ before the 20th, so before you leave would be great. If you hit a snag I can ask Amy as a backup. I'm so excited! We have someone coming to see the house in an hour, too. It would be funny to find a buyer as soon as the pressure was off.

Subject: mornin'
Date: Tue, 3 Aug 2010 7:05 AM
From: Mark
To: Lisa

Few moments alone since yesterday . . .

Berkeley house key pick-up no problem. Let me know when I can go. Sounded like you were shooting for the second week of August.

Two appointments this morning. Trying to pace things so I don't get in over my head or leave someone hanging before going to the Meade retreat. Try again tonight for chat.

Subject: mornin'
Date: Tue, 3 Aug 2010 2:44 PM
From: Lisa
To: Mark

Movin' and groovin' here:

Cd's sorted and packed. *bang!*
Much more stuff purged for yard sale. *bang!*
0% credit card granted for moving expenses to get miles. *bang!*
First movers quote is for $3K door to door complete. *bang! (great guy, too)*
Contract signed for Berkeley house. *bang!*
A/C to be fixed tomorrow for $800. *bang!*
Session w/Kathy confirming the Universe is smiling upon it all. *bang! bang!*
Life is *good* . . . let's chat.

Subject: re: mornin'
Date: Tue, 3 Aug 2010 2:59 PM
From: Mark
To: Lisa

So call me already. . .

Subject: mornin'

Date: Wed, 4 Aug 2010 6:33 AM
From: Lisa
To: Mark

Rainy morning. Nice, but still really humid, though better than last night
when it felt like living in a greenhouse. More done last night and cut
clothes in closet by half! Where did all this stuff come from?? Geez. Feels
great to lighten the load.

I'll be prepping for the yard sale all day. I have one, maybe two client
calls, two moving estimates, and A/C repair. Hour-long gaps between all
of it, so check in. I love having company via my headset while I sort all
my crap.

_____

Subject: Berkeleychat. . .
Date: Wed, 4 Aug 2010 4:20 PM
From: Mark
To: Lisa

Just getting home . . .

I went by the Berkeley house this morning. All the charm must be
concentrated on the inside. The small yard has been ignored for a while,
which is a shame because you can see the house's potential: cool shape,
plenty of space for plants and cool garden art, and quiet, woodsy
neighborhood. You'll dig it. I did . . .

Sat in the truck for a bit. Pulled out my journal and then wrote for two
hours. Here's some of it:

*There's not much more to say about the coming changes. I've filled page
upon page in my last several journals with the personal hell that has been
my marriage, but now I'm beginning to let all of that go and start creating
the life I'd rather be living. I've wanted out of this relationship for years,
but it was my young daughter I couldn't bear to walk out on, regardless of
the rightness or the justification.*

*All the 'Mister-Hang-In-There' stories have been documented in twenty
years-worth of journals, and now that Savannah is, at sixteen and-a-half,
old enough to understand why this separation needs to happen, I feel like
the ground has been watered and fertilized enough to allow The Natural
Order Of Things to work it's organic magic. No need for me to tug at the
shoots and sprouts which are just now appearing: The fact that there is
visible new growth is all the reassurance I need.*

I no longer feel the need to figure out what to do, how to do it, or when. All signs point to a promising growing season ahead, and I need only extend a loving, nurturing kindness towards the garden I've been working in to insure its productivity.

I feel like the proof that God resides in me is showing up in the intention behind the creative things I do. These hands of mine have channeled a lot of beautiful, nourishing things through the years: music, writing, food, massage, photos, carpentry, money, sign language, heartfelt handshakes and hugs, and the driving of vehicles to places of great beauty and soul-making. These were places I felt drawn to, in search of a better understanding of the relationship between myself, the Great Spirit, and what it was that I came into this world to accomplish . . . and contribute.

The wounds and personal tragedies I've drawn to me are best thought of as necessary and appropriate. I've come to believe that alchemy, not psychology, is the best means of distilling from them any meaning or healing. There may well be clues and/or understanding to be derived from dissecting and examining each and every hurtful, damaging event of my life, but I suspect that an entirely different perspective can be gained through the mixing and combining of any number of the pivotal, initiatory experiences of my life. I have reason to believe that they are all related, that a common denominator exists which connects them, serving to guide and inform the trajectory of my life . . .

Never have I been so at peace with the notion of altering the lives of so many by choosing to live my own life authentically.

Subject: re: Berkeleychat. . .
Date: Wed, 4 Aug 2010 4:32 PM
From: Lisa
To: Mark

Awww. . . that's beautiful. Cool that you went to the house. Chat?

Subject: re: Berkeleychat. . .
Date: Wed, 4 Aug 2010 4:34 PM
From: Mark
To: Lisa

Sure

Subject: Zac chat. . .
Date: Wed, 4 Aug 2010 8:41 PM
From: Lisa
To: Mark

sigh . . .

Zac was so sweet tonight. He came home after his dinner out, which he tells me included this new girl he really likes. He gives me a hug goodnight and as he heads downstairs (he's been sleeping in the basement on the couch while the A/C is out), he turns around in the doorway and says:

"It kills me that I am leaving."
Why honey?
"Because there's a lot I will miss."
I know. What are you thinking you want to do?
"I have to go and make the most of it at Dad's in Tennessee. I have to do this."
You will meet so many new people and it could be really be great.
"I know. It'll be fine. Love you, Mom, good night."

Aww.

We are all in a place of being on the edge and leaping in faith. Wow. This on the heels of a chat with Rene' in which she said that she loved how I live on the edge more than she could (though she has ways of pushing the envelope that I wouldn't).

You mean being 6 inches from the edge instead of 6 feet?

Exactly.

Subject: re: Berkeleychat. . .
Date: Thu, 5 Aug 2010 1:29 PM
From: Mark
To: Lisa

Ugh . . . rough morning with new client. Just coming out of it feeling like shit. Ugh . . .

Got all the emails re: house key. Thanks.

Subject: re: Berkeleychat . . .
Date: Thu, 5 Aug 2010 2:36 PM
From: Lisa
To: Mark

Argh . . . it'll be OK

Subject: re: Berkeleychat . . .

Date: Thu, 5 Aug 2010 2:58 PM
From: Mark
To: Lisa

I need to hear more about how it'll be okay . . . :-(

chat?

_____
Subject: ugh
Date: Sat, 7 Aug 2010 6:57 AM
From: Mark
To: Lisa

It's a little rough, here inside of my head. Needing to fall back on my hang-in-there skills to get through my days . . .

Not much money or work happening. Small-time jobs bring food and gas money, but then comes a day or two or three with nothing. Mariah keeps talking about house-building on the property up north, buying houses around here, a car for Savannah, getting her insured, horse trainer bills, horse shows. It's tough to even go for a walk with her, having to listen to her plans and ideas about doing things together, on and on, while I nod and smile, giving the most non-committal answers I can, knowing that none of the things she's talking about are going to happen.

And then something happened last night that made me *really* sad . . .

We'd gone for a walk by the lake while Savannah had a piano lesson, and once back home I felt drained and conflicted. Didn't get out of the car right away. Just sat there, with the door open, looking at my feet, weary and a bit depressed from the events of the week. Ugh.

Finally went into the (messy, disorganized) house. We all agreed on what dinner would be, and I thought: *You know . . . I'm gonna just soak in the tub for a while, and let them handle dinner. It's my turn to chill out while someone else handles the food thing.*

So I announce I'm taking a bath. Run the water. I open the bathroom window all the way - fresh air and a hot soak, right? - close the door all the way (not *partially* open, which sends a different message), pull the shower curtain closed, and drop into the water . . .

Let go, let go . . . still your mind . . . take a break from the worry, the concern, the effort . . . just . . . take . . . a . . . break . . . Breathe. Rest. Shhhh now . . . shhhh . . . Five minutes. Ten minutes . . . and then:

Door opens. Mariah comes in.

Is that my soap I smell?

As she's talking she's getting undressed. She closes the window, pulls the shower curtain back:

Aren't you going to let me in?

Huh? Taking baths together ended a long time ago (duh), it's been a rough week, and the door was closed, so . . . but . . . but . . . *ugh.*

I sit up, move down towards the drain, turn sideways and hang my knees over the side to make room for her.

I don't remember what was said after that. I lasted about three minutes, then got out of the tub. Bath over.

Fuck.

And it plunges me into a really sad place. Can't get the moment of rest I need. Can't get the time to nourish myself a bit, to heal from the week I've had. Mariah has taken over my bath. *She's* now getting the long soak before dinner . . . which I ended up making.

I'm not angry. I'm really, really sad. I feel like I've been treated badly for no good reason. Not cared about. Not seen.

And I'm pretty sure she's been feeling that way for some time, which is kind of the point for separating. But that whole bath interruption thing just seemed *cruel* . . . Jesus, I can't imagine treating someone that way, just walking all over their private moment.

So, you know . . . There's no shortage of reasons to leave, but these days leading up to the Meade retreat are almost unbearable. I'm just relying on grace to pull me through, and give me the moment and the words to move on.

Subject: re:
Date: Sat, 7 Aug 2010 7:18 AM
From: Lisa
To: Mark

Oh, Mark . . .

I am in tears reading your story. I cannot even fathom that kind of intrusion. It is unbearable to imagine being forced to give up all solace in your own home. I could not live like that. I am such a creature of sanctuary. I love the space of quiet moments and retreat and the only reference I have is if I were writing in the yard and Mom would come out to chat. Argh. But in my *bath*? . . . to join, uninvited, someone's bath? I can't even . . .

Try to get some time on your own today. I will be sending you all the warm energy and care that I can while I part with all this meaningless stuff and head there soon to give you a hug.

Subject: re:
Date: Sat, 7 Aug 2010 7:33 AM
From: Mark
To: Lisa

Yeah, well, thanks. Everyone up now, so won't have much contact today. Thanks for the support. You're a sweetie.

Subject: Rhymes & reasons
Date: Sat, 7 Aug 2010 9:24 AM
From: Mark
To: Lisa

It's quiet and calm here for the moment, and writing to you helps my head.

Pardon me while I ramble . . .

After sending that quick response to your email, I sat here at the computer, listening to music, staring out the window with my face in my hands . . .

"Rhymes And Reasons" came on a while ago and brought up a familiar yearning to be way, *way* out in the middle of nowhere, and get back to a life where I can take care of these deeper, moody needs in whatever way seems fitting. Just the freedom to disappear for a few days seems like a luxury, a gift. And that wandering, drifting thing? That gypsy life? I'm really good at it.

It's not a running away *from,* but a running *to* . . . to those places that nourish me and make me feel better . . . a citizen-of-the-world thing, where home is a place inside of me, not a 1,500 square-foot house in a decent neighborhood. It must be that my love of road trips with bands and horse shows are evidence of a deeply important need be out in the world in a way that helps me feel expansive and large, where all this internalized passion and creativity can expand outward and roam. Tears come now as I look out my window, picturing wide-open desert landscapes . . .

And that moment of wet eyes and yearning brings up a whole-body sensation of calling out, from way down deep, to be delivered to the Other Side. It *has* to be that God sees me right now, sees the sincerity of this need, and can feel me reaching out for a hand to make it up these last few treacherous steps, so close to making it to the top, having come so far, for so long. I do not want to fall.

I am not angry. I do not wish ill on the lives of others.

But I cannot stay here.

It's painful to continue living in this world where neglected houses fall into disrepair, creativity struggles for full expression, and spontaneous acts of loving kindness are few. Year after year of efforting this square marriage into a round hole has been an admirable spiritual practice, but I no longer feel nourished by it. I can't imagine anyone else under this roof feeling nourished by it either.

But out there, beyond the glass, the yard, and the neighborhood, is a place which mirrors what's in *here* - inside of *me* - where harmony and wholeness can happen, and I can get back to the business of showing up in the world as the man I'm *supposed* to be, the one I signed up for.

———

Subject: re: Rhymes & reasons
Date: Sat, 7 Aug 2010 9:48 AM
From: Lisa
To: Mark

God is watching, nodding, hand extended. Trust the walk and know the tears will come and that's okay. He wants you to feel this deeply. You have to. Know that your depth is what makes this meaningful. Know that your daughter will thrive with a father who is true to who he is here to be. Then she gets to see that and *be* that, too.

———

Subject: re: Rhymes & reasons
Date: Sat, 7 Aug 2010 9:53 AM
From: Mark
To: Lisa

(sigh) . . . thanks . . .

thirty-four

Subject: signs. . .
Date: Sat, 7 Aug 2010 1:39 PM
From: Lisa
To: Mark

When I moved to California the first time in 1982 I went to the bank a few days before I left to take out all my money, a bit less than $500. I sat there in the drive-thru feeling anxious with anticipation . . . *am I doing the right thing? Is it going to be OK?* I offered up a prayer to God to give me a sign, please. Within moments *Going to California* by Led Zepplin came on the radio. Ah, yes. OK, it's all OK. Smile. Shivers. And I moved to San Francisco and had a wonderful nine years . . . leading to the life I have now.

Lately I have been looking for the signs again every time I turn on the radio, thinking maybe I will hear that song again.

Today, as I was surveying the rest of all my stuff, thinking that someone could come and take it all away in a dumpster and I would be fine, I would be *free* . . . I leaned over to turn off the radio just as *California Dreamin'* came on.

Ah, yes. OK, it's all OK.

The signs are coming to us. Beckoning us. Urging us, pushing us. Keep watching for signs.

Subject: we have lift off. . .
Date: Sat, 7 Aug 2010 4:06 PM
From: Lisa
To: Mark

Just booked my plane ticket to my new life. Sunday, August 29 arriving at 10:10am to SFO

Subject: re: we have lift off. . .
Date: Sun, 8 Aug 2010 5:58 AM
From: Mark
To: Lisa

Gigging with Calico in Sacramento that day, an outdoor country concert in front of the Capitol building. Not sure of the start time. We'll figure out the key thing.

———

Subject: re: we have lift off. . .
Date: Sun, 8 Aug 2010 6:07 AM
From: Lisa
To: Mark

How are you today? Better?

———

Subject: re: we have lift off. . .
Date: Sun, 8 Aug 2010 6:18 AM
From: Mark
To: Lisa

Eh, just okay. Answering ads on Craigslist. Spent yesterday around home, then to the coast after dropping Savannah at an overnight horse thingy. Dinner w/ Mariah in Half Moon Bay, then home.

oooff. . .

———

Subject: re: we have lift off. . .
Date: Sun, 8 Aug 2010 6:24 AM
From: Lisa
To: Mark

I know. It's so hard. It's recent enough for me to remember that sinking feeling just being around Dave and knowing that when he was talking about the Iowa reunion trip that year, or whatever, I wouldn't be going. I also remember feeling like I could throw up when I actually uttered the words: *you need to go*. It was not easy at all, and yet everything now is so much better for all of us. The perspective is really something, looking at it through your lens today, remembering it then and seeing how well we are all doing now. Much happier, and especially the boys are better off.

Wow. It's good to look back one year later. Another *One Year*.

It will really help to be doing some tiny thing that moves you forward to your new place, any small thing that makes you feel like you are preparing physically. Seems when I finally started purging and packing, the energy shifted to *moving*.

———

Subject: re: we have lift off. . .
Date: Sun, 8 Aug 2010 6:28 AM

From: Mark
To: Lisa

Ah, good idea. Priority now is work. Next to nothing in the coming week. My old remodeling boss Mike called me last week. Haven't returned his call yet.

_____
Subject: re: we have lift off. . .
Date: Sun, 8 Aug 2010 6:32 AM
From: Lisa
To: Mark

Yes, work is good. Interesting that your old boss should resurface now. Good if nothing else shows up, I guess.

_____
Subject: re: we have lift off. . .
Date: Sun, 8 Aug 2010 9:48 AM
From: Mark
To: Lisa

Had to get away from here . . .

Went to the lake for a walk a little after 7am while Mariah was still in bed. Needed to have some nature, some quiet, and just let stuff go . . .

She just left for the barn. We had a chat when I came back from my walk, and I deflected my crappy mood to being about the lack of work . . . which still ended up being a downer, talking about it with her. *Ugh.*

Wanna chat?

_____
Subject: oh!
Date: Sun, 8 Aug 2010 7:03 PM
From: Lisa
To: Mark

I forget to tell you on the phone . . .

Eat Pray Love comes out next week. As tempted as I am, I won't see it if you don't, and we can go together. Can't believe the timing really worked out on that one!

_____
Subject: re: oh!
Date: Mon, 9 Aug 2010 6:10 AM
From: Mark
To: Lisa

It's a date.

_____

Subject: re: oh!
Date: Mon, 9 Aug 2010 10:30 AM
From: Mark
To: Lisa

you there? I'm at the library . . .

_____

Subject: oh!
Date: Mon, 9 Aug 2010 10:34 AM
From: Lisa
To: Mark

Yeah. (huge sigh) Just finished my Master Coach oral exam.

_____

Subject:
Date: Mon, 9 Aug 2010 10:37 AM
From: Mark
To: Lisa

. . . *AND?* . . .

_____

Subject: re:
Date: Mon, 9 Aug 2010 10:34 AM
From: Lisa
To: Mark

It was daunting, but I was confident and the examiner's issue was one I could handle. She got to her desired conclusion, which doesn't even get scored, and I have to believe that I was masterful. I'm glad it's over. I get my results within 30 days at which point I will be in California. It does not define me as a coach or as a person.

_____

Subject:
Date: Mon, 9 Aug 2010 11:17 AM
From: Mark
To: Lisa

Cool. Nice attitude. Sounds like the results won't make or break you . . . but if you DO pass, the little gold star on your cred sheet will look nice.

I'm on another page, writing my drummer buddy in France - Danny - about my lack of passion for being a *more* successful contractor. Haven't gotten very far, but it's where I'm at, and there's a tremendous amount of back story to fill him in on. It's all leading to the coming separation . . .

After a day of yard work yesterday I took a break to endure Mariah's Q and A about our relationship, money, etc. This while sitting in the sun in the backyard, her doing most of the talking, and me pausing to check in with myself to see if *the moment* and *the words* were going to show up.

Nope.

It ended with an agreement to at least be kinder to one another. No mention of the bath incident. Yeah, well, whatever, so we go pick blackberries in the pasture before Savannah gets home from the horse thingy . . .

Things mellowed after blackberries. In fact, Mariah poured it on thick for the rest of the evening, made a cobbler, and in all ways played nicey-nice which didn't surprise me since, early in the backyard chat, when she asked about making an effort to heal things, I said bluntly: "Actually, I'm thinking more about giving up."

I didn't have to say much after that (my talking-to-listening ratio with her has always felt like a consistent 20/80, respectively), and, like I said, I waited to see if the "words for change" would come to me, but: no. Clearly, though, she's getting the message in small doses as a prelude to what's coming, hence the stress-free evening.

Interesting moment last night while barbecuing. Had a wine buzz going and felt a real strong pull to go back to the Kevin and Cody story. Missing them, actually . . .

Time to go. I'll check in later.

Subject: re:
Date: Mon, 9 Aug 2010 11:34 AM
From: Lisa
To: Mark

Nice.

Next challenge of my day: selecting a car mover. The auto transport industry is riddled with charlatans so I am being cautious and wary. (more sighing). Later . . .

Subject: ohmygodohmygodohmygod . . . . . . !!!!!!!!!!!!
Date: Mon, 9 Aug 2010 4:08 PM

From: Mark
To: Lisa

Just finished a spontaneous, out-of-nowhere 3-hour lunch with my sister. Holy shit. Divorce talk led to stories about the divorce of our parents. And guess what I learned that I knew nothing about?

My mom was thinking of divorcing my dad even before he left. She was going to wait til after my sister - the youngest - *had graduated high school before saying anything.*

What the- . . . ?

So now I have to do a whole reset with the way I've been holding my family history in my head. This news - and the timing of it - are so goddamn perfect that I almost don't believe it. This is HUGE for me, and in a GOOD way! Not to mention how I never would have heard this if I'd been working today, and hadn't seen my sister this morning for just a few minutes to pass along a birthday gift.

This is awesome . . .

Gotta go. Old boss wants to hire me back to help him run the company. Band rehearsal tonight. Winechat a maybe. Home with Savannah in 2 hours . . .

holy shit . . .!

———
Subject: ohmygodohmygodohmygod . . . . . . !!!!!!!!!!!!
Date: Mon, 9 Aug 2010 4:08 PM
From: Lisa
To: Mark

Wow. Buh-bye guilt over *I'm just like my Dad.*

I am here packing. I'll check back for chat.

wow

———
Subject: got chat?
Date: Mon, 9 Aug 2010 6:35 PM
From: Mark
To: Lisa

Band arriving for rehearsal soon, and gotta get dinner happening. Short chat while I bang pots and pans if you like . . .

Subject: tightropes
Date: Wed, 11 Aug 2010 4:40 AM
From: Lisa
To: Mark

Did bit of writing in my journal about this little journey we are on . . . here is a piece of it:

As we embark on our individual moves to a new life, supporting one another with each wrinkle and discovery, we catch glimpses of what is to come. It is a beautiful, delicate dance and a huge, scary leap. Both bold and trepidacious, we are walking this path on our own separate tightropes, close enough sometimes to occasionally reach out to the other's hand to steady us. At times the gap widens and we are unable to touch; it is then that our pace slows and becomes more perilous. It is then that faith takes hold of our hands and the invisible threads that connect us provide the needed balance to move another inch forward. We are almost at our destinations now, facing both endings and beginnings. In honoring the endings we will provide a lovely welcoming for the beginnings to come, trusting that we have conquered our fear of heights and will not fall.

Subject: help wanted . . .
Date: Wed, 11 Aug 2010 12:08 PM
From: Mark
To: Lisa

At the library, with news about the remodel company, after a meeting with the boss and the friend of mine he hired . . .

I'm being offered a weekly salary - beginning the Monday I return from the retreat - to help organize the shop operations, and create a more efficient system of ordering and delivering products.

The "shop", I learned, is a barn-like building on a remote back road, where workers of questionable immigration status make the kitchen reface products needed. The building couldn't be further from OSHA-compliant, which is another cost-cutting manifestation of the company's "business model".

It's a big mess, with plenty of problems and headaches to go around. The money would at least be a guarantee of covering things like rent, food and gas. I wouldn't even consider this job if I didn't feel so . . . desperate. Not a whole lot of integrity there, unless there's integrity in doing what needs to be done, under the current circumstances.

What say you?

Subject: re: help wanted. . .
Date: Wed, 11 Aug 2010 12:10 PM
From: Lisa
To: Mark

Not desperate. *Smart*. With nothing else coming in, it will carry you
through until you can quit whenever it makes sense. I suggest that you
make sure there is some flexibility in the job for you. Hardcore hours?

There IS integrity in doing what needs to be done, under the current
circumstances . . . which, by the way, are temporary.

Subject: re: help wanted. . .
Date: Wed, 11 Aug 2010 1:16 PM
From: Mark
To: Lisa

hmmm . . . home now, re-working my head space . . .

got chat?

Subject: mornin'
Date: Thu, 12 Aug 2010 6:06 AM
From: Mark
To: Lisa

After talking with you I cleaned the kitchen and scrubbed it's filthy floor, a
way of moving energy as I continued to talk myself into taking the new
job: *It's a gift, it's fine, there's plenty of money,* etc. The girls came home
and Mariah wasn't exactly supportive when I gave her details about the job
offer, the working conditions, etc. I added that I was probably going to
take the job since my boss threw a little more money at me, asking me to
start being the first guy to arrive at the new jobs, bringing the workers the
initial materials they need to get under way. He's essentially wanting me
to be the "face" of the company, reassuring the customer on Day One of
their remodel.

You should have heard the 'whoop' from my friend at the office when I
told him I'll take the job.

Subject: re: mornin'
Date: Thu, 12 Aug 2010 6:56 AM
From: Lisa
To: Mark

Love it. Nicely done! One step closer.

_____
Subject:
Date: Fri, 13 Aug 2010 2:19 AM
From: Mark
To: Lisa

2 a.m. here. Just got in from a gig. I'll get a few hours sleep, then leave at 6:30 to take Savannah to horse thingy. Work all day, then home in the eve. *oooff* . . .

_____
Subject: Mornin'
Date: Fri, 13 Aug 2010 5:49 AM
From: Lisa
To: Mark

Long day for you . . . hope it goes well. I have 6 clients today! That's a long day for me; nearly back-to-back. Catch you when you come up for air. I am here all weekend packing. Still a bit mesmerized by it all. The Universe clearly approves of your plans, doesn't it? So many proofs . . .

_____
Subject:
Date: Sun, 15 Aug 2010 2:36 PM
From: Mark
To: Lisa

Everybody home for the moment. Limited writing time . . .

Yesterday Mariah saw *Eat, Pray, Love* with the woman who lives next door. They pulled up as I was leaving for the gig, both of them in high spirits, saying their goodbyes and promising to go to Italy together in 2 years . . .

. . . funny somehow . . .

_____
Subject: gettin' ready
Date: Sun, 15 Aug 2010 4:06 PM
From: Mark
To: Lisa

Cleaning out desk here, getting organized . . . getting *ready*. Going through the drawer with my writing stuff, misc. projects, and my folder of dream collage clippings (2 year's worth).

Currently burning *thousands* of pics from the home computer onto discs . .

. *HA!*

Subject: re: gettin' ready
Date: Mon, 16 Aug 2010 6:51 AM
From: Lisa
To: Mark

Speaking of burning things . . . there was a marriage certificate that I made when I married Dave, so that the wedding felt more *official* (since we didn't file a license). After my office purge it ended up in a folder at the top of a box of old papers I had labeled BURN. While Dave was over to pick up a few things yesterday we were down in the yard and I made a fire. Unbeknownst to him, the Pergo marriage certificate was the first thing I placed on the inferno, watching the edges curl as it disappeared, slowly, till it was gone.

Like our marriage.

Subject: hey
Date: Mon, 16 Aug 2010 7:17 PM
From: Lisa
To: Mark

Hope you're ready for your Meade journey . . . should we not talk before you leave, have an amazing experience. It will be extraordinary.

hug.

Subject: mornin'
Date: Tue, 17 Aug 2010 5:33 AM
From: Mark
To: Lisa

Yeah, I'm ready. Leaving around 10.

Subject: re: mornin'
Date: Tue, 17 Aug 2010 5:43 AM
From: Lisa
To: Mark

Karen is driving up from Nashville today to help me pack and take some of Zac's stuff down to Tennessee. I love her.

Home stretch . . .

Subject: re: mornin'

Date: Tue, 17 Aug 2010 6:06 AM
From: Mark
To: Lisa

You know how when you're engaged in a project, just working, and your mind kind of goes off on these streams of consciousness, turning over and over in your head different ideas, or somehow another part of your mind is trying to work something out? Anyway, as I worked yesterday I observed my mind turn over this whole scenario of calmly telling Mariah about leaving, but in this case there was this whole thing about how there's no reason for anyone to freak or declare some kind of war. We'll still stay in touch, communicate about Savannah's needs, and everyone lives a new life based on the new arrangement.

Well, there were a lot more details, but I marveled at how simple it all seemed. Very plausible . . . or not. :-)

See ya later.

thirty-five

Subject: archeological treasures. . .
Date: Sat, 21 Aug 2010 3:57 PM
From: Lisa
To: Mark

Getting down to the bottom of drawers and the back of closets. Today's finds were precious. Among them, in separate places, I found the attached photos of you circa 1987 doing dream collages at my apartment. I also found the little *"For when you need . . ."* notes you wrote and attached to the items in the Survival Kit you gave me at my 30th birthday/going away party, just before I left San Francisco for Nashville with Jimmy 20 years ago.

Thinking of you big today and hoping you are having a wonderful retreat.

_____
Subject: mornin'
Date: Mon, 23 Aug 2010 5:30 AM
From: Lisa

To: Mark

Sending Zac off to college this morning. His car is packed and my sister will be here in an hour to drive down to Tennessee with him. Bittersweet, but mostly just a really great and proud moment.

How was Meade? How are *you*?

_____

Subject: re: mornin'
Date: Mon, 23 Aug 2010 5:43 AM
From: Mark
To: Lisa

I'm good. Meade retreat was awesome. Many stories, of course. Lots on my plate today. Start new job with the remodel company. The pics you sent are great. What a trip to see myself again with long, dark hair.

_____

Subject: re: mornin'
Date: Mon, 23 Aug 2010 5:30 AM
From: Lisa
To: Mark

I'll forward the email with details about getting the Berkeley house key. Thanks much. That means I will see you on Sunday, huh? :-)

_____

Subject: re: mornin'
Date: Mon, 23 Aug 2010 5:56 AM
From: Mark
To: Lisa

Girls away all that weekend at a horse show, and the Calico gig in Sacramento is off, so Sunday is still a go at this point.

Adjusting to modern world after deep, deep nature connection and daily rituals. Going for a pre-dawn walk . . . to keep the channel open.

Don't let the quicky notes here fool you; all is well. : -)

_____

Subject: re: mornin'
Date: Mon, 23 Aug 2010 6:30 AM
From: Lisa
To: Mark

Enjoy. I know it is. I feel it.

I am in deep transition here. Lots to share.

Subject: Meade snippets. . .
Date: Mon, 23 Aug 2010 9:11 PM
From: Mark
To: Lisa

The African medicine man I'd met and received a blessing from some 6 or 8 years ago was at the Meade retreat, instructing me on rituals to help and guide me in the 'next life' . . .

Lots of tears, for various reasons, mostly just from witnessing other men tell the most moving stories, or in response to the incredible compassion in the room . . . *whew* .

Subject: re: Meade snippets...
Date: Tue, 24 Aug 2010 5:46 AM
From: Lisa
To: Mark

Hey, good mornin'. . .

While you were gone I'd listen to Meade and imagine you there, close to the flame, soaking it all up like a sponge and wringing it out when you need it most . . .

I can hardly believe that I will be moving there in just days.

Subject: re-entry
Date: Tue, 24 Aug 2010 5:58 AM
From: Mark
To: Lisa

Buon giorno, dolcezza . . .

First day of new job yesterday, ending with going out to the cabinet shop, loaded down with soft drinks and cookies for the dozen or so workers, and spending a half hour with the head guy out there, him telling me about all the little things they could use to make things nicer for them, like, say, *water to drink,* a table to eat their lunch at, a first aid kit . . . I mean, *c'mon.*

So I'm heading out soon to bring these guys a bunch of stuff, and will end the day with going to the house in Berkeley to pick up your key.

Subject: re: re-entry
Date: Tue, 24 Aug 2010 6:00 AM

Sounds like a hero's day to me . . .

I've missed you.

_____
Subject: re: re-entry
Date: Tue, 24 Aug 2010 6:06 AM
From: Mark
To: Lisa

Mi manchi, anche . . .

Devo correre. Ciao.

_____
Subject: Hey . . .
Date: Wed, 25 Aug 2010 5:41 AM
From: Lisa
To: Mark

Anxious to hear about the Berkeley place. Down to the wire here. A little overwhelmed and it's so weird with Zac gone.

_____
Subject: re: Hey…
Date: Wed, 25 Aug 2010 6:31 AM
From: Mark
To: Lisa

This new work schedule means I now don't get home before 5, and with Savannah still on vacation it's now a random thing about who's home and when. Savannah came home yesterday soon after me and I finally had a moment to pass on some information the medicine man at the retreat had for her.

I spent a lot of time with this guy getting instructions about spirits, ancestors, and ritual. I was sitting outside with him the morning of the last day and showed him a picture of Savannah. As soon as I put it in his hands he said, "The water spirits are very strong with her," and ". . . she has healing in her hands . . . she will do much healing with her hands in her life."

So there was this moment last night when Savannah came in the door, sat down and told me about her barn day, and the moment arrived when it felt right to pass on the info the medicine man had given me about her. I emphasized the healing hands thing, especially regarding her mare. She related a few stories about how quickly the horse responds to her touch, especially during events when the horse gets a little jacked up from the work she's being asked to do. Savannah notices how quickly the horse calms down when she gets petted and patted while being ridden. I encouraged her to start *believing* she has a real gift - an African medicine man sure thinks she does - and to maybe start taking it more seriously.

It was so great, that talk. She really let it in. I tried passing on the info in a way where she didn't think it was a bunch of woo-woo bullshit from her goofy dad; I think I accomplished that, because she really listened.

I picked up your key yesterday. Met the woman. Lovely. She leaves Friday night. I thought I might stop by the house - kinda look in on things - on my way to the Calico gig on Saturday afternoon. Remind me of your arrival details.

Gotta leave soon, but I'm still here . . .

_____
Subject: re: Hey...
Date: Wed, 25 Aug 2010 6:41 AM
From: Lisa
To: Mark

So sweet about Savannah. Great about the place. I arrive Sunday at 10am, get a car and come *home*. I am in a mess here and a little freaked out. Please tell me it is all gonna come together, in the cool way you do.

_____
Subject: Pretend
Date: Wed, 25 Aug 2010 6:53 AM
From: Mark
To: Lisa

Just pretend you're coming out here to have breakfast with me as part of your new life, where you have the time, the money, and the power to live your life any way you want to. Then pretend that you know how much better you'll feel after we have a breakfastchat; then pretend you can count on me to remind you what a great idea it was to move back here, and how the gods and the universe and the angels and your tribe and your ancestors are totally behind you on this, and that there's nothing but love and support waiting for you when you get here . . .

Breathe that in for a moment . . . and think of how cool it is that it's all true.

Thursday chat. Count on it. Gotta run.

Don't forget to pretend . . .

_____

Subject: re: Pretend
Date: Wed, 25 Aug 2010 9:30 AM
From: Lisa
To: Mark

OK (tears) . . . It's getting out of *here* that overwhelms me.

How about we cook brunch, hang on the couch and chat and share music and food and wine and talk, talk, talk? The kinda day you have talked about for, like, 5 years. You up for that?

_____

Subject: re: Pretend
Date: Wed, 25 Aug 2010 12:53 PM
From: Mark
To: Lisa

home for a sec, then running right back out . . .

cooking brunch it is.

see ya . . .

_____

Subject: re: Pretend
Date: Wed, 25 Aug 2010 1:33 PM
From: Lisa
To: Mark

Lovely, can't wait.

Oh! Good news: My car will be picked up by Friday and get to Berkeley on Wednesday.

_____

Subject: down to the wire. . .
Date: Wed, 25 Aug 2010 8:00 PM
From: Lisa
To: Mark

Finally, I can see this all done and out the door. What an exhausting day made worse by awful allergies from the dust of a decade under Zac's bed. Took my folks out to dinner and it was nice, not too emotional. I talked with my juju girls in the Bay Area and I'm really on my way. Thanks for the 'pretend' today that felt so very real. You know just what to say. . . but you always did.

Ever since *Welcome to California* . . .

Subject: Mornin'. . .
Date: Thu, 26 Aug 2010 6:36 AM
From: Mark
To: Lisa

cleaning the kitchen before heading out . . .

how you doing?

Subject: re: Mornin'. . .
Date: Thu, 26 Aug 2010 6:36 AM
From: Lisa
To: Mark

Better. Can breathe, finally. Exhausted and amped at the same time. Car being picked up at 1pm. Talk later?

Subject: re: Mornin'. . .
Date: Thu, 26 Aug 2010 7:10 AM
From: Mark
To: Lisa

Yeah. Winechat tonight. About 8 your time?

Subject: re: Mornin'. . .
Date: Thu, 26 Aug 2010 9:00 AM
From: Lisa
To: Mark

Yeah, good. Talk to you tonight.

Subject: goodbyes
Date: Fri, 27 Aug 2010 1:55 PM
From: Lisa
To: Mark

Mom was here to say goodbye . . .

Dave just left . . .

My sister is on her way over . . .

It's emotional but I am really ready to leave. Amy just called and it was great to hear a tribal voice. I will call you tonight to hear yours.

Wow. Moving company comes *tomorrow*.

Subject: Here I come
Date: Sun, 29 Aug 2010 4:05 AM
From: Lisa
To: Mark

Leaving for the airport. See you at noon.

thirty-six

Subject: homecoming
Date: Sun, 29 Aug 2010 9:29 PM
From: Lisa
To: Mark

I have settled in and am mostly unpacked, making it feel a bit more like home. I brought a few fridge magnets to put up family pix and the Meade stuff to remind me that I *live* here. The view of the City below at night is incredible . . . oh, man. Watched a beautiful sunset over the bay and now the lights are stunning. Alice has truly landed in Wonderland. Talked with Rene' (fun) and then called Zac to wish him a great first day at college tomorrow. What a beautiful day. I'll finish packing then read some. I thought I would journal but there are no words yet to write. No words for how good it feels to be *home*.

Subject: Mornin'
Date: Mon, 30 Aug 2010 4:59 AM
From: Lisa
To: Mark

. . . from Berkeley :-)

Great sleep except for the 2am call from Australia, from the woman who lives here, who did some seriously bad time zone math LOL I told her all is well . . . really well.

Free all day to explore, still ridiculously excited!

___

Subject: re: Mornin'
Date: Mon, 30 Aug 2010 6:51 AM
From: Mark
To: Lisa

Got home last night and had a good dinner ready when the girls came home, but boy, after my visit with you it was like being in another world . . . like returning to the modern world after a week in the redwoods with the Meade retreat . . . a little disorienting.

Heading out soon. Enjoy your day.

___

Subject: I got wine. . .
Date: Mon, 30 Aug 2010 5:32 PM
From: Lisa
To: Mark

You got chat?

___

Subject: re: I got wine. . .
Date: Mon, 30 Aug 2010 8:54 PM
From: Mark
To: Lisa

not tonight . . . :-(

___

Subject: Mornin'. . .
Date: Tue, 31 Aug 2010 6:18 AM
From: Lisa
To: Mark

I wrote *something* (finally!) in an email to my friend in Georgia after reading her newsletter. I thought you might like to read it.

Good morning, April . . .

I am sharing my cup of freshly brewed French Roast with you from the top of the Berkeley, California hills. It is 5:30am here and I have been up for an hour since calling my son in Tennessee with an 18th birthday wakeup call before he heads off to his second day of college. Our babies grow up fast, my friend, and without a few more left in the nest, like you have, I was able to fly the coup and go on to my own adventure. And what an adventure this is.

After much talk for years about returning to my beloved California, a series of Divinely-inspired events brought me here, as if by magic. Last fall I shared the true conviction of my desire to be here with my oldest and dearest of friends. That I actually find myself here now is astonishing. As I write this I know that magic only takes us so far, and yes, God opened all the doors (or held them ajar, at least) but I had to step through them. One after the other I have leaped, sauntered or sometimes crawled over each threshold, leading me to this moment of grace, watching the lights below sparkle over beautiful San Francisco, anticipating the sun greeting another new day over the Bay.

Life is good.

There is much important work for me to do here. I want to inspire and guide people to seek out their own doors, to contemplate what lies behind them, and support them as they cross thresholds. A true collaboration with that same friend awaits behind one of my doors and I am excited about working with a trusted, wise counterpart. The writer in me seems to be what called me here most. She lies behind a lovely etched glass door that beckons me to open it, though the key keeps getting misplaced. I have pressed my nose against its smooth surface and peered through it a thousand times. I know the part of me that hides behind that door is waiting to be discovered.

I've been unable to write a word since arriving on Sunday, yet your beautiful words inspired me, so here I am. Thank you. How lovely that our brief connection at a Dallas conference became such a lasting friendship.

So about that phone call . . . I'm here and would love to hear from you. I will look forward to a great chat.

Hugs and love,
Lisa

Subject: re: Mornin'. . .
Date: Tue, 31 Aug 2010 6:31 AM
From: Mark
To: Lisa

Nice life you've got there . . . Love the image of pressing your nose against the glass door, peering in, and seeing your writer self inside, doing her thing.

House waking up.

Later.

Subject: re: Mornin'. . .
Date: Tue, 31 Aug 2010 6:42 AM
From: Mark
To: Lisa

Another minute . . .

Where will you be today? I'm doing a lot of running around . . . not a great
day yesterday, mostly because I have too much time and not enough
direction from on high. The office seems to be fine with me figuring out
what to do with myself . . . no complaints, but I'm trying to be effective
without putting things on their existing workload. So . . . how 'bout you
ride with me and help me get some perspective? Plus it will be fun.

Yes?

Subject: re: Mornin'. . .
Date: Tue, 31 Aug 2010 6:44 AM
From: Lisa
To: Mark

Yes

Subject: hi . . .
Date: Wed, 1 Sep 2010 5:01 PM
From: Lisa
To: Mark

how was your day?

Subject: re: hi . . .
Date: Wed, 1 Sep 2010 7:42 PM
From: Mark
To: Lisa

oooff . . . heavy heart . . . mostly about work. So many angry customers . . .
broken promises (fucking salesmen!) . . .

It's not the workers. Jesus, such good hearts out there, making the best of
their fucked up jobs. LOVE those guys. Problem: Designers, getting SO
many things wrong, only to have the office believing there's a rip-off going
on. Nope. The big money leak is coming from the designers.

Heartbreaking to know the workers are being falsely accused. You should
see the great work they're doing . . . Jesus . . . (tears . .) it's so wrong . . . .

so backwards . . .

gotta go. but you get the idea. (sigh) girls home soon.

Fond memories of riding around with you yesterday . . . Thank you.

Subject: re: hi . . .
Date: Wed, 1 Sep 2010 7:50 PM
From: Lisa
To: Mark

Aww. . .

Had an unexpected invitation for dinner from my client, Doug. Nice time at a cool Italian place in Berkeley. Loved the clothesline of laundry draped through the place.

Subject: mornin' . . .
Date: Thu, 2 Sep 2010 6:07 AM
From: Mark
To: Lisa

Sounds like a cool place . . .

Went to bed early last night after being wiped out from so much crying. Some of that was one of those God-infused episodes, where I'm bent over, eyes tightly closed, and from the inside I see a lot of light. It feels beautiful and deeply sad at the same time.

Lots of driving yesterday. More today. Going to the shop first thing, not sure after that.

Subject: re: mornin' . . .
Date: Thu, 2 Sep 2010 6:09 AM
From: Lisa
To: Mark

Mornin' . . .

I am free today and will be out and about to look at places to live. If you think there may be a window to meet up for a bit, call me.

Subject: heads up
Date: Sat, 4 Sep 2010 6:40 AM
From: Mark
To: Lisa

Hold off on emails til further notice. I'll be having The Talk with Mariah this morning . . . time to shut down for the day. No more emails til I get back to you . . .

here we go . . .

_____

Subject: morning
Date: Wed, 8 Sep 2010 6:02 AM
From: Mark
To: Lisa

Blues band playing tonight . . .

Not feeling so shiny. Long, long day yesterday, up to my neck in phone calls and demands. Sorry to have to cut things short with you during those phone calls. I had to push aside all my personal issues to handle the workload. One minute after getting home the horn band started arriving for a rehearsal, followed by a couple of hours of helping get the girls packed for their road trip. Ugh . . . wiped me out. In the middle of all this: a cloud of grief about the looming separation. And by the way . . . all the I Chings and juju in the world doesn't make me feel any better about what Savannah will go through. Being in the same room with her, hearing about the great time she had over the weekend, is quite a bit different than chatting in a rose garden with you, wanting to believe she'll "be fine". It's just fucking heart-wrenching. Makes me feel like a selfish dick: *I want to be able to come and go as I please, doing what I want, whenever I want to do it. . .* ugh. *Really?*

So, a few days of space and having the house to myself til the weekend. Still a full plate, though: Gotta get drums to the gig early tonight; turn the car in for repairs tomorrow morning; no second vehicle secured as yet - perhaps a company van - to get me through the next few days, which includes the horn band gig on Friday; former customers calling to book side jobs, but I can't think straight enough to commit to anything yet; money, moving, doubt, fear, pain. Jesus . . . up, down, grounded, then not . . . what a fucking shit storm. High point of the day: The look on one of the installers face as I took away a cabinet he'd been installing, which had to get back to the shop for touch-up ASAP so he could keep his job moving along. This new job has me riding in and out on a white horse every now and then . . . feels good.

More of the same today: lots of driving and phone calls, right up until having to set up for tonight's gig.

Happy to hear of your new life coming together. Really. I'm sure we'll find time to do "Eat, Pray . ." this week. I'm still in.

One day at a time, one thing at a time . . . (sigh). I keep eating and praying. Thanks for holding the space.

_____
Subject: morning
Date: Wed, 8 Sep 2010 6:38 AM
From: Lisa
To: Mark

Hey there. I know, things aren't even as rosy up here on the hill as they were in the rose garden that day. That was a nice moment. Move through it with all the grace you can muster. It's there for you.

I am eating and praying, too. And loving many souls. Settling into my new life and moving through all the feelings that are coming up for me. Holding space for Zac, for you. Looking forward to my new place coming together - my stuff will be here sometime next week. I am going over to sign the lease at noon today.

_____
Subject: morning
Date: Mon, 13 Sep 2010 10:32 PM
From: Lisa
To: Mark

I appreciate you indulging my rambling phone messages and what may sound like an awkward attempt to connect (which maybe it is?) but there is real content behind most of them. Sometime I may call just to hear your voice. Please let that be OK, too. As I move through this time there is a need to share what's showing up for me and it's great to be able to call you. Gotta share as we go, right?

_____
Subject: re: morning
Date: Tue, 14 Sep 2010 5:55 AM
From: Mark
To: Lisa

It's *all* okay. Every bit of it . . .
Had a one-on-one talk with Savannah in her room last night about the coming divorce . . .

Over a week ago I made it clear to Mariah that the divorce was for real, and I suspected that Savannah had been getting a one-sided view about this from her mom during their daily drives to the barn. I asked Savannah what she knew, how she felt, what she'd been told, and wanted to answer any questions. I made an effort to assure her that I wasn't angry or feeling

365

hateful towards her mom, and that, in my heart, I was doing what felt like the right thing by putting an end to a dysfunctional, unhappy marriage. I didn't bring up God, life purpose, or the idea of being *called,* but I did use the example of the boyfriend she broke up with earlier this year, asking: *What do you think it would have felt like to stay with him, pretending everything was fine because you were afraid of hurting his feelings? How long do you think you could keep that up?* She understood my point, but it didn't seem to give her much comfort.

She was calmly sitting up in bed as we discussed all of this. After everything had been said I asked her if she felt afraid . . .

"A little," she said.
Are you angry?
"A little."
Fair enough. That sounds about right, I said.

And that was pretty much it. Mariah tried to come into the room three times, wanting to know what was being said, but I shooed her away, sensing that this might be the only opportunity I would ever have to talk privately with Savannah about what was taking place. Also, I felt strongly that there was something right about having this conversation with her *before* the day comes when I'm no longer living there. It won't lessen the hurt, but at least we will have talked about it, and I got to have my moment of looking her in the eye when I said how sorry I was that things should turn out this way.

Ugh. Heartbreaking . . .

Subject: hmmm… maybe
Date: Tue, 14 Sep 2010 6:50 PM
From: Mark
To: Lisa

Sitting here, sipping wine, cruising Craigslist for places to live . . .
thinking: *Shit, I need a garage . . . houses are gonna be too expensive . . .*
and then I find an affordable cottage right here in town . . . with a *garage!*

Think I'll check it out tomorrow.

Subject: juju attack
Date: Tue, 14 Sep 2010 7:12 PM
From: Mark
To: Lisa

Just threw the I Ching after looking at those rental places, the cottage with the garage in particular . . .

Where to live? When and how to move? I need to get out of here . . .

#40, LIBERATION - No changing lines. Check it out.

Total juju . . .

Subject: re: hmmm... maybe
Date: Tue, 14 Sep 2010 7:48 PM
From: Lisa
To: Mark

hmmm . . . wow, yeah. You will find just the right place now that you have really started to look. Trust that. The I Ching: Liberation to the . . . *new normal* . . . wow. It is, as they say. . . all good.

Dude on.

Subject: movin' in
Date: Thu, 16 Sep 2010 10:25 PM
From: Lisa
To: Mark

When hauling all the bed frame pieces into my new place I accepted the help of my neighbor. Nice guy. Showed me all the work they have done on their 126 year-old Victorian; what a beautiful place. Good to have them next door.

Get to see that cottage yet?

Subject: cottage report
Date: Fri, 17 Sep 2010 7:33 PM
From: Mark
To: Lisa

Just got home after checking it out . . . interesting . . .

Small, clean, newly-painted, bars on some windows, end unit, no vent or fan over the gas stove, washer and dryer in the kitchen, dining area to one side of the kitchen at a window, back door in the kitchen has a screen door to a very narrow "yard" in the back: three feet to the fence behind, forty feet long, with neighbors right on the other side. Good-sized attached garage - perfect for drums, tools, and workshop space.

Met one of the neighbors, a guy who works for PG&E in the city. Told me his story (twice divorced) . . . very sweet guy, knows all the neighbors . . . nice vibe from him. Seems like a quiet, low-key little community of one-bedroom cottages.

And . . . the place has been available for almost two months; no takers for almost a month. Just on an energy/vibe level I think I'd fit right in. But the place has a funky vibe to it, mostly from the backyard neighbors being able to look right into the place.

So, took an application. Other prospects for this place have flunked the credit check. Hmmm . . .

_____
Subject: re: cottage report
Date: Fri, 17 Sep 2010 8:08 PM
From: Lisa
To: Mark

Hmmm, well, it sounds like it's yours if it works for you and the price is right. The washer/dryer kitchen thing is weird but I saw a lot of that actually and it's great that it even has them. Think I'd like that better than my plywood floor laundry outhouse. LOL There are a lot of things about my new place that feel really funky but somehow the place is still good.

A garage, laundry, in town . . . all pluses for that rent. But you have to not hate it. Remember that wherever you land right now is temporary. And you can always keep looking while you decide to apply or not.

_____
Subject: writing assignment
Date: Wed, 22 Sep 2010 8:51 PM
From: Mark
To: Lisa

Asked the I Ching: *What would be the result of moving into the new place by Oct 1st?*

53 *Development* (Gradual Progress) and # 49 *Revolution*. Look them up, please. I'd like your life coach perspective on the info. I'll read it in the morning . . .

_____
Subject: re: writing assignment
Date: Thu, 23 Sep 2010 4:03 AM
From: Lisa
To: Mark

You will have to call me for it. Only have internet on my phone since I stayed in my new place last night.

Subject: re: writing assignment
Date: Thu, 23 Sep 2010 5:11 AM
From: Mark
To: Lisa

whoa . . . 4am? You up? I'll call you.

Subject:
Date: Sun, 26 Sep 2010 5:12 AM
From: Lisa
To: Mark

Mornin . . . Another early one, I love it. Thinking about a dawn beach stroll.

Subject: re:
Date: Mon, 27 Sep 2010 5:44 AM
From: Mark
To: Lisa

Holy shit . . . gotta move out of here. *Today*. Rough night last night, with Mariah coming unglued. A real first class rant about . . . *ugh* . . . never mind. It was awful.

Don't bother responding to this. I'll be gone. I'll call later.

thirty-seven

Subject: writing assignment from you
Date: Sun, 10 Oct 2010 9:10 AM
From: Lisa

To: Mark

How did you get to be who you are?, he asked . . . *tell me in 500 words or less . . .*

Wow. OK . . .

It seems to me that I am the sum total of all the choices I have ever made, all the people I have known and all the places I have seen. I became me with each step I took, each challenge I chose to overcome and even more so by the ones I didn't. I have been shaped by each moment of joy, each painful decision, each meaningful conversation and seemingly meaningless encounter. The shape of my heart is a mirror of those I have loved and who love me. The shape of my body reflects the food that I eat and how I move through the world. My mind has been shaped by all my thoughts, the random and brilliant, the fearful and brave. I have gleaned wisdom and information from at least a thousand books and more from the company I keep. After all that, I am still not really who I am without my *soul.* For it is my soul, shaped by God, that recognizes all that I am here to be, to *become.* My soul watches as I spin through all my life experiences, then gently steadies me and points me in the direction I need most to go. She is my compass on the journey of becoming who I am. She holds the map.

Are we there yet?

Not even close.

_____
Subject: look who's online!
Date: Fri, 15 Oct 2010 5:55 AM
From: Mark
To: Lisa

I did it! Thanks for your help getting me wi-fied . . .

Been up since 3am. Started right in on setting up the wi-fi thing and am now in a Starbucks at the end of my block.

Can't believe my place still looks like I moved in yesterday. Wow. I have my laptop on my desk for the first time after a couple weeks of sitting on the floor with it perched on an empty cardboard box.

Jesus, this is such a strange, wonderful time . . .

_____
Subject: re: look who's online!
Date: Fri, 15 Oct 2010 6:05 AM

From: Lisa
To: Mark

Cool. I've been printing out our emails. Big stack printed already . . . wow.
Lots, lots, lots more. How fun it will be to read them together this
weekend.

_____
Subject: aftermath . . .
Date: Mon, 18 Oct 2010 10:57 PM
From: Lisa
To: Mark

The kitchen is clean and the house straightened up from our live-out-loud
day. What a joy to wash the dishes from the meals we shared while knee
deep in reading the *story of us*. In each room I could feel bits of this
magical day, a little in awe of the relaxed ease with which two people
could share a space, a vision, themselves. It feels as if the whole place
should be damp from the tears that we shed. Wow-wee.

Thank you for spending this day with me. I will never forget it.

love,
Lis

_____
Subject: re: aftermath . . .
Date: Tue, 19 Oct 2010 6:01 AM
From: Mark
To: Lisa

As for me . . .

I went to bed immediately when I got home, slept like a stone til 4 am.
Came here to Starbucks and was the first one in the door when they
opened at 4:30am. As soon as I walked in the song "Hallelujah" came on.

Hallelujah indeed.

I'm sitting back in my chair, staring dumbly at my laptop screen, exhausted
and bewildered. Yesterday has to be the most connected I've been to my
heart in quite some time. I suppose this is what I get for trusting in God
and the Universe and all the *ju ju magica* I've called out to through the
years, pleading to know and connect with why I'm here and what exactly it
is that I'm supposed to do with this life. I have no memory of previous
lives, so I can't be sure if I'm picking up where I left off from the last one,
or spontaneously making this shit up on a day-to-day basis. And I most
certainly cannot explain why, over these past weeks, I should tear up so

easily and so often. Like now . . .

It's one thing to have a divinely-inspired love given to you to experience and share; it's something else altogether to recognize it when it appears. It's tempting to reach for something poetic and profound to say about such a gift, but I think maybe it's best to just leave it be and let it speak for itself. Our job is to go on being humbled and grateful that we should get to experience such a thing in our lifetimes, and preserve its magic by doing the most responsible thing possible to keep it alive . . .

Just keep saying *yes*.

gratitude

Support and encouragement came to us in many forms over many years. We'd like to express the deepest gratitude to those people who, whether they were aware of it or not, played a role in the creation of this story . . .

To the JuJu Girls, who have been there for us through it all, we give our love and appreciation beyond measure. We thank Mary for her gracious friendship, brutal honesty, and incredible holiday dinners. You guys are family to us. Thanks to "Chick On" Amy for decades of friendship, laughs, and her keen perspective. Rene' you are a treasure. We appreciate how much you love our story and how much you love us. And to Kathy there are barely words for how you have held the space for both of us. Your love, support and insight have carried us over the threshold to where we are today. We love you, Kathy JuJu.

Lisa's sister, Denise, read our story late in the game but was one of our best readers. Thanks, Den. The way you related to our story has brought us closer. You'll be a JuJu girl yet. Karen, your friendship means the world to me. You are loved, near or far, by me and my son.

Bill, whose friendship and brotherly love has consistently exemplified what it means to be the kind of man that God likes working through. Your support and compassion for those in need has earned you a position as the lead singer in His band. Mitch, a music brother since high school, has never been anything less than inspirational when it came to making lemonade from life's lemons. Heartfelt thanks to you and Sandra for your nourishing, uplifting friendship.

To Mosaic Voices founder Michael Meade, whose wisdom and insight regarding the Soul's journey became a lifeline during the worst of inner storms. Your grounded male leadership is honored and deeply respected.

We are very grateful to those who have encouraged us and cheered us on by reading our words, listening to our stories, and/or supporting our relationship: Lilan, Laurie, Sarah S., Cynthia, Sherri, Nan, Robbie, Deb, Sarah T., Joelle, Julio, Gini, Elenna, Garner, Linda, Kim, Valerie and our book coach Catharine who pointed us in the right direction from the beginning of this project, helping us to see that our emails really do tell the whole story.

Our families have loved us and tolerated us even though we didn't always fit in with the rest of the family. We know we're whack jobs. Love to all of you for your support and understanding. Our heartfelt thanks go out to our Italian moms from Chicago, Patt and Eleanor; Lisa's dad, Ron; and Mark's sisters, Ellen and Susan.

Our kids have inspired not just words in our book, but chunks of our lives. We love them most of all and hope our story can model for them the profound importance of being true to who you are. Be brave enough to find out who that is, and connect with someone who loves you for it. If you read closely enough you will find within this book are love letters to both of you.

And to each other we offer profound gratitude for bringing out the best in one another for over 30 years. Our deep and wide connection grows deeper still as we navigate the Divine waters our boat sails on.

We are loved.